THE AMERICAN TAX DOLLAR & BAILOUTS

2011 TAXES, LIQUIDITY, & BAILOUTS OF AMERICAN BUSINESS & GOVERNMENT

JAYSON REEVES

IUNIVERSE, INC.
BLOOMINGTON

THE AMERICAN TAX DOLLAR & BAILOUTS 2011 TAXES, LIQUIDITY, & BAILOUTS OF AMERICAN BUSINESS & GOVERNMENT

iUniverse books may be ordered through booksellers or by contacting:

iUniverse
1663 Liberty Drive
Bloomington, IN 47403
www.iuniverse.com
1-800-Authors (1-800-288-4677)

ISBN: 978-1-4502-8808-8 (sc)
ISBN: 978-1-4502-8809-5 (ebk)

Printed in the United States of America

iUniverse rev. date: 1/27/2011

CONTENTS

INTRODUCTION

The American society consisting of all the individual states, and the United States federal government including the citizens was established in a diversified format. These conflicts and issues exist considering the businesses, and people's lawful resource to pay taxes. The American issue of taxes, business, and government liquidity including the format of various government financial bailout's has been a troublesome economic issue during this first decade of 2000. A relevant fact is that the American people are the human citizen factor that makes up all of the American system of government, and businesses apart from taxation, and some foreign markets. Every year sense, and even during the beginning of most established governments (c/o1776) within the United States of America, these collected tax currencies, and money helped pay for government services with accumulated tax revenue dollars. These are certain provisions of services that are supported for a vast amount of government issues which includes the concept of tax funded government enterprises, insured U.S. Anti-Trust laws of liability, the infrastructure, and all logical resources of American government duties, and liquidity. Therefore this becomes the relevant financial operating funds considered for all levels of American government supported by the Treasury of all state governments, and the United States federal government.

Another perceptional tax currency management concern within American government that was established with format during the 1930s, and 1940s was government enterprises, and government corporations to manage, and enforce regulated liquidity. This tax dollar issue within government securities, and diversified project funds became important just as most values where established within U.S. Savings Bonds. This is also factored for certain government sponsored enterprises, and different U.S. corporate entities to insure the liability of certain industries, and markets. Some of the issues of government tax liquidity can be observed in these certain United States government sponsored enterprise's that are used for the promoting of the American general welfare. Those U.S. government enterprises, and corporations such as Sallie Mae, Fannie Mae, Freddie Mac, Ginnie Mea and even the Federal Deposit Insurance Corporation (FDIC) where established, and operated with tax dollars and government invested dollars for secured debt to manage, and appropriate liquidity.

In large "Government Sponsored Enterprise's" (c/o corporate duties) consist of government liquidity within securities are valuable to American citizens, and governed assets which includes the format of certain business, and government duties. Certain United States government securities are established as, Sallie Mae; is the Student Loan Marketing Association. Fannie Mae; is the Federal National Mortgage Loan Association. Freddie Mac; is the Federal Home Mortgage Loan Corporation. Then Ginnie Mae; is the Government National Mortgage Association. Considering these government enterprise's it is important to remember that this divides the lawful support of individual, and business income earnings. This is similar to U.S. Savings Bonds, and Treasury Securities which also helps establish equity, and liquidity. This factor of government support is vital in most assets that are purchased within long term agreements. Therefore this becomes the important factor within how the individual states, and the United States federal government manages the liquidity, and equity in most all American established tax supported enterprises, and most factual assets of insured liability.

This book; The American Tax Dollar and Bailout's by the "Author" Jayson Reeves will outline some of the physical, and economic damages that certain local, state, and federal government issues including businesses in the United States have suffered with during the recent years. This is partly why the U.S. government established the "Troubled Asset Relief Program" (TARP) during 2008 from the George Bush Presidential administration. These liability issues of TARP, and the struggling American economy have now in 2009 and 2010 became some of the tax dollar spending issued conflicts of the U.S. Presidential Barrack Obama administration. Throughout this composition of writing it will include historical facts that where part of business liquidation subjects, and government emergency financial bailouts (c/o TARP) that have been an important taxpaying corporate compromise issue of liability. Observing this, the good corporate citizenship values of American business that occasionally saves the existence of small, and more so large corporate businesses is relevant when the businesspeople, and government work together. Considering these, and other conflicts our well developed American society may not be as well as it could, and therefore these issues are factored within the past, and how it will possibly effect the future of American people, businesses, and government.

A list of good concerns (c/o relevant bad issues) factored within certain corporations, and government failures can be one thing on the outside of valued indifference, and then from the inside of business pondered with accumulated managed debt, and worries. Considering the best management decisions these are the factors of good, and bad issues of managing tax revenue, taxable earnings, and business! These few resources upon other corporate, and government failures apart from progress to pursue good management have been the center point of worries in the American society. Public corporate businesses such as United Airlines Corporation, American Airlines Corporation, American

International Group Inc, Bear Sterns Investments Inc., Merrill Lynch and a vast amount of local or commercial banks have suffered the need of U.S. government TARP bailouts. This includes the relevant understanding of whether or not they deserve a rescue from the U.S. government's bailout plan. One consideration of why some businesses require funded help of this nature is because the 9-11 Terrorist Attacks, Hurricane Katrina, and a few other disasters have cost citizens, and businesses severely from something government could have prevented.

Other U.S. government bailout concerns are included within the indifferent problems suffered at the Ford Motor Company, Chrysler Corporation, and General Motors Corporation. This includes their CEO's that pursued bailout, and special government lending factors of most business concerns to help their corporate America duties of value. Ford Motor Company decided to stop asking for U.S. government bailout money during 2009, and this left the U.S. government with the other American automobile company's in a complex restructuring process. It is vital to observe, and consider this good, and bad format of most American corporations that have limited assets, and a constructive resource of liability that is managed properly. Within the concept of this managed liability the United States Constitutional values of America are, and can be established as relevant due to business predictions, and planning. Considering these limitations that seem unlimited within the Corporate America values that effect the rich, and poor of the American tax paying society, this therefore is valued with these subjects, and a great deal more trying to exclude corporate welfare, or poverty.

Observing, and understanding the American system of tax collections in the United States that is occasionally similar, but different in most other countries, these factors of property taxes, sales taxes, and payroll taxes within industry factors of importance become relevant within business, government, and a well developed society. Over the decades, and centuries these taxable concerns for the people that usually require helpful government subjects of discipline with duties of lawful concern, we find the executive, legislative, and judicial branches of government applicable. Within these facts of good, bad, or irrelevant tax notices these economic, and financial statements occasionally become an issue of the legislature, and the courts to maintain the enforcement of discipline. This is relevant even more so if the individual state court, or the U.S. Supreme Court has been fairly active just as some of the lower courts that observe these subjects of taxable property, sales items, and diversified income tax earnings that are values of American prosperity.

The observation of this book will also explain how the people, corporations, and government are valued within the tax structured system of America. This also considerably includes churches, religious organizations, certain professional organizations, and most foundations that offer support to the American society. These are the tax bracket conditional factor's that provides an equation between businesses, organizations, and even the government with values to helpfully appropriate the discipline of people, places such as national parks, and certain values of research including various facilities. From time to time this becomes relevant of how society receives charitable donations, and support for extra-curricular activities for the young, and old in America. These donations of cash, and or equipment help increase the effort of certain productive groups of people that are facilitated as in schools, churches, theater's, children's sports organizations, and hospitals considering certain values of research, athletics, and other advanced studies.

Understanding professional studies, and taxable characteristics within the profession of engineering in the United States it is factually vital to observe the problems of the aging utilization (utility & component) infrastructure's. The bailout of the city of New Orleans, Louisiana is a vital tax appropriated example with issues of expenditures that will require years of professional engineering studies, and various geological social evaluations to rebuild the city after hurricane Katrina. This also includes a vast amount of damages to southern Mississippi. Because of the 2005 Hurricane Katrina including this government, and engineering disaster this is the largest regional, and city government bailout, and rescue in America recent times. This will consist of United States tax dollar expenditures, appropriations, enterprise disciplines, and certain public, private investments extending the process of government, and societal renovation, and construction issues. Then managing these factors should be appropriately considered in the tax dollar currency circulation of money from government in various parts of New Orleans, various cities, and towns throughout Mississippi, Texas, Florida, Georgia, and a few other regions of the United States.

New Orleans, Louisiana, and now the 2008 floods in the state's of Indiana, and more so Iowa will be a part of a tax bailout "government Declared Disaster". This Federal Emergency Management Agency (FEMA) and various U.S. Department of Interior issues geographically will require the repair of infrastructures, and upgrades to certain bridges, dams, sewer systems, and levees for all waterway (c/o also bridge and roadway) systems. In addition this includes the losses to vast amounts of households which the Federal Emergency Management Agency try's to stabilize a percentage of the damage that occurs. These are severely dangerous issues within the American general public upon safe conditions of the consideration, and developing of new infrastructure concerns throughout the American society. Considering these American tax dollar issues with State of Emergency factors within most all cities, and state taxable budgets, this will require factors of budget planning to value the restructuring of these major American regions.

The timing, and effect of these sad levels of disaster are at a time in America where banking institutions, and investment banks are part of bailouts, and bankruptcies. This also includes conflicting federal funds rates, and therefore borrowing money is a complex consideration. These conflicting problems implement additional conflicts in the American government system of grants, and loans which makes collage studies, and productive activities slightly difficult for various people. Our American society has gotten to the point that things should have been fixed, before these "things even more so became very expensive disasters" at the taxable, and livable expense of most local citizens. These expense items, and factors also include the relevance within businesses, and even the conditional value of important duties of our American system of government with tax revenue.

Within these changing times of the American society that we live in concerning the banking industry, it is vital, but more so relevant to evaluate these issues that have become a very complex problem to the format within observed managed liquidity, and most occurred debt. This vitally includes the liquidity within productive, but economically complex growth in America that occurred during this first decade of 2000. Banking, tax dollars, and the liquidity within government funds is the basic concern of "business, and social survival" that will considerably be discussed in this book. How public, private, small, and large business conditions are part of these changing times will also be considered for its discussed relevance. These vital issues are applicable to the approaching years of 2009, 2010, and up to 2020.

Liquidity in these American banking establishments including federal funds are also at the rate of competitive problems against good, and more so bad foreign relations. An important consolidation is that America did not properly except the govern global economy with national security factors of most diversified effects during the years of the 1990s, and 2000. Not taking this exception serious we now have an economic recession that is giving use some of the worse indicators in history from international business, and various United States national security concerns. This includes the worse losses of tax revenue advancements from most all logical regions of American business, and some of the worse social, economic, and business problems of resource's in U.S. history. Also these years of 2009 being a time of war for America, there is a large commitment of expenses that apply from our tax revenue system into federal banking, treasury, and government. As this applies to the American economy including taxes, business, and government liquidity "considering" so many bailout's, this is a fighting subject that is only slightly indifferent from this time of war in Iraq, and Afghanistan (c/o the September 11, 2001 attacks) concerning America. Therefore this resource of our American format of liquidity is applied within the characteristic, and ability to meet all maturing obligations, and contingencies promptly with beneficial factors to the American society of taxes, commitment's, and the people.

CHAPTER ONE

THE TAX DOLLAR ACCUMULATION FROM AMERICAN WORKERS & BUSINESSES

The accumulation of American tax dollars is a valuable resource of government tax revenue within all forms of government in the United States of America which applies to the people that are employees, employers, and even board of directors. These are the vast majority of people installed with the powers, and duties observing the disciplines of all citizens, and businesses that pay taxes at logical, and with accountable rates of income earning issues, and wages. This accumulation process of tax revenue is vitally important to all cities, towns, states, and the United States federal government. Then this becomes the government format of economic balance of disciplines within the establishment of local, state, and the federal tax system that appropriates expenditures to operate government in a developed society. These tax revenue conditions to the American system of government are then held together "by logical enforcement" of the individual states, and United States Constitutional laws.

Considering recent corporate bailouts some state, and federal government subjects such as a state of Emergency or Declared Disaster's is nearly the same (without loan agreements) observing the format of similarities as a United States government "Bailout Corporate" lending agreement process. This also includes various evaluated decisions, and termed agreements within procedures. Considering these are a few reasons why we as Americans pay taxes, our conclusive evaluation is vital that all conditions of logical management apply. This process with certain other conflicts has went through many good, and bad changes over the last few centuries with government tax revenue dollars.

Observing the years, and decades of today the people of individual American states like Louisiana, New York, Iowa, Michigan, Indiana, North Carolina, West Virginia, and a vast amount of others have witnessed certain tax bailouts that have emerged. A reluctant subject is that most earthquakes, mudslides, and wildfires applied by nature, and with conditions of danger to people has been applicable to disasters in California. These west-coast disasters are mostly insured, but they are contingent with liabilities by tax dollar useful appropriations. Contrary to this fact of insured property, these are still concerned American tax dollar issues, and with inflation this occasionally becomes vital, and applicable for the best discipline, and evaluated results. These become the tax dollar input, and output evaluated factors of citizens, all type of employees, and the employers of the American society we live in.

Considering the accumulation of taxes in the United States during the early 1900s that was about $17.34 per person annually most things expand with economics, infrastructure development, and social growth. Now, and during the early 1980s the taxes per person a year average was at about $1,400.00 annually representing the population, labor laws, and certain subjects of inflation. This is the compounded inflationary process of a nation's economy. Within those years of the 1980s (c/o the late 1970s) the state, and local tax dollar totals had accumulated to about $121.0 million dollars, and the federal government collected more than $165 million dollars of taxes. This accumulated a combined total of $285.0 million dollars (c/o asset liquidity) throughout the entire country, contrary to the sales taxes from small items like books or food, and other items like house, cars, boats, and other products. These levels of tax dollar accumulated issues with inflation is compounded by the advancement of infrastructure roadways, bridges, and other assets such as schools, and other government institutions and buildings.

During these years of the 1990s our American system of government accumulated tax dollar values that are at about $3,724,100,000.00 (c/o billions of dollars) is making the per person annual tax average at about $12,483.55 a year. This average becomes conflicting for young people that have been unemployed or even laid off for over 10 years, whom haven't filed, or paid taxes. This conflict includes taxes that people on welfare, or that are homeless don't pay considering this large part of the American population are counted, or are a valued concern within citizens. Now during 2007, and 2008 the valued probability issue is that bailing out the citizens has reached about $93 billion dollars of tax payment stimulus to all tax filing citizens. The years of 2009, and 2010 consist of similar problems with hopes of improvements. Within these tax liquidity government liability issues, and factors that the citizens of the United States where observing with inflation, the government provided stimulus checks during 2008, and this helped a perceptional bit. This being an idea from the George Bush Presidential administration becomes something that was appropriately acceptable by most all American taxpaying citizens.

When the American society observes complicated economic hard times such as during the 1929 Great Depression most all citizens, and government find this issue of created concern with valued opinions to become wise within manageable budgets. This is the format of workers, and businesses including investors to have vital awareness from the top to the bottom of most social values. The Internal Revenue Services (IRS) is factored as a public monopoly contractor for the United States Department of Treasury, and government. Taking this issue serious within good, and bad economic times for the citizens that appropriate government tax dollars, most American people, and the government have found many days to correct the govern tax system. This is part of the Separation of Powers (c/o the Executive, Legislative, and Judicial branch's of government) that most logical citizens value with resourceful decisions. American businesses, and their employees find command ground for taxation with certain decisions of voiced opinions, and calculated numbers that are factored on these quarterly, and annually subjective tax rates, and payments of concern.

When American tax payers value certain effective issues, a vast amount of tax liquidity factors are based around certain programs of a government enterprise capacity with various activities. A couple of these programs are Medicare, and Medicade from the tax dollar values between government, and the citizens that help the cost of maintaining the American people's health. The tax dollars that are appropriated for American taxpaying retired or disabled citizens, and their families are managed as another large enterprise or government program entity of vital importance. Observing the taxpayers healthcare concerns the term Medicare is from the United States federal government. This U.S. federal tax funded program is established to the appropriated larger factors of medicine, and medical care for the sick, retired, and or disabled citizens that need medicine, hospital stay requirements, and certain other insured disciplines. The term Medicade is a federal sponsored program for all individual state governments to provide healthcare funding for all citizens (c/o certain qualifications) of the individual states with healthcare matters, and concerns. Understanding these two government funded enterprises, or government program factors within the American system of government, it also is relevant to having provisions for the medically indigent to afford their health care issues.

Making fact of the large commitment of Medicare, and Medicade this is the funding logic of the Social Security Administration of the United States government. The Social

Security Administration of the United States government that sponsors, and manages the discipline of Medicare, and Medicade operating system standards are valuable for the American people. The logic of healthcare, and funding is a small percentage of the overall tax dollar values that is deducted, and or collected from the American wage, and business earned tax dollars within government revenues. Understanding the U.S. governments Social Security Administration, and policy conditions considering certain values of managing, this applies to legislature that consist of various financial resources of lawful discipline. Then observing this administration from time to time, it has been a vital consideration of concern that this government agency can become insolvent if the executive, and legislative government branch decisions are not pursued properly in the future. This inadequate funding issue of possible insolvency in the American system of government is the concern that misappropriated or mismanaged government budgets will be the cause of a future problem. If the Social Security funding of the United States suddenly requires a bailout this would be an American failure worse than the Great Depression, but factored differently with concern, and relative madness. Upon this relevant concern it becomes important to remember that during the Great Depression of 1929 there was no Social Security among other financial enterprise concerns. Also in 1929 no unions existed to help the quality of pay, and issues of job safety, security, and healthcare.

Considering unusual commits, and issues of insolvency, people get fired from certain jobs, and or prosecuted to protect the innocents of the old, and some very young taxpaying Americans. When these factors of crime, and money play a role the observation of anyone can, and has to be considered liable with judgment, which means it can be a union member, management official, or a government official. This becomes the fact of when good government officials (c/o accountants, lawyers, and other professionals) have a unified discipline or a vital commitment to the innocence of people. Therefore these issues of taxes, and tax dollars of liability within the U.S. government including decisions of liquidity are factored with understanding, and then taken as a very serious subject within disciplines of responsibility.

The relative consideration of vital decisions of tax dollar concerns has consisted of the largest city bailout in United States history which was the disastrous effects of the 2005 Hurricane Katrina in New Orleans, Louisiana. Now the Gulf of Mexico, and off the shores of New Orleans has suffered with an expensive deepwater oil well leak from a British Petroleum Company accident that has paralyzed this southern regions $2.1 billion dollar fishing industry until cleanup is effective. Louisiana's fishing industry has an average revenue of around $270 million a year (c/o 2008) with them losing estimate's of around $150 million's dollars with the 2010 oil disaster. There was also a considerable comparison within the 1871 disastrous fire of the city of Chicago when we observe the New Orleans Katrina hurricane & flooding disaster. This 1871 Chicago, Illinois fire before the turn of the century caused the death of about 300 people, and destroyed about $200 million dollars worth of property. Within this recently observed factor the subjects with the city, counties (c/o parish's), and states including the federal governments declaration of a region as a disaster the U.S. government has tax dollar vital support to provide its citizens. These levels of support are important to relieve the failures of a lack of professional responsibilities (c/o 1990 & 2005) that lead to the billions, "but maybe less than a trillion dollars in damage" in New Orleans contrary to problems in other regions of America.

Both Chicago, and New Orleans had scientific engineering faults, and conditions that where contingently accessible as it applies to the common features of wood, and concrete. Theoretically Hurricane Katrina effected Mississippi, Louisiana, and slightly some parts of Texas including a few other U.S. governed states. Hurricane Katrina during 2005 also effected islands off the bordered coast of the United States throughout the Gulf of Mexico, the Caribbean Sea, and the Atlantic Ocean. Understanding this sad fact within the American loss of lives, assets, and most normal conditions of livable standards, the city of New Orleans suffered in the after mass of flooding from a weak concrete levee system to contain the water. This massive compound of "ocean waters, and flood waters" in New Orleans came from the resources of Lake Pontchartran, the Mississippi River, and the Gulf of Mexico which activated real concern for the Federal Emergency Management Agency (FEMA) of the U.S. government. The tax dollar cost of FEMA, and recovering damages is, and was an increasing factor (c/o exceeding $50 to $100 billion dollars) with certain other increasingly destructive disasters that must be stabilized. Our American government, and most logical professionals especially with appropriated United States government tax dollar funded engineering, and construction projects has very few excuses (c/o contingencies) not to consist of better levels of liability.

The American regions of the Gulf States having a percentage of land compounded within the Gulf of Mexico waters, the vast amount of tax paying industries such as American offshore oil drilling rigs, wild sea life fishing, and other industry's within shipping ports suffered damages during the 2005 Hurricane Katrina. A vast amount of these damages where financially insured except for the logical fact that most homes near the shores, and on the land suffered tremendous damage as well. It also consisted of vast amounts of uninsured American citizen owned properties, and taxpayers losing their lives, and assets. These tax dollar, and tax payer issues have implemented stressful times from this American disaster that some people could not survive living thru due to the massive paper work requirements. Considering this, the restructuring will be tremendous. The city of New Orleans resides below sea level, and therefore the factual logic that occurred is that a majority of houses, and some business facilities where under water, and or relocated by water with the highest level of wind, contamination, and water damages.

American accumulated tax dollars, and liquidity has been a troublesome factor in other regions of the United States including with certain factors of Corporate America. When the term

Corporate America is used it's a working factor of massive business earnings, tax filing procedures, and societal responsibilities. At this time the term, and concept is near bankruptcy, or in the mist of cash liquidity problems (c/o tolerance) within business, and government restructuring from the severely "bad factors of markets, and decisions". This has become the formal logic that the United States government can not bailout all businesses, or corporations especially within those that do not do so good, or that don't maintain productive business values. Bad business is like bad government that is factored "with" some things that must go, and some people that must be dealt with or replaced to maintain business or corporate American stability. This becomes vital when the proper capacity of others including people within issues is to correct any wrong doing, or issues of abuse to a government office, or the business that is inevitable to survival. These become issues that are shared by the good, bad, rich, poor, educated or uneducated of all people making the best effort not to destroy the American values of our society, businesses, and government.

Upon these government issues, and considerations just as Ray Nagan the former Mayor of New Orleans, and Mike Brown formerly of FEMA, and others missed something important with "hurricane Katrina" most every near-by taxpaying citizen suffered including some plans of their retirement. This also includes how the cost of gas, and oil went up in cost severely after this hurricane damage had effected certain oil producing American regional states. The tax dollar funding for the Federal Emergency Management Agency (FEMA) disciplines of procedures should not have failed with other government offices, and professionals concerning this subject. FEMA's Mike Brown, and Ray Nagan the former mayor are government officials separately, but both of these people, and others where part of the American society of complacent officials that did not care to worry until things had totally went bad. We may as well include a few company's like the BP Company, and a certain amount of their corporate officials like Tony Hayward their Chief Executive, whom understands the oil business, but he could not control safety, and other oil production issues in American. Although after BP's 2nd very serious fatal accident in 5 years (2005 & 2010) causing America grief they also did not seem to worry until the disaster was imminent to all, but they stayed committed to the problem. The consideration of other disasters includes banks, and airline company's filing bankruptcy, and seeking bailouts from the United States federal government. Contrary to complacent problems these are part of the millions of hard working Americans pushing the work to restructure what they can to have a retirement, a safer workplace, and environment with a productive future.

Other problems effecting Texas, and Mississippi besides hurricanes where the issues of the Enron Corporation, and the WorldCom Corporations worker's including investor's that lost all their invested money, and retirement savings from the company. A theoretical fact is that these two company's only operated for about 10 years with $10s of billions of dollars "each" from corporate American cash holdings from various corporate mergers. Social Security might help the suffering of the taxpayers that qualify, but others may be a long way from that point, especially considering the taxes normal people pay apart from the equation of corporate merged dollars that defaulted. Also this means tax revenue for government became a default of liquidity. This is part of the 2000 decade which consist of these factored problems upon the observation of what government can do, or should do upon observing that financial losses continued. Therefore it will mean the stakes are high, almost at the capacity of life, or death that describes what is "now" a bad economic recession.

Understanding these concerns one statement by the U.S. Supreme Court Justice William Brennan Jr. provided in a conclusion becomes relevant for the conflicts within the taxpaying American society. His observation had a valued concern for taxpaying Americans, and the American society that is balanced with the United States Constitution as he stated; the United States Constitution Grants Power, Limits Power, and Protects

Against the Abuse of Power. Surely before the 2008 recession Abuse of Power was rapid. During 2006 the Chief Justice of the U.S. Supreme Court John Roberts acknowledged a statement that the United States Supreme Court is a place for the common people of America to have prosperity, not just for the rich, and powerful. Contrary to this considerate statement unemployment has reached a percentage that is only to be compared to the Great Depression, and that includes certain veterans of foreign war.

Observing these concerns even the concept of the U.S. Department of Defense solder's, sailors, air patrol, and other officers including various civilians from time to time not earning the most money in America are occasionally suffering. These people like others occasionally are to be recognized by the highest courts in government, but some have become a loss within opportunities of being productive taxpaying citizens. This is vital to understand within how it applies to other citizens that can be valued with justice helping the American society become more prosperous with business stability. Therefore the highest courts have a duty if certain legal issues with damages occur, but this is the concern where lawyers don't care to work for free unless the reward is valuable. Considering these issues it is vital that the American small businesses are included in this valid concern due to sacrifices, and commitments that are invested in their business to survive these economic times, and pay taxes.

These factual issues within business, and government are also becoming a long term tax payer financial bailout issue. In addition this includes most factors upon the relatively important issue of social restructuring which consist of the U.S. Constitutional rights of citizens, and their sacrifices to achieve social progress. This was a relevant conflict even to the extent of Ken Lay, and the Enron Corporation which left American citizens, and it's employees including investors suffering before his prosecution, and death. Considering this, the taxable workers of the American society has had to share the cost effect of this, and other corporate losses within being very expensive social problems upon taxable progress. All working Americans including military personal, and the valued concept of family's have a duty to observe, and at most times pay taxes. Therefore this became the format to settle these social economic problems including those connected to company's like Enron Corporation, WorldCom Corporation, and a few others.

Taxable income, and tax appropriations are vital factors of important subjects within defending the United States during the years of the 1990s, and 2000s upon which vitally includes other times, and the present. Observing the Persian Gulf War that America is fighting, and funding between 2003, and 2007 upon which $85 billion dollars has been spent on "Defense Contractors" and this is not including the pay earnings that the military personal receive for their services, this is part of America's budget crisis. Also an observation of (c/o 1978) the percentage of the estimated American population within 219,103,000 people that paid income taxes, and other types of taxes becomes the formal logic of accumulated government revenue, and a surplus of savings. Then this is observed within how so many important things in government are financially managed, and funded. The population today during 2009 is more than 310,500,000 with unemployment at about 9.5% of working aged citizens. Between the executive, legislative, and judicial branches of government this is a large concept within the budgets, planning, estimates, and other appropriate decisions by the American system of government, and some business officials.

The United States population has increased, but it is relevant to say that the amount of tax dollars paid into the system during 2000 has increased with various consolidated conflicts, and numbers. This factual consideration is due to the fact that millions of illegal aliens have migrated to America especially from Mexico with certain complex good, and bad agendas being pursued against the American society. In 2005 the Mexican immigration estimated population was about 10,000,000 (millions) new Mexican's illegally in America working, and some being an illegal burden to society. Some of these Mexicans where even heavily involved in crime, "contrary" to the fact that some became American citizens. A discreet observation within Mexican immigrants is that, the taxable earned income they made consisted of a vast amount of these people that paid no taxes with no Social Security numbers. Considering this acquired fact they were part of a problem that they rarely ever provided an economic positive adjustment into the state, and or federal tax base, and accumulated tax funds with lawful observation.

During the last thirty to forty years the United States has established the International Monetary Fund from American tax dollars which helped certain international concerns. Observing international support funded money, this problem of illegal immigrants has "defeated the logical purpose" of tax contributions that the American society has appropriated money for. Another problem is immigrants that get involved only in crime is a problem, but even more so terrorist acts that destroy American assets, and people become a serious tax dollar burden as well. Therefore within these good, and bad international concerns, and valued tax dollar resources to support the American economy, the U.S. government must enforce the laws that will protect this American issue of equity.

American small, and large businesses including public or private corporations throughout the United States have organized, and provided diversified leadership within tax dollar values of accumulation, and growth for decades, and some concerns over a few centuries. How corporations more so then some small businesses provide value to the tax base in America is the diversified concentration of providing secured employment (c/o even in government) to millions of citizens that may start, and operate their own business productively becomes vital to the future. In addition the United States government, and all individual state governments receive tax revenue from this gross income of established resources within net accumulated earnings. These tax resources also include certain things such as inventory, and various property that the American people as citizens, and others such as businesses own. Considering these issues of tax rates, and payments from public, and private businesses, corporations, and others, the government receives adequate funds to operate, and govern the American people, society, and diversified business issues in a lawful way.

During the 1990s, and the years of 2000 to 2009 the American corporate atmosphere has achieved certain up's, and down's in their marketing procedures. Observing the small businesses of America these times considering the bad economy within markets, and government issues has cause problems for business to expand. This also gives acknowledgement that tax accumulated dollars within currency are compiling a loss. The more American people, and property ownership values that exist, this is factored with the increase of more tax dollars that are a valuable concern with management duty's for the American society discipline within productive growth, and earnings. During the better times of American economic discipline, and prosperity the small, and large corporations, and businesses find themselves working productively together, and this offers value to all the people involved. We must remember that some of the better corporations such as, General Electric Corporation, United States Steel Corporation, Ely Lilly Corporation, Marathon Oil Corporation, Hess Corporation, Del Monte Food Company, McDonalds Corporation, and other businesses invest money for future expansion to increase financial stability, and prosperous business resources. Considering the "American Banking" society including these, and other establishments this has been a time of complicated issues to achieve any type of business expansion where tax revenue dollars can provide prosperous resources of government. This formal concept of product, and or financial expansion, and stability is a worrisome factor that must improve for small businesses as well as it exist for large businesses. Contrary to the complex business atmosphere some small, and large companies have achieved efficiency.

Understanding American investment banking, and local commerce banking establishments most all have accumulated vast amounts of problems during their 2007-2008 quarterly taxable income values of profitable earnings. This also includes losses on annual income earnings within reviews due to delinquent credit, and mortgage lending which is also valued thru market resources. This vitally includes certain foreign business, and social issues of concern. These factual issues are part of the American employees, and citizen losses with issues of business slow down's within lawful prosperity, and economic agreements of manageable income. The investment bank Bear Stearns and its investment banking establishment was the 84 year old financial brokerage firm that has accumulated hundreds of millions of dollars in losses during 2007. These Bear Stearns "investment bank" business losses came from delinquent bank credit issues, and mortgage lending conflicts with "Mortgage Backed Securities" that was recently managed improperly.

Observing January of 2008 Bear Stearns the investment bank had to disclose a $1.9 billion dollar quarterly loss of write downs. Within the format of procedures during the next 6 months James Cayne the Chief Executive Officer of Bear Stearns investments would step down, and then a vast amount of layoffs started to become the process of restructuring. Understanding the investment banking business this may have consisted of the company buying out their existing broker employee contracts that becomes very expensive, and complex. Therefore the increase in taxable commitments becomes applicable to earnings that consist of too many extensively combined losses. This process of implementation was a problem from the bottom to the top of the taxpaying employees that where then subjected to looking for other means of employment. Then the conclusive result is that financial relief to compensate their employment corporate loss values, and individual livable standards, had to be restructured.

Understanding the employees of Bear Stearns Investment Bank needing helpful decisions, and the consideration as taxpaying citizens, the company Bear Stearns was now in the corporate trouble of their life by needing to ask the United States government for a financial bailout. This was something that they all knew they totally could not depend on; "similar" to a business partner or their investor's concept of opinions, and the occasional good, and sometimes bad decisions they made. The United States government, and most local governments are not big on bailing out (c/o some bankruptcies) most of the financially troubled businesses of America easily. The Federal Deposit Insurance Corporation (FDIC) only bails out local member bank customers to a guaranteed limit of liability to all account depositors of the failing insolvent banks. These are funded deposits "Backed By The Full Faith & Credit Of The United States Congress", and Government. Stock brokers, and their firm's are not guaranteed and backed by the Full Faith and Credit of the U.S. Congress, and government which it's applicable commitment with the FDIC is conditionally different.

Ten years before June, and December of 2007, and 2008 large brokerage firms where paying most top professional brokers large bonus's ($10,000.00, $100,000.00, to $1,000,000.00 +) but now a vast amount are lucky to have a job. Directly behind Bear Stearns was Merrill Lynch and their ex-CEO Stan O'Neal. Then within these bailout issues of hard times this overwhelmed Citigroup, and their ex-CEO Charles Prince with his resignation, and this was repeated with other bankers that also suffered from these bad credit market conditions. Therefore with these massive corporate banking losses, and massive financial fraud conditions, the American economy for a large percentage of people has lately provided a depressed environment with struggles to overcome.

The United States credit markets, mortgage markets, and financial markets upon others (c/o the 2000s) have dealt the American economy, and system of taxation subjective concerns for years to come. A valuable consolidation of business in America is that if most large businesses suffer a vast amount of the time the small business, and citizens will suffer also. Local government throughout the United States of America within small towns, and cities are finding this problem critical to their money circulation, and taxable incentives. Small banks are represented in a regulated professional government lending capacity by the same issues as large banks (c/o Articles of Incorporation), and the United States Federal Reserve Bank system considering this can slightly be observed (c/o the FDIC) in most all rural cities, and town banks.

It is important that small to large towns with productive businesses maintain banking, and tax dollar circulations so that the security of equity is protected, and managed. This is also true in large metropolitan areas with larger issues of unlawful business competition, and then this routinely causes disruption in most stable markets, and secured taxable businesses. Understanding this, a vast amount of markets (c/o U.S. Anti-Trust law concerns) within markets such as in real estate, and mortgage bank lending during the first part of 2000 have suffered conditions of diversified, and rational financial manipulation. This has put a lack of trust in most banking, and business consumer issues of productive concern, and other factual long term financial complex issues including conflicting equity. The resource within consumers is one important consideration, but investors have been occasionally misguided as well due to tax issues, and foreign conflicts pursuing matters to penetrate control of various American investments, properties, and certain diversified businesses. Therefore the tax dollar accumulations, and support is valued to certain foreign businesses including people, and then Americans are left behind unless the American system of government including the vital nature of the courts, and judiciary enforce the laws.

Suffering has been inevitable within various American businesses including the American people as taxpaying constituents being the observation of foreign control taking up American tax dollar valued corporations. Businesses such as Zenith Corporation, Amoco Oil Corporation, Bethlehem Steel Corporation, and Inland Steel Corporation suddenly became part of an American tax revenue issue of losses. This also vitally included coal mining companies, and more so certain retail department stores such as Montgomery Ward's, and Service Merchandise which have been vital factors within appropriated losses to the American tax revenue values of accumulated support. These two retail stores where more than likely part of an Endless Loop Crisis with "maybe" Anti-Trust law violations that seem to even put Best Buy Corporation, Circuit City Corporation, and others on the American map of businesses before they failed. Actually them, and a few others looked more so like incompetent market manipulators or cheaters, but their businesses had relevance. Considering these issues another vital example is the (Mittal Steel) International Steel Group, the International Coal Group, and the proprietorship of owners within Wilber Ross, Lakshmi Mittal, and a few others. These Corporate American (c/o more so foreign business) within people made a vast amount of business sales, or purchases (c/o business transactions or corporate takeovers), which were slightly out of regulated control in America.

Wilber Ross bough into American steel manufacturing, and coal mining, but he did not have strong interest in managing or restructuring a steel manufacturing business with troubles. From Wilber Ross with International Coal Group to Lakshmi Mittal (c/o Inland Steel, LTV, & Bethlehem Steel) with both of their merger creation of International Steel Group gave Lakshmi Mittal opportunity to gain control of various American steel manufacturing companies that became questionable. Lakshmi Mittal then had more concern to control international business assets, and then leveraged $40 billion dollars on these American business assets (c/o bank lending) to purchase another foreign steel maker. This was the accumulated reduction conflict of American tax revenue including other things that existed from LTV Steel Corporation, Inland Steel Corporation, and Bethlehem Steel Corporation. Upon this concept of considerations within their good, or bad U.S. domestic and international conditions of value that have partly caused government conflict, certain U.S.

national security matters where evident, considering also very few American investors made money from the transaction.

Considering this taxable business format within issues, these factors of taxable business in the United States also consist of a vast amount of Americans working for these taxable groups, or businesses whom have a strong foreign interest that is dangerously complex. It's also important to remember that some of these company's do business with certain state governments, and the United States federal government as defense, and other subjective contractors. Believing certain conflicts, this support is constantly valued with these businesses, or their complex constituency now appropriating their corporate headquarters in other countries other than some located in the United States. Considering this tax dollar diversion with all small nonpublic businesses making effort to increase earnings, and tax revenue that is supporting a foreign consideration of facts, the American society is now losing what use to be large components of support from the American tax base of resources. This looks like the International Monetary Fund, and certain foreign groups of people have conducted, and achieved a "Corporate Hostel Takeover" of a vast amount of corporate American small, and large (c/o some franchise) businesses. The corporate takeovers have consisted of certain retail stores, petroleum businesses, and manufacturing business entities with American products, and commodities such as gas, oil, steel, and communication systems. In addition, this therefore also consist of ownership values at boardroom, and business (c/o stock ownership) controlling stakes. This puts most common taxpaying citizens, and some local governments in financial worries that you might comparably discover in other countries. Upon these factors, American's have consolidated less accumulated tax dollars, and are suffering bad conflicts within their format of government, and the American economy.

Our American tax dollars, and economy that combines all of the American resources of logical income, and commodities consist of certain values of established disciplines upon understanding the observed workers, commodities, and businesses. Considering this outline of factual conditions, theoretically the American society, and world will consist of changes, but due to accumulated American tax dollars, "hopefully" it will always be for the better of governed duties, and not the governed wrongful worse of conditions.

CHAPTER TWO

TAX DOLLARS APPROPRIATED FOR THE STATE'S & THE U.S. FEDERAL GOVERNMENT

The state, and federal tax dollars of the American system of government within the United States are appropriated for the many important, and valued government subjects within all aspects of society, and American life. Understanding the American government tax funds, and accounts that are important to pay expenses, purchase product supply's, and render service's including pay government wages, and salaries, lately it has also consisted of bailing out citizens, and more so corporate businesses, and certain banking institutions. This is done by the managed tax dollars from the diversified concept of citizens, all types of businesses, and surplus budgets from the U.S. federal government. These are the vital input, and output of tax dollar revenue issues upon resources throughout the American society that the President and the U.S. Congress had to pass a bill, and agree to the terms of this process, and transaction. These terms consisted of the businesses, banks, and corporations that the U.S. government (c/o the Congress) approved for bailout money, and the procedures within how they must pay the money back in good terms. Therefore this money, and lending terms of conditional agreements would put money back into the United States federal governments conditions of Treasury similar to tax revenue.

All the American cities, towns, states, and the U.S. federal government including a few other territorial bounders consist of the people paying these tax duty resources of a governed money circulation. These issue's of government money is part of the accumulated values of government liquidity. No lawful part of the American system of government in the United States is denied these considerations of appropriated money, and support especially when the regional government is applicable, and involved. This becomes one of the many logical reasons of format that politics, and government must work properly with agreeable terms, and the logic of disagreeable concerns that apply solutions. Observing these corporate businesses that did receive bailout government loans of money most all have provided business resource conditions throughout the United States, and some parts of the world. These issues within ethical government decisions, and commitments for the American society where considered to help the U.S. economy and certain lawful business prosperity survive.

Observing the geography of the United States not to mention the world that we live in, the American system of taxation is appropriated federally for 48 mainland U.S. individual state governments. Also Alaska, Hawaii, the Virgin Islands, and other overseas (U.S. island and possession) territories are governed in a taxable capacity from the United States federal government. Considering the format of taxes, liquidity, and bailouts all these levels of government concern are conditional to a State of Emergency. The state of Emergency issues are valued when disaster strikes in its many different conditions, and capacity of contingent damages. This important tax dollar output resource concern within tax appropriations of money to support local or regional liquidity during the 1990s, and 2000s has tapped this factual priority, and problem many times. Observing these social, and business issues of an emergency the concept of government liquidity could have been more stable if more public, private businesses, and government would have kept more markets, and resources productive. Therefore businesses, wages, taxable income, and other lawful opportunities where governed, and this caused a lack of productive, and prosperous values in America and its circulation of money.

Tax appropriations, expenditures of money, and services for disasters with most State of Emergencies, and a normal rate of government business has consisted of watching, and warning the people of nature that can be harmful or dangerous to society, and the infrastructure. These levels of caution consist of issues within the effects of flooding, tornados, mudslides, earthquakes, hurricanes, and other problems in our society of natures atmosphere . See, how we value this in the American society of public, private businesses, and various government concerns is that a vast amount of subjects, and events can become unsafe, and dangerous in a relatively short amount of time. Making judgment as concerned citizens or even employees of certain businesses to help each other is a vitally productive factor, but the tax appropriations, and deductible items from the state, and federal government makes these helpful efforts part of the responsible liability that American's depend on. Throughout some neighborly or helpful issues of recovering from severe problems of weather, or social problems are valued as being part of a "good corporate or business citizenship" capacity of public duties when appropriate.

Most occasions within disasters, and recovery this includes insurance on some very complex or expensive items, and assets, but this can be a vital resource for the citizenship or taxpayer values that American's are appropriated! We also recognize this consideration of tax duties within the good, and more so bad roadway, waterway, or utility infrastructures, and equipment that lately have been part of the problem of an obsolete U.S. infrastructure. These utility infrastructure issues have been helpful, but with conflicts during various disasters, or conflicting weather. This is the necessity for most all government appropriations, and expenditures, but local governments, individual states, and the U.S. federal system of taxation is part of this money circulation. Considering this government tax revenue income, this keeps valued assets including various residential, and commercial business resource's astute as the American society cannot exist without these tax economic issues of value.

Within the total observation of state, and federal income taxes during the 1990s, and the years of 2000 most all issues of tax expenditures, and appropriations including tax deductible items are relevant concerns established from gross income. These are values within the American system of government where the state and federal Department's of Treasury, and the Internal Revenue Service compile tax collections for the "Governments base of Revenue". As we observe more detail within businesses (as well occasional personal tax percentages) the issue of the itemized tax, and the standard tax deductions becomes vitally important within gross income earnings if business activities are more than the estimations by government (c/o IRS), and tax revenue collections. During the years between 2005 thru 2010, government tax revenue have decreased similar to corporate, and small business losses in revenue which is observed by the U.S. Treasury, the U.S. Federal Reserve, and various people. Understanding this, the consolidation of businesses, and citizen's providing government tax revenue is vital, but the equations are relevant for all things of substance. This was conflicting due to the loss of various businesses between the 1990s throughout 2008. This then has forced tax payable citizens into a correctional format of lawful, and unlawful equations.

Observing the IRS, and the U.S. government system of tax exemptions, and tax deductible items most conditions of business, and American social issues are reasonably considered, and observed by businesses, and individuals with tax concerned resources. Upon this reliable factor this is vitally considered because between business, and personal tax deductions a person's state, and federal income taxes can be lower when claiming various itemized deductions. This makes the standard tax deduction an appropriate consideration with valued decisions by most all taxpaying citizens. Within the evaluated review for itemized deductions these issues are financially applied to the economics of tax filing preparation by claiming your standard deductions, this can and must be evaluated for having a positive logical financial tax refund. This is relevant upon what may be a productive small business resource of citizenship duties consolidated with or observed as normal taxable income, and earnings.

Some of the relevant American "Internal Revenue Service" (IRS) issues of itemized deductions consist of investment interest, and expense deductions including charitable contributions. In addition other important deductions consist of casualties, and or theft conditions, but this is not to forget various employee business expenses. To go further with understanding the different definitions between "tax deductions", and tax incentives" becomes very helpful. The Tax Deduction; is a subtraction from gross income in arriving at taxable income. A deduction differs from a tax credit in the perception that a deduction reduces taxable income, and a credit reduces tax liability. The "Tax Incentive"; is a government taxing policy intended to encourage a particular activity (c/o mortgage financing of real estate) which becomes valuable to both individuals, and businesses. Therefore these tax planning evaluated factors are within certain guild line details of the American system of government which apply to people, and even businesses with various tax beneficial resources.

The concept of mortgage financing within real estate including the sale's of property is a tax manageable concern due to the fact that real estate is occasionally an investment due the type of equity that may have a certain agenda. Various taxes are paid on the purchase of new, and or existing real estate, and this is a formal value within government tax revenue. As tax credits are involved, an investment tax credit provides a diverse issue of relevance. The type of equity in a house is slightly different from the equity in a business. Considering the Investment Tax Credit it was established as a reduction in federal taxes for purchasing certain property, which was primarily for equipment. The objective in providing the investment credit was created to encourage companies to make acquisitions resulting in a stronger economy. The Tax Reform Act of 1986 repealed the investment tax credit for property acquired after January 1, 1986 with some exceptions for transition property. Most of these tax filing disciplines, and procedures changed a certain part of the process of filing taxes which took place between 1988, and 1995.

The reason why government has duties besides most all executive, legislative, and judicial branches of American government is for various values including the importance of government services like explaining taxes, and even improvements to the infrastructures. This is the logic applied to a well developed, and lawfully productive society. These government assets, and issues of discipline have all kinds of resources which continuously need tax dollar expenditures. Some of these factual duties, and assets within the managing of roadways, railroads, bridges, dams, shipping ports, street lights, and other structures with material's, or supply's are valued as important details. These infrastructure components are required within government regulation to be observed as safe, and managed with professional minded citizens. This applies to most conditions of a logical format concerning the up grading or maintenance process procedures.

The U.S. Army Corps of Engineers have been an important part of dams and river waterway resources in America, but their work with others have been in conflict similar to the U.S. Department of Energy, and the U.S. Department Interior duties which have a logical need of improvements. There is rarely any misguided discrepancies besides complacent government that occurs because this becomes the vital concern of liability by the people as citizens just as concerns existed with the electrical blackout that effected most all the citizens of the east coast during 2003. Estimate's of this U.S. regional blackout where around $6 billion dollars in losses in 8 states for citizens, businesses, and government applicable to utility companies. The enormous amount of storm water issues is factored with the U.S. Department of Interior, and U.S. Army Corps of Engineers. This is the fact within events of how we have observed a lack of utilities, roadway specifications, building codes, and government engineering duties applicable to danger or inadequate liability. All levels of the cities, towns, states, and the federal government usually apply the maintenance cost in their annual, or emergency budget expenses.

Upon this format within dangerous building codes, and conditional government structures which including infrastructure assets, this can make certain subdivision communities of houses vulnerable within liabilities. These issues of liability keep people, and their assets safe from various activities such as high wind causing damages, or flooding that overcomes the logical use of the roads, houses, or buildings that should withstand acts of nature. This is a logical evaluation of most building codes in most regional cities, and towns which are applicable to state, and federal government guild-lines where citizens can be vulnerable to problems. Considering so many obsolete infrastructures that apply to water, and storm water this American society of today did not withstand certain weather conditions considering this was a loss in liquidity for various people including the government. A circumference of tax dollar currencies, and the professional or occupational disciplines of government codes, and specifications from engineering, architecture, and construction levels of efficiency are vitally important in these concerns. Upon a format of logic, this helps to save, and or adjust these property, public health, and casualty concerned issues of most American communities. Therefore this applies also to a certain capacity of the rich, poor, insured, and uninsured people of America, and their contingent liability factors of liquidity, and livable standards.

Observing the state of Illinois (c/o other states) within certain new subdivisions of houses, and some renovation projects that were severely overlooked within the importance of building codes, and the evaluation of proper government specifications, a vast amount of regulatory problems occurred. South of the city of Chicago, Illinois for about five years or so during the late 1990s, numerous residential subdivisions of new houses were destroyed by tornados. This was factual due to certain inadequate geographical building standard codes, and various problems that became evident. Another resource of problems occurred which was factually observed when certain mid-west thunderstorms, and tornados occurred, and destroyed everything possible in various regional areas. Thunderstorm's, and tornado's are a lot more complex to withstand even with certain building requirements applied geographically. Considering this concern which caused certain facilitated, and asset damages within disasters the result of this natural storm system of nature is relevant to every precaution necessary to stay out of the way which becomes important. It's vital to remember that these storms can be very dangerous, but some American built structures have been able to withstand some of these forceful winds, winding twisters, and high and low temperatures of weather including thunder storm conditions. The quality of material is a factor with construction company disciplines working with professionals to provide building codes with quality standards that is also a considerable problem with government values of these factual levels of disaster.

Then in certain locations (with occasional government conflicts) building ordinance issues observing certain structure's, and facility use concerns became considerably dangerous. A concept of this factual problem vitally included a variation of conflicts within residential and commercial establishments within the city of Chicago which their mayor Richard Daley did not enforce properly with city administrators. One severe problem occurred when an outside porch collapsed, and killed more than 20 people. They had also exceeded the maximum amount of people, and load specifications that the porch could hold during a party. This was a problem that repeated its self a vast amount of times no matter if the specified weight capacity was observed. Also this government problem existed more than the normal logic of timing, and with dependable "looking" structures having logical long-term need of structural liability. This then became a vital tax payer issue that should have been observed before this fatal problem became a subject to be corrected. These residential and commercial building code problems became out of control due to complicated government officials not pursuing the best possible solutions, and duties. Considering this the city government of Chicago had to crack down on as many of these facility structures with their building inspectors as much as possible, but the lack of good, and more so bad issues of structural work still lingered in remote areas. Therefore tax dollar liabilities became an expensive, and dangerous issue no matter where, and who may be effected, but all facilities with building permits "which is local government revenue" should have been reviewed, outlined, and considered better. This was a vital duty by the occupants, owners, and occasionally more so the city government of Chicago.

These factors of inappropriate building code duties also include when certain nightclub fatalities, and their businesses, and customers suffered with damages from buildings occupied within the maximum level of people required by law. Enormous tax dollars are appropriated to insure the American society that these bad conflicts don't occur which was part of massive fatalities in an environment of entertainment, and social comfort. Over twenty people died after a fight, and a stamped of people rushing to the door when a Chicago Southside (E2) nightclub entertained more people in their facility then the city law requires. Theoretically these are conditions of liability, and a full lack of protecting the liquidity of the American society of assets, and people that are relevant to the tax appropriated decisions of local, state, and some federal government concerns. Considering these unusual facts, there where tax dollars appropriated, but a lack of government inspections became dangerously late for citizens. The logical concept of business liquidity was threatened, and destroyed upon which therefore liability was not valued with lawful significance.

Considering small, and large local governments, and their tax appropriation processes, liability between the businesses, and citizens consist of a vast amount of calculated equations for most all government duties. Usually this has budget disciplines that are reviewed in a legislative, and government format. Most city, county, state, and U.S. federal legislative objectives require the executive office's administration to use, and manage these tax dollar appropriated funds to protect asset liquidity, and the liability of citizens, government, and how it applies to most all property. The consideration of government, and it's Separation of Powers most times make decisions from the valued opinions of the required people as citizens. This becomes the factor within American local, and or state tax paying citizens that should be guided, and provided with the best possible services (c/o the U.S. federal government) along with their citizenship duties.

The United States is divided into regional jurisdictions that geographically consist of state governments that are equal in duties, and powers of authority. All levels of individual state government's have interventions from the United States federal government which is the highest levels of formal government, and their jurisdiction of power for the "American society, and system of government". Each state government supports the many cities, and towns understanding that this becomes the format to appropriate, and manage all levels of tax dollars received, invested, and put to lawful use. Legislative decisions for the rate of taxes to be paid, and the diversified tax funds that are accumulated, are done so with providing budgets within legislative factors by elected officials, and the people. These issues are important to observe considering how the tax dollars, and liquidity will prevent government, and business bailouts that qualify.

The highest to the lowest types of bailouts in America has been the format of severe problems where people, property, and the laws have been effected with severe damage, or issued problems. The wars that America has had before the 1800s (c/o 2001) was a start to understand vital, and important government bailout's. The major fire that destroyed a vast amount of buildings with fatalities, and people in the city of Chicago during 1871 was another major disaster that can be compared to a bailout. This is where certain levels of society, and constituents of government had to step in with certain appropriate funds. The hurricane and flooding of Galveston, Texas during 1900 killed 6000 people which had to be rebuilt for the survival of American human life existence, which enhanced the oil industry, and shipping distribution was a similar disaster. During the 1940s the Pearl Harbor attacks on United States Naval ships, and American civilians at the naval base in Hawaii accumulated a severe amount of problems within injuries, fatalities, and damage of all kinds. The Pearl Harbor attack was resolved with an executive order, and war which covered more than a bailout, even more so if you observe September 11, 2001. Government appropriations of tax dollar liquidity have helped these type of issues for well over 2 century's, but liquidity losses apply, and should be recognized.

Considering the Pearl Harbor attacks by Japanese war fighter planes, this was part of World War II, and government tax dollars that had to be used to fund another war, and defense for the citizens which included the national security of the United States "which was" eminent to American defense. Also the city, and government assets including the people had to be cared for with medical treatment during the fighting defense of this violent attack against America. This was different from the supportive cost, and parts of the city, and state including the United States Naval equipment that had to be replaced although the U.S.S. Arizona that still stands, is evident of American defense, and it's tax funded liabilities. Also following the Pearl Harbor attacks in 1941 the United States government put forth more tax dollars with the establishing of the U.S. Central Intelligence Agency (CIA) to secure, and defend America. Upon complacent government the CIA fail to prevent both World Trade Center terrorist attacks, (c/o 1992, and 2001) with other conflicts on September 11, 2001. These facts considering other things that were destroyed concerning the American liquidity that needed protective support, and manageable disciplines became a relevant consideration of tax dollar valued duties thru government.

Observing, and considering the defense of the United States certain war's, and attacks against America are not the only tax appropriated issues observing special engineering, and construction projects that certain regions in America required. Roadways that connect to state, and federal highways is one vital example including toll roads, bridges, and drainage systems. These are the issues of city, county, state, and more so the United States federal government assets of liquidity that are built, and managed by engineers, geologist, construction workers, and a few others. Understanding large structures like the Hoover Dam between the State's of Arizona, and Nevada which includes thousands of other dams these federal tax dollar funded projects where done to serve certain special utility needs such as electricity, and water retention conditional resources. Between Boston, and going towards New York during 1991 to 2003 a large highway tunnel project (I-90) was built underwater through Massachusetts, and to other states due to some other aging roadway travel concerns of safety. Considering how safe you would like to be riding in a car, or truck deep underwater in a tunnel, some government funded projects will find a logical, and professional way for appropriate existence. This was a tax dollar project costing around $14.6 billion dollars; considering it had $10 billion dollars in cost overruns. Observing this professionally in a responsible government capacity for all levels of government from the local to the state support of the tax liquidity, these projects become part of the money circulation, and government duty to provide efficient roadways, and infrastructures.

For the last 100 years different tax dollar liability, and liquidity issues of taxation within the concern of engineering, and construction projects has been part of the good, and bad of inflation, and technology to improve society. Within what was observed during these decades, and years including some of the issues observed within the U.S. Presidencies of Bill Clinton, and George Bush a vast amount of technology was considered, but not to the most needed concerns. Besides the floods of New Orleans, there was more than 20 other states with vast amounts of flood problems that at one time years ago the American society of property owners where protected from better. To consistently appropriate the tax liquidity dollars into highways seemed good, but not "up-dating" waterway retention basin walls, and highway drainage systems caused severe flooding at various times. Therefore theoretically, and considerably the fish on the land, and in certain houses where surviving better then the people contrary to some new housing developments built on the banks of waterways.

The bulk of mid-west flooding vitally includes the waterways of the Great Lakes region upon which the accumulated water (c/o river and lake conditions) is occasionally growing out of control. A vital infrastructure consideration consisted of water retention levees, and retention basins which during 2008 lacked operating efficiency, and destroyed hundreds of millions of dollars of assets, and tens of thousands of people's property. Some of the other saddest flooding issues observed was throughout Indiana, and certain parts of the state of Kansas. Also Iowa has gotten hit bad along with certain parts of New Jersey that include some parts of Pennsylvania. The liquidity factor within the damage, and factual issues of liquidation where hard to consume economically, therefore the people had to find, and consider another process (c/o FEMA) of reorganizing their assets, and lives.

The more America builds new homes, manufacturing facilities, and even construct roads or highways with the concern of engineers, and constructors the more they take away, and arrange different cut and fill land component quantities from the earth. Also the rain water (c/o Army Corps of Engineers & Department of Interior) on land with accumulation's of compounded water increases every season, and year which includes these facts of concern where ignored geographically during the 1990s, and throughout the years of 2000. This is where government asset liquidity could have been used more effective before the expenses of the people needed additional help from the government to overcome a disaster. Even if you try to understand environmentalist with certain economic, and land remediation activity in America it becomes a bad balance when the fish are living better in people's homes, more so than the taxpaying property owners. These flood damages also leave contamination that can be dangerous for small children, and very tuff, and exhausting for senior citizens to clean up.

A few levels of caution are applicable to our American concern for safety is within the determination of "Professionals of Engineering and Construction" which have had days, and projects that loss liquidity, and the life of various people. A very important observation was the government funded project, and disaster of the Buffalo Creek Dam of West Virginia. This process within American infrastructure issues had a vital purpose, but the large dam collapsed killing more than 120 people, and destroying numerous homes in a small West Virginia coal mining valley, and community. Another federal government funded project that had trouble was the collapse of the Cline Avenue toll-way bridges in Northwest Indiana during the process of construction. During this 1984 construction accident of bridges that span over 100 feet in height in various places near certain steel mill operations, this area included certain wet lands where at least 15 workers were killed, with others injured. The United States Anti-Trust laws (c/o labor laws) holds taxes between business (c/o Engineering & Construction Contractors) logical, with "liability" so that infrastructures can be a productive circuit braking process against nature to keep citizens safe. Therefore dangerous anti-competitive practices should or could be eliminated.

Considering these problems of flooding, and roadway bridge issues that have taken people's lives, and cause damage (c/o being very helpful and logical to construction workers) all over the United States this is a collaboration of liability between the people, certain businesses, and government. Then this helpful concern of governed infrastructures is relevant, especially in certain regions where they are just beginning to figure out new, and different solutions of how to solve the rain water accumulation problems with expanding communities. Usually new developed communities have new roads, and sewers, but older areas usually require roadway and infrastructure maintenance, and up-graded new roadways which includes even sewer drainage components. Considering this, perfection in the individual states of America, and certain infrastructure improvements are vitally important subjects in the past, as well as the critical future of today.

Tax dollars appropriated to certain levels of government research, and how that research is applied to the many different parts of America occasionally has vital importance including safety. One thing that vast amounts of people may observe is that research conducted by scientist, professionals like engineers, doctors of internal medicine, and others such as geologist, and metallurgist usually have a direction of study to achieve a solution to a scientific problem. These solutions are then based on relevant factors of the Constitution of the United States, and lately the conflicting appropriations concerning liquidity within the logical Anti-Trust laws of liability within business, and contingent liability's to the general public.

A vast amount of the time the United States government, and sometimes a few other countries have observed, and outlined factors of research with certain colleges, universities, and certain businesses that work to create a format of the conditional solutions of that research. This provides products or services to be used with logical disciplines within the general public in a lawful, and or safe capacity. Such government tax dollar funded research projects like stem cell research, atom smashing compounds, and geological evaluated conditions of earthquakes, and hurricanes becomes important to the American general public as well. Also this valued research includes volcanic eruptions, and certain variations of tornados, and hurricanes that gives professionals, and the general public including government a provision of how to preserve, and protect the American society. Most people in this principal format, and concern of logical effect's, use's, and preventative resources of discipline consist of valued levels of awareness. These are matters to take into consideration when various subjects of possible danger will become helpful in society. Therefore this becomes the good, and more so bad within liability of American protected issues of asset valued liquidity unless things are not done in a rightful capacity.

Managing the liquidity within the American society has valuable concerns even as it applies to the 1st Amendment rights of religion, and free speech which also includes places of worship, and most logical organizations maintaining certain American values. The valued consideration, and moral establishments of church, and how it applies to the state, and federal government are factually considered, and observed within most family values. These family values are maintained, managed, and valued with these moral establishments of worship for all people. A factor of governed liability that is highly relevant with liable resources is the logical condition of marriage, and birth rights with certificates, and even death certificates. These American values of congregations in the church, and most civic organizations with clergy members, and government leadership provides enormous support with citizenship, and taxpayer duties that include the concerns of a well developed American society.

The basic format within church establishments that usually have a low to any effective tax rate factor due to nonprofit organization statues is a justifiable resource from the American society, and government respectfully. The beneficial obligations that church establishment's provide within children, senior citizens, and all others within their member congregation provides religious supported values, and guidance. Although the variation of religious studies, and opinions are broad, and sometimes aggressively different to a vast majority of the people, this nonprofit tax concern is relevant for social values, and identity. This also is relevant within the format applied to the lawful religious values that can be observed when these personal identity issues are found within the U.S. Congress not making or prohibiting law on logical religious establishments. Observing this the people find, and value the importance of solitude, and certain values of command ground with the laws including the 1st Amendment of the United States Constitution. These 1st Amendment issues provide governed disciplines of prosperous living in the American society that becomes relevant for most all religious worship upon which also includes logical free speech.

Some of the American religious scholars, and pastors such as Reverend Martin Luther King, Reverend Billy Graham, Reverend Robert Lowery, Reverend Pat Robertson, Pope John Paul (c/o Italy & the U.S.), Bishop Desmond Tutu (c/o South Africa & the U.S.) , and a few others used their first Amendment rights to express peace, and wisdom for all man-kind including human rights. A vast amount of these leaders of "Religious" establishments, and government have also served in the United States Armed Forces or at the capacity of Reverend Jesse Jackson, Andrew Young, or lawyers like Justice - Thurgood Marshall, and others as it applies to the American Civil Rights movement. Some even understand these issues from the atrocity of the Holocaust throughout Germany, and Poland during the years around 1943. These are values that the American government works hard to lawfully evaluate, and support within studies of moral, and war time atrocity. Therefore all of these people of the church (c/o government) applied leadership as it became their lawful concern to balance the American society of respectful culture, morals, and educational values. This was factored from the U.S. concentration of tax dollar supportive measures that gave most of them (tax-exempt) lawful opportunities within donations to do so as it applies to the U.S. Constitution.

The values of most conditions of church, and religious organizations from time to time also work, and support scholarships for dependable people, and the continued American studies of religion in a lawful capacity. Considering the different American state governments these concerns of religious values in the United States include certain studies which are retained for moral values. The concentration of these studies may be observed within certain logical establishments that are saturated in different parts of the world. This appropriates the disciplines, and concerns of religious scholars, and what they do to apply their duties as a clergy to the citizens, the American society, other countries, and more so their local congregations lawfully. Upon the nonprofit tax exemptions of money managed within religion, and the tax issues of these establishments, they are not highly taxable due to the provisions of contributions, and the activities that are not being considered taxable earned income. This important awareness is very different within the values of most every establishment in America, and most all of the public, or private businesses with the exceptions that church establishments also pay utility bills, and other expenses. Managing duties therefore becomes the distinct value of the commitment to any organization establishment including most households. Understanding this there are various conditions that apply to the taxable, and non-taxable resources of establishments in the American society.

As it is understood, and observed a church or business is not always the most likely social constituencies that any form of American government will easily bailout. Within the different rights of these establishments of more so religious values that are secrete, and solemn to peoples religious beliefs, their survival is thru contributions of grace, and church ties. This becomes relevant when there is overwhelming probable cause, and concern for the life of a church, and it's congregation to exist lawfully. Considering the governments logical understanding of most all religious establishments within America that are considered to be safe, and moral establishments, they usually have activity that exist without bad problems or conflicting fatalities. This occurs occasionally in other environments, and some businesses which have a lawful amount of different government issues that are applicable to government regulation. Upon this observation they have support from congregation members, and their resource within logical volunteers to support appropriate causes.

During this first decade of 2000 consisting of the new millennium certain business bailout issues have been factored with issues surrounding various church establishments with good members that need work in diversified social conditions that are applicable to various industries. Understanding this with disturbing evidence, and even the people that most all the time where negatively effected in society, the outreach of the church is usually were they most times find moral, and local support to overcome. Within the various levels of American social problems these people depending on the church also had to deal with these tuff economic times. Then some local businesses had an appropriate presence within time to occasionally recover. This decade within terrorizing evidence of harmful events consisted of most parts of the American society of business, and religious establishments finding certain ways to work hard, and appropriate their agenda to go forward. This was even more evident in the state of Texas with the Enron Corporation's former employees that had to occasionally depend on the church for food, and support after the Enron Corporation bankruptcy. In addition the level of determination of these people also includes how most businesses are separate from the church by its members, but moral appreciation is a very powerful concept of social discipline for most levels of respectful integrity.

Issues of things such as the weather not being completely a religious subject this format within American social problems is determined from the "force of nature", not completely an act of God. This is a conditional issue of concern because of the massive infrastructure conditions of America that have loss control over certain regional developments to deal with nature. These levels of control include issues of safety that where developed by man, and must be reconstructed with maintenance by man when obsolete. Man verses "Mother Nature" is full of these challenges. This also includes the ability for people, assets, and facilities to survive volatile weather conditions. Bad weather conditions mixed with foreign, and U.S. domestic threats to the American society is a tragic burden upon which this then applies to good observation, and hopefully not the bad of people including government decision making. These decisions apart from threats have been an array of issues to control, some bad religious issues, and more so government opinions. This is where "We The People" must support the good of American citizens with determination to survive productively apart from some bad foreign relation factors.

Upon this determination, it also applies to the other relevant issues of not being able to advance forward in the American society of today unless local government has served it's tax revenue appropriated duties, and therefore a managed resource within a well developed society is protected.

Observing a severe factor in the state government tax liquidity issues of today is how during 2008 the state capital building of Iowa suffered tremendously by floods, and was submerged underwater for 2 or 3 days. This State Capital facility of Dos Monies, Iowa is the vital concern of all taxpaying citizens of the State of Iowa, and a concentration of other resources of government. The Iowa flooded regions was some of the worse during 2008 which Indiana, and Illinois suffered also. This was the after mass from hurricane (Ike), and a storm surge that effected American southern states such as Louisiana, and Mississippi before coming to the northern states. This problem of government asset liquidity values to other citizens, and states including the U.S. government's valuable concern is to be corrected in the future with cost ranging from $10 to $80 billion dollars. Considering our American society, the problem that occurred in Dos Monies, Iowa has the American society, and states like Iowa, and Kansas concerned about future safety, and public health. There are some very important government, engineering, and geological details that have or will continue to destroy the American society that we live in if they are not detailed, and revised properly. This therefore means that certain regions of the United States are consistently facing a crisis from year to year. Therefore if someone says don't worry; they where occasionally, and severely wrong, "then" and now. Theoretically even more so they may be saying don't worry because they have a working process or level of ignorance for an enemy country to destroy America. Therefore more American professionals properly training other Americans will be one of the best solutions without conflict.

Now these issues of the United States government, and it's liquidity of future existence are factored with short term possible damages to a vast amount of expensive assets. Upon most complacent issues, this also means that not too many long-term stable conditions exist within these concerns that should provide safety, and equity. Then from any bad conditions of nature, and other problem's these are only a comfortable looking threat that requires levels of security, and good decision making. Understanding these observed factual conditions of losses in America, the government is also observing a loss, and this includes insurance companies that are also losing at severely high rates. Some local governments, and more so insurance companies will restructure productively if they maintain discipline in the economic budgets, and financial balance sheets of discipline with better levels of professionalism. Therefore this means that the tax dollar liquidity must be restructured by local, and state government for public, private businesses, and "yours truly" most all levels of the United States federal government.

CHAPTER THREE

SMALL & LARGE BUSINESS LIQUIDITY IN AMERICA

Considering the business liquidity of small, and large public, or private businesses of America, the concept of government bailouts, mergers, and even bankruptcies are major concerns during the first decade of 2000. These business, and government issues that have been around during the last century of changes throughout American businesses consist of various industry formats, and disciplines throughout society. Most American's and business owners are concerned about what will these values of economic liquidity in the American society consist of in the future. Public, and private corporations, and other small or large business issues that are regulated, and supported by the United States federal government are part of the local governments observation of prosperity. This includes the individual states that have suffered with the obligations of tax revenue, and budgets to financially survive. The rate of business survival, and successful disciplines for, and by Americans need to drastically improve with some adjustments to the laws concerning the years of 1995 thru 2000, and the future. Therefore the future good years will have to make up for the bad years or more so determine solutions from business years of the past to improve for the future. This vitally depends on if the best decisions are made by the American system of government with American business owners that are committed to lawful, and productive prosperity.

Business survival in America including most existing market competitive factors, and paying taxes is the relevant consideration of any successful financial bailouts, mergers, bankruptcies, and even prosperous earnings that will accomplish business, and government prosperity of solitude. This is also vital to the managing of certain issues within business, and government disciplines that gives us certain levels of socially productive values, and expanded opportunities of business success. Two large business issues of trying to maintain success during 2009 was Bank of America, and the Goldman Sachs Company upon which these banking institutions received $45 billion dollars each with the U.S. governments Troubled Asset Relief Program (TARP) funds. Money as Department of Treasury debt, and budget issues including the U.S. Federal Reserve lending policy to these, and other businesses (c/o Bank Holdings) to survive, "implies" that somewhere a vast amount of business planning objectives were not accomplished. Those banking business objectives that were not accomplished was mortgage lending projected earnings, and the Mortgage Backed Securities in investment banking that failed. Therefore considering the American market of mortgages with people, households, and small businesses failed due to an enormous amount of asset liquidity that was not accomplished!

Within the discipline of hard work, education, and other values to achieve the better parts of life, and business prosperity, the American society of business, and government could have done better maintaining liquidity. This is consistently based on the system of American "Constitutional" laws, and the prosperous conditions of certain businesses, and markets. After most all of these conflicting distractions a vast amount of corporate, and government constituents went to work truly trying to solve these problems. These banking and business values can, and should be evaluated in most all troubled businesses although some corporate lending from TARP funds have been paid back to the U.S. government in good timing. This does not mean all is well and done, but these values are appropriated with the necessary business, and social functions to maintain future good business planning, and earnings. Therefore with hopeful business, and employment expansion this becomes vital to all small, and large business factors of liquidity.

The issue, and term corporate merger is part of the logical concept of taxable businesses with procedures of factual "agreements and decisions to purchase", and then control the stock, and ownership of various combined company's. Our American society of the people, and businesses sometimes has been a factor of the good, bad, and occasionally out of control issues within employee factors of this management change, or leveled business procedure's within merger process discipline's. The investment underwriting of these merger / buyout issues that consist of large amounts of asset liquidity are partly observed by the U.S. Securities & Exchange Commission due to some conflicts of illegal greed. Within observing every obligation of business earning income that includes earning a taxable wage, and or salary the corporate equity, and cash values must be held steady. Then these certain values of change are consistent upon management changes within some corporate mergers, and buyouts.

The issues of tax matters exist, but investments in the "stock, and bond market exchanges" are a diverse tax issue including the American people whom find additional valued earnings within corporate mergers. Corporate buyouts of small or large American publicly held company's become money making issues that include taxable activity within various capital gain earnings, and taxable procedures. Even certain mom, pop, family businesses on occasions should consider thinking big or expanding with appropriate caution. Contrary to the fact, this format of mergers (c/o small or large investors or businesses) has been a financial issue that is occasionally out of control lately. This becomes the good, and bad discrepancy within corporate leveraging components of assets valued with liquidity.

Part of the real problem to the U.S. government, and various business society concerns is that American "Assets and Commodities" are being controlled and even damaged occasionally by too much foreign interest including certain enemy's of America. This concept of American commodities including mergers, and buyouts recently also puts discrepancy in most valued American employees of today, and into the future! Concerning these factors the employees of these involved businesses with their effort is to be organized in tax paying, and filing responsibilities is important, but the lack of some U.S. Constitutional laws being enforced have often become an overall "tax revenue issue, and employee downfall"! These relevant issues become the format of management business controlled values of ownership, and or issues of reorganizing business. Therefore the business consist of substantial government tax values, and most times this is observed in the principal market price of a company's stock, but the American people effect becomes the other vital subject.

Small, and large company's including their capacity of liquidity, and asset management values are clearly observed on occasions for the merger, corporate buyout, or business purchase procedures they may consider. This becomes the business concerns of the American society that have diversified effects. When this obligation of corporate, individual business, and or personal spending is a factor or concern within responsible future earnings, the new ownership acquires a set of diverse problems. These problems are consistent most all the time for the new ownership understanding within most legal, and business duties of managing this new business venture in a lawful capacity.

There is not many good examples lately of small business expansions which include mergers if you observe the business transactions between (SBC) Southern Bell Company, Ameritech, and the Bell Laboratory of (AT&T) American Telephone & Telegraph Corporation. Considering the business start of

Ameritech Corporation, this regional agreement concept of duties, and a certain percentage of assets that where acquired from American Telephone and Telegraph Corporation consisted of company owned stocks, bonds, and other assets including facilities. In addition this important fact consisted of certain equipment which maintained value within an agreement to service a regional telecommunication market with budget values of the FCC, and other government professionals. Most regional markets with tax issues, and other subjects become a complex reality of liability, liquidity, and professional disciplines. This also consisted of legal factors within SBC, AT&T and the government including corporate management conflicts to be reorganized that needed some consideration of corrections.

Before Ameritech the regional telephone service providers where Indiana Bell, Illinois Bell, Michigan Bell, Minnesota Bell, and a few more of around 23 other individual Bell Companies with different region disciplines including the Western Electric Company. This vitally included Bell Laboratories which was the research, and technical division of this monopoly of phone companies with duties to maintain, and establish product, and service liability. These technical issues of a large company like AT&T being reconsolidated into certain company's such as Ameritech (c/o SBC) were the format of strong business liquidity, and their asset management for expansion. This business with divesture concerns should have had more lawfully aggressive corporate decisions within planning for lawful progress in business. Considering their lack of lawful discipline, and certain business decisions the liquidity of assets after Ameritech's failure where relinquished back to the large dispute of AT&T, and SBC which cost the government less than some other conflicts that still have not been resolved.

The issue of liquidity expansion with certain internet companies have on occasion's monopolized certain markets which only vast amounts of other businesses have maintained prosperous growth expansion. The American society of business has a relevant consideration of most factors to advance their business quality, or increase assets, upon which this applies to most utility companies, and certain other tax dollar generating issues of America. Observing the prosperity of the U.S. Constitution, the citizens and their tax paying duties have only been shifted from one market strongly within information technology, and the internet. The internet, and utility companies are factual to be productive when they started with strong liquidity, and certain asset's. Understanding the expansion of most internet businesses, a vast amount of American's turn on the internet, just as much as they turn on the light's in their homes. This is the logic within understanding to manage, and increase their personal or business assets which is supportive liquidity in a productively expanding market.

Additional values, and liquidity are considered vitally when various corporate, or professional businesses include the format to lawfully protect themselves, and client's productively. These monopoly protection values within a lawful resource of any possible conditions of bankruptcy, and liquidation for the business, or clients are then the subjects upon research that creates part of the solution. This becomes the U.S. Anti-Trust law disciplines (c/o the Public Utility Company Holding Act.) that vitally include the utility company's within communication, gas, electricity, water, and some sewage concerns. Now the internet has additional legislative concerns to correct their holding company disciplines. Liquidity, and issues of any bailout has been very low to none for most utility companies, and their monopolized business service duties to the general public. Some internet communication companies have only began to start to just seem to come, and go arbitrarily before the best lawful, and legislative correction.

Enron Corporation was an example of a company with no chance for a bailout consideration from a troubled American society. The Enron Corporation was started from a corporate merged buyout of a public utility company in Texas named the Houston Natural Gas Company. Upon this factor the Enron

Corporation did not stay the course of most regulated disciplines of the U.S. Public Utility Company Holding Act, and certain valued concerns of professionalism. The operating liquidity of these public utility company's usually consist of gas, water, or even wastewater with pumping machinery (c/o synthetics & liquid) including equipment. Another public utility operating standard is electrical transformers (c/o distributing electricity) with other equipment such as gauges, meters, and even satellites. This electric utility concern was capitalized in one region when Enron bought-out Portland GE; a well funded utility company with strong steady liquidity, but Enron's part was fraudulent with failure. The combination of these materials, equipment, and businesses at full capacity operating management levels of resource provides liability conditions of professionalism which is hopefully passed on to the general public, and customers. Therefore these processes that have a cost but also applies vitally to the public health, and livable standard needs of the citizens become relevant in the public monopolies lawful responsibilities. These business, and liability issues are relevant to the American tax dollar circulation to manage liquidity productively, and this is a vital part of the developed American society of government, and business.

Utility companies have liability conditions as monopolies. These monopoly disciplines within occasionally considering the telephone companies become part of the slightly complex business operations of duties to provide vital public utility services. This factor of business lately consisted of various up's, and down's during the 1990s, and 2000s upon which certain reorganizing business asset liquidity concerns of utility service distribution business operations where relevant to the monopolies stability. Companies such as (NIPSCO) Northern Indiana Public Service Company (c/o their status as a monopoly) at one time would provide gas, and electric utility service's combined. Although NIPSCO continued to bill the customers for both gas, and electricity, this public utility company has excepted complex energy partners such as

"NISOURCE". These business taxable factors have relevance, but the business format has severe difference's within all utilities.

Considering NIPSCO, and certain economic values of discipline within whole sale, and retail service price issues of things such as natural gas apart from electricity they created or *established a parent company of (not 1 business but 2) utility companies. NIPSCO the utility company went from one which has now become NISOURCE, and NIPSCO as the subsidiary that consisted of a taxable expansion, and this was to possibly help industry values of consideration. Truly this more looked like another Enron "type" business transaction with NISOURCE conducting a corporate buyout of NIPSCO, but very little changed with NIPSCO's public utility business activities as a northern Indiana monopoly business holder. This was done during a time that companies where involved heavily in the "Junk Bond" financial markets to create additional investor cash (including businesses) if it was necessary or not. Considering this also consisted of who controls the entire company (c/o monopolies), this becomes important to their diversified business duties, and decisions of progress for concerned relevance.

The liquidity of stock, and bond rate values of the company NIPSCO was strong with good earnings during the late 1980s, and early 1990s. Considering factors of management to achieve business stability with most service duties recognized by the general public citizens of America this means the company had strong liquidity factors of valued responsibilities. During these times of the American future with the economic recession of 2007, 2008, and 2009 public utilities, and their liquidity consist of important tax rate issues. The liquidity, and tax rate issues are maintained for the company's management of bond market rates consisting of credit, assets, and even mortgage's from their managed procedures within Banking, and investment bank underwriting.

NIPSCO as an American utility company may not be financially hurt as bad as some like Commonwealth Edison of Chicago, Detroit, California, and more so New York due to the cost effect of terrorism, and or a questionable banking market with various concerns. Most industry values of discipline are important to utility companies, and other businesses, but negative issues occur and then the right corrections are vital, contrary to which market is larger or smaller. Otherwise the corporate public utility business factors of applicable commitment and discipline are relevant to commercial banks, and investment bank underwriting. Sometimes these factual conflicts occur because, "the bigger the utility regional market, the bigger the fraudulent problems within managing may become if financial disaster, or a conflicting crisis occurs. Therefore all duties, and technical details must be reviewed, and upgraded when necessary. This becomes important from the chief executives priority of decision making observing the taxable profit values of the changing markets for any type of manageable advancement with most all details, to the entry level employees working to learn the business productively.

Small businesses, and how they work with utility companies, the government, and their customers are factual concerns within managing liquidity. Some people would observe that when residential, and commercial property foreclosures occur there is less utility company customers to factor liquidity asset values that are, and must be evaluated. The small evaluated outlook of productive businesses of America usually are not large corporate, or government bond holders (c/o liquid investments), but this includes utility, and mortgage markets that are within their relevant consideration. Although considering small businesses that may consist of these or other types of investments, most times this is part of a well planned expansion of business which improves economic resources. Observing bond market rate troubles such as within "Mortgage, and Asset Backed Securities" during 2007 this has made small businesses evaluate things to cut back on because of certain inflationary factors. These factors of destructive inflation also consist of issues from the credit markets or their resources of lenders now tightening or restricting credit lending opportunities upon most business issues of affordability. Therefore government enforced regulation becomes important just like hard work, and the long term commitment of most business operations, and some personal items like homes with or without a mortgage.

Government on occasions seeking solutions upon concerns with, and for small businesses, and their taxable commitments to find themselves in the capacity of having a stronger business in competitive markets have suffered during tuff times. Throughout American business this has become the uncomfortable capacity to work together to solve financial problems that is vitally important. These problems can be observed within how during the late 1980s small businesses where advancing into the larger capacity of public ownership investments at good (or interesting) rates of turnover. Understanding this a level of comfort, and trust was established upon which the American economy was strong or consisted of more stability. Now 20 years later small business issues upon resource have become very cautious about illegal, or destructive management control of their business concerns, and certain public opportunity investments. Another concerned problem within business ownership thru investment dollars is the vast amount of foreign investors that are now controlling American businesses, and corporations that are a discharged opinion by, and for the American tax payers. This means a certain level of tax dollar concerns, and appropriations from the United States government have factored a diversion throughout individual states that are benefiting foreign business people occasionally more than some American born citizens as business owners.

As people in America have observed for the many years of their life, they sometimes can remember certain small, and large businesses they have observed with some role of important likes, and occasional dislikes. These are the factored issues that produce the good, and bad history that is observed in business, and government, but all have a tax equation that appropriates the future of the citizens of the United States. This becomes the caution of limitations on how, and why a financial bailout, or other certain hard working people, and businesses considered these factors that are important. When these subjects of business, and government are considered if it is based on the money earning disciplines of decisions, they are sometimes made for a productive adjustment. This includes taxable employees, assets of "dependable services and products", and then the relevant equation is applied to the format of budgets similar to the ones in all levels of government. If a budget short fall is detected in a company, or business that has been around for over 50 to 100 years it usually opens up within the eyes, and the concerned attention of employees, and a massive amount of other people. Therefore these issues including taxes become important with the format of their agreeable terms, and conditions, but more so workable solutions.

Understanding the up's, and down's that are considered within the complex years of Civil Rights in America between black, and white Americans including other ethnic groups of nationality within businesses, and opportunities there has been expansion, but some have lacked stability. Most of these Civil Rights corrections of employment, and business issues have expanded with good, and bad levels of diversity upon trying to maintain these appropriate corrections. One level of small business diversity within Civil Rights is the improvements of restructured businesses that no longer (c/o the 1950s) discriminate strongly on race. This means a taxable business can work productively serving, and respecting people which includes more establishments with black, white, and other American's working productively together. Tax dollars, and the public relations or civil obedience that includes factors of education are part of these values that the people observe, and stand up for as logical citizens. Occasionally this also is where the good, and more so bad foreign relation issues have effects on the American hard working constitutes, and their humbled logical ambitions. Some corporations have loss due to bad foreign related business dealings, and this is factored with the small supportive businesses, and losses to government tax collected dollars that may have been supportive to the overall American society. The tax appropriated American dollars to government that then supports every man, woman, and child within the many diversified American conditions that may exist, has appropriate relevance.

Upon even what's considered the good, bad, evil, or ignorant that applies to Americans is mostly valued within ownership in business, but all people must conduct themselves within the boundaries of the law. Considering the diversity of American taxpaying businesses of logic this is valued within also the format of international business matters of a large or small capacity applicable to the regulation of lawful business factors. Corporate America, and the well developed American society of the United States has consideration on the good, bad, or what can be lawfully governed within the consideration of businesses, and all people upon how they conduct certain activities. Undeveloped, and developed international business concerns are a vital consideration of all taxable facts within what is lawfully compensated in the form of productive values between business, and government. Otherwise the courts, and government enforcing most all of the state, and federal regulative issues most times helps American business improve the subjects of taxable earnings, and employment factors with the general public.

During the 1990s, and the first part of the 2000s certain social values became complex for small business owners with their employee payrolls, and deductions from employee pay checks that are a workable, and important process of knowledge, and decisions. Contrary to the wages for salary or hourly work production this is part of the strict evaluation that provides a balance to small, and large business accounting, and bookkeeping as it applies to most levels of production. A valid example of a dollar ($1.00), to a dollar and a half ($1.50) per hour (c/o addition) which did equate to a minimum wage rate of $5.50 an hour, and now headed to $6.50 an hour means a business must pay this labor cost, and maintain the management of that cost factor of efficiency. Then on the upper side of certain Wall Street investment banks a $100,000.00 bonus with a salary exceeding occasionally $200,000.00 has become too common of a subject with these banks that failed along with the American economy. This also means that apart from bankruptcies (c/o bailouts) the businesses must keep, or improve business standards, and do business that is profitable to insure any overhead cost, and contingent liabilities. A high percentage of newly started businesses throughout America critically consider these government wage standards, including business wage liabilities of liquidity during their first few years. This is the long-term capacity to earn what money was originally spent on the business opening, and the start of hopefully a prosperous, and productive business with good operating business procedures being something harsh to consider. Therefore new, old, small, or large businesses have disciplines to follow, and or to be aware of within working to achieve business expanded progress, or logical success.

Understanding the many business issues of cost, labor, stored inventory, and the outside business expenses such as from factors of accounting, law, and or insurance with other details, these things are a consistent, and vital responsibility of decisions to avoid contingent bankruptcies, and bailouts. Labor unions, and even excessive spending in management have been some of the details that banks, and manufactures are factored with in bankruptcy, but in some businesses it's the hard work of management that can bring business out of bankruptcy. Both bankruptcies, and business bailouts are similar to the activities of the Federal Deposit Insurance Corporation which cost almost everyone something. The losing cost includes the applied bank savings, and some assets of the tax payers, the government, and the people including employees, and various business owners. This means also that the operating cash liquidity of business is not available to be a productive business. Observing this American business format is struggling with different matters besides labor cost, and excessive inventory is similar to record losses of new business start ups during 2008, and 2009.

Upon this problem the supporting concept of the products, services, and or the workforce employment issues have suffered, but only to value government liquidity support. Too compare Enron, WorldCom, and certain other businesses such as Continental Illinois Bank of Chicago (1982), and the Chrysler Corporation the term corporate fraud may become important. Theoretically, observing these corporate businesses which have been the important subjects of American large company bankruptcies, and considered bailouts lack of sales, earnings, and manipulative fraud has been a liquidity conflict that effects the American economy. These bankruptcies, contrary to the hard work to restructure an American company, and various businesses consist of disciplines that occasionally work. Most businesses just don't qualify for any bailout, and the restructuring seems hopeless to the overall region, or certain local economy's, and therefore various other businesses fail within future business existence.

The same format of business restructuring was done for General Electric Corporation during the mid 1970s. Restructuring General Electric Corporation like other corporations took a number of years to work productively. This process also consisted of business earnings, product improvements, customer values, and employees to restructure an entire companies business operation. Jack Welch the former CEO of General Electric Corporation was one of the main people credited with improving, and keeping this company very productive coming out of the 1970s, and especially the late 1980s. The Enron, and WorldCom Corporation's problem of bankruptcy with, hardly no consideration of a rightful bailout considering the format of business executives did not have logical guidance of earning business income. Considering this, employees, investors, and customers suffered all together. Both Enron, and WorldCom where businesses started from corporate mergers, and healthy conditions of "financed asset equity" as it applies to most lawful corporations with a large concentration of cash liquidity. This means that Enron, and WorldCom Corp where well financed businesses for years after their merger activity, but unlike General Electric they were not productively expanding or growing businesses.

A bailout was considered out of the question if you compare the Chrysler Corporation business matters of the 1970s that suffered different product, and business complex failures. This observation also consisted of their established inventory, and the commitment of Lee Iacocca; the Chrysler CEO, and others to manage the liquidity, and asset values of the business. The upper management officials of Enron, WorldCom, and a few other corporations did not have productive plans to restructure, but only to earn the highest wages agreed on without productive business outcomes. Sadly, but with productive effort, Lee Iacocca lowered his salary to $1.00 a year with stock incentives until Chrysler Corporation restructured. These factors of restored liquidity consisted of productive earnings, and the good products to be put back into the company's business plan of marketing. Considering this type of effect within the small, and large businesses associated with the automobile company, and even other industries these management subjects can increase liquidity overtime.

Within issues of a holding company, and the restructuring of Harris Bank that suffered liquidity values of growth from delinquent loans, hard working evaluations, and with certain decisions was part of an important solution to stay valued with bank production matters. Continental Illinois Bank, and other banking institutions consist of totally different stored inventory, and labor or operating cost issues with management decision making. Understanding some of these issues is different than that of a consumer electronics business, or an automobile manufacture. The automobile industry was restructuring (c/o 1980), and the steel industry consisted of employee layoff issues, and therefore Continental Illinois Bank of Chicago had a duty to hold strength within the "cash and operating liquidity" of the bank. The U.S. Bank Company Holding Act is relatively important to the business of banking, but other vital aspects exist within how good, or bad businesses and companies do with earned income to balance out a regional economy. With vast amounts of small and large businesses having more economic gains than losses this becomes the better prosperity of an economic, and tax dollar generating cycle. Considering all the products (c/o GDP), and services this money circulation is vital to be managed by government, and most all other concerned citizens.

Observing small, and large businesses including banks such as Harris Bank, Citicorp (c/o Citigroup) Bank and a few other businesses that are publicly owned have different market values of concern to consider on a day by day base. Considering this, both public, and privately owned businesses have worked hard not to suffer financially in a bad business, and regional markets economy, and capacity. Observing the years of the 1990s I slightly considered it a bad time for some growing private companies to provide public stock offerings of their company's investment opportunities due to the discipline needed within enforcing United States Securities and Exchange laws, and United States Anti-Trust laws. Understanding small, and large American businesses, and certain issues of government some American investments in corporations was consolidated with increased foreign investors. Besides good, and more so bad foreign relations the original law's of America, and the United States Constitution can, and has been a factor of occasionally destructive manipulation. This vitally takes away from their responsible duties to the American people, various business owners, and various opportunities including a well governed American society with innocent people involved. Businesses such as Harris Bank, Citibank, certain oil companies, communication company's, and certain individual investors in business have recognized this issue.

Observing, and understanding American small, and large businesses, and corporation's that compete for business or even market share, the U.S. Anti-Trust laws with other issues of law are always an important concern. The government in the United States of America has worked for decades sense about 1910 to 1930 on establishing a format of laws that occasionally go back even further. Upon this observation during the years of 1990 thru 2000 if the state's, and federal government allowed certain laws to be violated including against certain citizens, and business owners, the bad economy, and a sad war is part of the results. Observing certain American people being victimized, this is what has created bad wealth, and insecurity within the American society, and laws that are suffering abusively.

American small, and large business conditions with hard working citizens, and the formal issues of respecting the laws is the vital part of American wealth, and security to apply prosperity which means people earn, and also businesses or organizations earn or expand with lawful opportunities. The American system of government maintains a balance of collected income tax revenue for the future of the American society, and this includes the many ways of prosperity, and opportunities which are to be resourceful to American's.

CHAPTER FOUR

GOOD & BAD FOREIGN INVESTMENTS & AMERICAN LIQUIDITY

The format of the American tax dollars with checks, balances, and investment issues have relevant concern when good, and bad foreign investments are controlling certain rates of liquidity applicable to American assets, and even certain American commodities. Considering America is a place, and country that excepts people, and certain commodities from many different parts of the world with investments, the liquidity of American business activity is the result of a well developed society. These resources of developments consist of tax revenue in the billon's of dollars obligated to the U.S. government which is a vital part of long term economic progress for U.S. Constitutional stability. The U.S. government liquidity base is valued around $5 to $8 trillion dollars, which means disciplinary budgets apply. This is also an important consideration of the business, and government facts of regulatory disciplines that are part of the global, and United States domestic relations as it applies to the economy. Therefore during this corporate crisis (c/o 2009) of businesses needing to be financially bailed-out, this also consisted of paying foreign businesses that had an invested interest.

Understanding business, and governed liquidity is a provision of liability within regulated products, services, and various tax funded projects that appropriate a well developed American society, and sometimes even in other diverse places surrounding the United States. Various issues of the United States National Security is part of this discipline to keep from advancing U.S. cash / currency liquidity, and valued commodities to foreign enemies. The bailout of AIG sent billions of dollars to at least 5 foreign companies. This is usually where national security is not a problem, and good foreign relations consist of prosperous business. Some of these issues have been a severe downfall, but lawful business is just as important as protecting American assets, businesses, and the people from terrorism, and other negative foreign, and occasionally domestic conflicts. These become some of the factual conditions that the American system of government, and society must value concerning the lawful issues of protection from logical tax dollar accumulations, and it's useful values of liquidity.

During decades of business in America, and even how the United States federal government spends money, the procurement of items related to things such as defense are, and become vital. This is a vital issue in times of war, which means a market, and society is born, or restructured over, and over again. The fact of this matter is that corporations are created from sometimes the small businesses that work productively with some value of large corporations in a lawfully productive capacity. American domestic, and international trade is an issue that's been around for a long time. This includes expensive U.S. military defense products occasionally form other select countries. During the year of 1914 the United States Congress established the U.S. Federal Trade Commission. Upon establishing the U.S. Federal Trade Commission, this considerably gave the U.S. government a direction as it applies to American, and more so foreign products, and agreements from other countries with good relations to the United States.

Managing the U.S. federal trade concerns throughout America are five trade commissioners appointed by the president of the United States government upon which information technology products have been some of most considerable trade items to review. This is slightly different form the arbitrarily new, good, and bad of computer internet systems, including other vital U.S. market systems of discipline. Upon this format of government duties the U.S. Federal Trade Commission has a responsibility to review a certain amount of governed business details, and provide aggressive observation of regulatory disciplines for these products that must be consistent within use to the U.S. Constitution. The concept of this process has even existed throughout different global good, bad, and foreign issues of relations, making the state, and federal Constitutional laws the American people's value of strength, and disciplinary resource against any conflict.

This duration of time, and business also has observed what American government worries about within international investments, and international terror. International investment's with terror have caused the American society destruction, and danger to U.S. Anti-Trust laws, and the economy. This can be seen in larger cities sense 1995 to 2009 where foreign people have outnumbered American's within business openings or ownership compared to born in America new business owners. Also there are different factors of when agriculture food items, or other products are even subsidized as aid for the poor, or disaster stricken regions of the world (c/o U.S. Commodities) and foreign trade which may apply. These become the issues of generosity from America, but the root of manageable American business, and good responsibilities still exist for earned income, and liquidity "especially avoiding foreign corruption.

The import, and export concept of business is also occasionally factored with some funded issues by the World Bank, and the International Monetary Fund. Upon values of the International Monetary Fund in comparison to close countries like Mexico, and Canada it's important to remember these international people sometimes retrieve support from Washington D.C., and the capitals of Ottawa, and Mexico City where the governed laws are slightly different. Considering one would explain the geographical business, and social factors of Mexicans maintaining business support from both Washington D.C., and Mexico City this consist of competitive economic issues. These international governed nations, and their capital cities have concerned factors for American businesses, and consumers similar to their own business issues including employment, and production of various products. These business activities cause foreign currency activity rates to also effect American liquidity expansion such as at Ford Motor Company's plant in Mexico that is trying to offset Japanese automobile manufacturing competitors. With factual monetary concern this lately has raised legal issues, wage issues, and business issues which include personal expense concerns. Observing these competitive expenses, and wage factors the American society must preserve monetary liabilities of caution, applicable to the U.S. Constitution, and American business standards that are different legally within these other country's from them having economic control in American markets.

Considering the American differences in Mexico there is a language, and currency conflict upon other social issues of diversity. The American difference in Canada is established from a parliamentary system of governed factors, and a society upon which most businesses endure certain international (c/o the U.S.) business governed conflicts of consideration. Observing America the enormous amount of new, and more so illegal citizens of immigration have been a business complex subject due to these culture conflicting issues. These things have applied cost to the American tax dollars currency rates within the added good, and bad culture conflict of import, and export business competitive issues. These diversified factors upon which American businesses, and people occasionally lose opportunities are vital to consider for most lawful issues of discipline.

The issue's of liquidity has also hit the American workers in a competitive concept that abridges their tax dollar values of opportunity. Observing these issues of near or far away foreign constituents, and sometimes enemy's, the tax dollar values of equity is part of this diversified issue of liquidity. These factors of liquidity applies to American's when maintaining employment, business, and investment prosperity which has a currency measure of equity issues within stability. This also includes millions, and billions of American dollars that are now being sent (c/o corporations and liquidity factors) to foreign countries eliminating certain values of equity, and liquidity within a variation of American markets, households, and businesses.

American currency with the format of gold leveraged thru the World Bank, and the U.S. Federal Reserve Bank system with commerce banking throughout the United States was at one time the equity process that appropriates liquidity leveraged values of cash in America. Although the "Gold Standard" in the United States was eliminated in 1971 which this was a way of controlling inflation investments in gold, and other precious metals which gold commodities as investments have did very good during the 2009 recession. The most valued currency of liquidity for the (U.S.) individual states, and the federal governments asset liquidity is the personal, and business tax revenue (c/o leveraging gold) when dollars are managed, invested, and controlled by government. Inflation, and more so the gold bullion, and silver markets that are leveraging bank assets is part of this relevant banking currency issue within "trade in America". This format of the "legal tender, and monetary support" is not valued without massive levels of American rates of production.

Observing this important concern within the value of the dollar that is relevant to most all American products, and services this includes most economic facts of income earning issues. In addition this is applicable to wages, or American investment returns, upon which then a slight bit of foreign business conflicts cannot "manipulate control" of U.S. economic or social prosperity.

A high demand of foreign products from these other countries including different currencies is part of the subject that makes the currency rate increase, or decrease. Considering the strength or weakness of the valued dollars currency rate, a validity of business, and personal spending is effected. Items, and products such as gas within a weak currency market of the dollar, the consumer will get less gas (c/o product) for the dollar. Within these good, and more so bad effects, we find the American people taking up the consolidation of how the concept of inflation, and taxation will somehow provide a balanced equation of living standards.

Observing the valuable commodity's existing geographically in the American society of markets such as within gold, silver, oil, wood, food crops, animal live stock, and even water becomes values for liquidity within the rate of the currency. Contrary to the values of public access in the United States, and certain other places the conditions of professions, and hobbies including agriculture, farms, and even home gardening is adjustable to business, and government liquidity in which future years of planning in America where a logical sacrifice. These are small personal household values that are even used in the massive resource of the farming industry, and other marketable products within businesses. This evaluation of business, and personal commitment is also part of a worldwide economic consideration of business factors that are productive in America, and other places. When people observe this consideration of "business and development", certain country's endure the lowest, and highest "commend and real denominator" of taxable liquidity that is normally considered. Understanding facts of research, and development these products that may include services such as a public or a governed utility's process of business, and industry procedures will, and should consist of liabilities. Considering markets, and government services this is the observation for a lawful level of public monopoly disciplines that are factored to appropriate the validity of leveraged liquidity within a productive developed society.

All levels of tax appropriated dollars, and the diversified concept of American values with certain international issues consist of the need for progress, and the ambition of the people. Within the American society as it applies to the United States Constitution this is valued with government appropriating the people's best, and most lawful solutions in a legally disciplined (c/o good and occasionally bad) way. This observation seems to get conflicting with education, and the educational issues that financially support Sallie Mae (the Student Loan Marketing Association), and the vast amount of good, and bad lending for college students, and people that is vital. The U.S. government has taken value to apply possibly more student loans (c/o grants) to foreign students that did not perform properly (c/o percentages) that added a loss of liquidity to loan opportunities, and funding. Observing a term, and commitment that appropriates the difference of investing in people, or in business these are the conflicting concerns to evaluate in both business, and the system of education. Therefore the issues concerning the discretionary rate of good, and bad American students, and various opportunities can have a logical subject within balance.

Student loans, and grants in factual comparison to the liquidity of the United States government that must be observant within the relevance of most student and residential housing, and certain asset market issues in America is a finance value of large cost responsibilities. College campuses, and the neighborhoods within most American communities consist of citizens, and the people's rights of financial commitments that must take issue of managing assets of liquidity serious that hold value for young, and old citizens alike. When the consideration of school buildings, houses, and other assets have good liability, these issues for college students that are similar to the general public are valued in American tax liquidity concerns for the priority that becomes important to the future equity for American families. Just as the best businesses, and businesspeople take assets, loans, and account liquidity serious it is vital for all citizens, and especially government to maintain the same discipline. Considering this, loans as it applies to liquidity is the comparison of budget issues which improves the opportunity of effort to some values to continue a college education by most students, and various older citizens. These are the important evaluated issues with considerations of where we have observed concern over the 1990 decade of valued, but delicate issues within the two home mortgage loan government sponsored enterprise's that suffered financial distress. This supports these relevant ambitions upon the business, and government transactions of Fannie Mae, and Freddie Mac. Therefore all government enterprise issues have good duties they perform, and occasionally this consist of some good and bad issues within years and corrections that must be evaluated for any arbitrary problems.

The government sponsored enterprises of Fannie Mae (the Federal National Mortgage Loan Association), and Freddie Mac (the Federal Home Mortgage Loan Corporation) upon which also consist of long term investment issues, and commerce bank matters have liquidity measures that serve vital duties. These government enterprises that compensate not only the state governments with up's, and down's, but they also consist of the sacrifices of the American people, and the society of banking to appropriate vital, and important liquidity adjustments. During the 1990s and the years of 2000 a vast amount of people where illegally manipulated victims, and or were excluded from certain opportunities due to income status, and other disadvantaged conditions within advancement opportunities. These issues of manipulation considering disadvantaged people caused certain conflicts of interest similar to a problem just like a low rate of marriage that effected the family household mortgage markets including various social values. Over the years Fannie Mae, and Freddie Mac have been government mortgage institutions of banking that have consisted of good, and occasionally bad years of lending economically.

During the last couple decades up to 2000 the enormous amount of foreign investments, and expanding markets with conflicts has consisted of limited liquidity assets. A majority of these markets has caused American people, and most American mortgage markets to suffer conflicts with long-term debt commitments that have been unfair or illogical to various consumers. A bailout, and takeover to control the finance issues of Fannie Mae, and Freddie Mac was established by the United States government, and therefore putting these institutions into receivership a vast amount of assets had to be reviewed. These institutional receivership concerns of capacity by the United States government also will consist of business procedures that become relevant upon the government enterprise process of restructuring. This has also hurt the housing market (c/o Fannie Mae and Freddie Mac) because of the loss of investment dollars that support American businesses, banking, the people, and mortgage business issues including investors. Observing the government and various social problems, the restructuring of these disciplines of business and government enterprise liquidity matters will consist of control, and U.S. Constitutional values that must be pursued to improve this overall economic outlook of operating issues.

Issues within the increase of foreign investments in American businesses are considered with good, and bad U.S. National Security which includes the state, and the U.S. federal Constitutional laws has effected resources of liquidity, and assets such as property. One consideration to observe is the compounded effects of Fannie Mae, and Freddie Mac which is mostly due to American investors, and applied to home ownership mortgages. Contrary to this resource, billions of dollars also have came from foreign ally banks that are among a vast amount of businesses that are filing bankruptcy, or they are having severe financial troubles. This means that these United States government sponsored enterprises have suffered to the losing value of foreign financial, and social problems. The U.S. government sponsored enterprise of Fannie Mae, and Freddie Mac lost in access of $100 billion dollars during 2008, and the

United States Department of Treasury (c/o Secretary Henry Paulson) said it would cost an estimated $25 billion dollars to keep the U.S. government's operational parts restored. This also consist of massive amounts of commercial facilities, and more so houses that where foreclosed on. Understanding this they went into receivership with a vast amount homes, and some commercial facilities not having any known owner, due more so to mortgage companies (c/o some banks) closing.

Within the format of more American investment dollars that are going to foreign businesses this means less American businesses consist of progress like in the supportive concept of mortgage, and banking businesses supported by Fannie Mae, and Freddie Mac. Due to the fact that vast amount's of people, and families have lately found trouble paying for new homes, and the banks that finance these loans have suffered the concept of losing equity to lend money during 2008 has factored tremendous conflicts. This banking issue consist of their lack of money making opportunities concerning this newly discovered problem as a severe consolidation of the past, and future. The issue of numerous businesses filing bankruptcy is also part of a problem for the government, the people, and even the banks that need extra money for the lending of each concern on taxable dollars of liquidity. This economic recession of 2007, and 2008 consist of not so much major corporations filing bankruptcy, but also small, and more so large banks that are now under the reorganizing control of the Federal Deposit Insurance Corporation, and the U.S. government.

The Federal Deposit Insurance Corporation (FDIC 1930s) has been around just as long as Fannie Mea, and Freddie Mac (upon their recently established nicknames), and they are all related in various way's to the American Banking industry. This format of banking is established as the U.S. Federal Home Loan Bank system. Also this is valued within the federal bank system which is managed in the 12 regional conditions of the United States. Upon any other federal bank concerns to raise money by issuing notes, bonds, and other service duties including the format of lending money becomes similar to commerce, and other logical bank business activities of loan requirements to improve liquidity. This outline of requirements is applied to select mortgage lenders, citizens, businesses, and the select bankers that are commissioned with their duties that consist of evaluating these procedures to make good, and lawful decisions. In addition this lending is based on most bank institutions liquidity of valued collateral. Therefore upon these government sponsored enterprises, and other asset values of protection, including the FDIC which was established to guarantee certain limits of deposits in member banks, conditional values of security where established. These become very good insured disciplines for the people whom made good decisions. Theoretically these good decisions usually consist of diversified banking.

How the good, and more so bad of foreign investments are in close contact with consolidation from American business, and government liquidity is based on the United States Constitutional laws, apart from some commerce, and international issues within laws. This is vitally considered within how greed from other country's whom can take control of American business must be held (c/o the U.S.) Constitutionally, and lawfully responsible. International and U.S. domestic greed apart from capitalism is a vital discretion if the American society including most all professional's are not careful with these good, and bad investments. Based on other duties, the FDIC also in complex times for banks, they will facilitate bank mergers that consist of some bad international banking matters. In doing this the FDIC will or can take full consideration of the American banks duties, and control of bank failures. Therefore the bank, and client liquidity is controlled, and regulated closely by the U.S. government without foreign or certain domestic conflicts or greed.

The banking, and corporate hard times of the American economy has suffered transitional banking, and market sector conditions of concern due to business, and employment effected by foreign, and some domestic business decisions that are high risk within contingent liabilities. When the American community of small, and large businesses including government take, and observe the business transactions of the Zenith Corporation (a former U.S. Defense contractor), Inland (now ArcelorMittal) Steel Corporation (a complex U.S. Defense contractor), a percentage of Chrysler (a U.S. Defense contractor), and even the Dow Jones Company, this so far outlines that America has loss a taxable stake of national security, and business liquidity.

The takeover (c/o other mergers) of Amoco Oil Corporation becoming a unit of British Petroleum Company is fairly within the same consideration of American tax base losses to an allied nation in valued liquidity. With respect, but aggressive observation this is the consolidation of various foreign business owners controlling trillions of dollars of American commodities, and soiled assets. This means Lakshmi Mittal (U.S., Europe, & India), Rupert Murdoch (U.S., & Europe), Kirk Kerkorian (U.S., & Europe), and a group of investors from Korea, and or Vietnam including a few other foreign wealthy investors are controlling a record amount of America corporate stock holdings. This is only part of the considered fact, and subject if you observed far South America, Canada, and Mexico we occasionally observe diversified conflicts. This also includes how certain nations such as Venezuela, China, and Japan has provided an increase of foreign people, and a decrease of American productive people which has applied economic changes to the American society. Also the same apply to complex taxable business matters with Great Britain, Africa, and some small conflicting or remote places like Indonesia. These corporate stock holding values of interest consist of American liquidity asset earning principal. Considering that these liquidity issues are valued within the perceptional American founded businesses with various U.S. commodities, and American employees most should or must be concerned about these matters in the future years to come.

Most times public, and private businesses of America have been as productive as possible paying taxes for, and by the American society, and people. Upon these tax issues, and endeavor's of every man, woman, and child in America these are the factors of established government concern, and duty to value the peoples lawful ways of life. Respect for certain foreign countries, and the consideration of the American people, and government that make the best effort with good foreign relations consist of a constant evaluation of global issues. These international, and American domestic decisions are valued within our American resources of future business, and social prosperity. Conditional decisions as most logical, and educated American's have value which is applied to the understanding of an individual person whom is sworn into a government office, and this is done for values of trust. Even though to swear is considered sinful, the term trust is a value that only goes as far as that one person (c/o occasional others), and a variation of political constituent's upon the logic that applied to government, and occasional business issues. This also includes business issues becoming the format valued concerns with disciplines to work with the American general public, and government. Therefore this value of lawfully governed trust is factored throughout most public, and private American businesses that work appropriately with most concerns of government, and the people.

Just as there is crime, and negligence with good, and bad decisions concerning the laws that must be enforced, or understood in most all places, this also includes the conditional issue of why taxes, and currencies are similar, but different in other countries. Considering this, and the format of public, private businesses, and government that views certain issues of good, and bad social concerns as important, this is the reality that consist of logic, and with certain revisions for a productively governed society. With people working productively together this improves good conditions of equitable liquidity. This vitally makes businesses outside of the United States which find themselves in bankruptcy with complex economic times similar to American good, and bad business values. This also consist of when certain business issue's become questionable with business, or market sector problems, but theoretically that is most times excluding U.S. government financial bailouts. The U.S. government during the bailout of AIG Inc. sent large sums of money to foreign business which was slightly considered a bad mistake, considering how these international issues were part of a conflict with American tax dollars, and how all of this applies to the bankruptcy court's, and other legal matters. Observing bankruptcy, and certain considerations of bailouts for businesses within this process of restructuring from financial crime, and or negligence this is occasionally a global economic problem all over the world. Upon these factors this is when a vast amount of businesses suffer the same (c/o currency rates), but most times with different factors of economics or product and service good, or improvable conditions. Then within business markets considering crime or negligence that is resolved in various duties "most solutions" consist of the best businesses having a responsible means to prevail or expand with discipline.

Considering financial investments are different from business products, and services this is the economic resource within a society, and it's developing businesses, diversified markets, and even government. This observation includes how even war time issue's with fighting, and conflicts occasionally somewhat destroy small, and large business operations which are a confined contradiction in a well governed society. Considering some businesses are protected, the hopeful ambition is a government resolution with agreements that will apply lawful ethics, and hard work to enforce the responsibilities of all lawful constituents involved. It is relevant for a governed society to lawfully comply with the business developing society, and the people upon considering most defense issues that becomes a part of that government's social duty.

This factor or war, and conflict has occurred on and off in Europe, and other country's which was the reasonable establishment of the North American Treaty Organization (NATO) to provide peace keeping missions to distressed places, or regions in conflict throughout the world. This was different, but with issues of relevance similar to the "9-11 Terrorist Report" during the President George Bush administration observing the United States government being attacked on September 11, 2001 is factually why the American, and Iraq / Afghanistan war was vitally declared. Some would offer comparison to that of the former Yugoslavia that was a tragic, and violent loss to European social concerns, and businesses. This was even more so a human rights tragedy pursued by Slobodan Milosevic in south-central Europe, but this consisted of the region throughout Sarajevo which was destroyed after hosting a set of worldwide Olympic games. Even throughout the continent of Africa during a 1997 civil war the vast amount of gold mines where part of business, and various diamonds became the atrocity of people being mutilated by the suspected forces of Foday Sankoh, and Jean Paul Akayesu. Therefore the government funded concerns of NATO and the United Nations serves a logical purpose of lawful, and disciplined order as much as they can see fit.

Apart from severe social, and business conflicts the American society consisted of a consolidation of liquidity that was supportive of American prosperity. In the Midwest of the United States some steelworkers during the peak of the Vietnam War where earning $60,000.00 to $80,000.00 dollars a year from (war time steel production) overtime at U.S. Steel Corp. This level of business production included other U.S. defense business contractors such as LTV, Inland Steel Corp, Amoco Oil Corp, and Zenith Corp whom as businesses have changed drastically from U.S. to foreign ownership. With these factors that vitally includes war, and or defense production, and non-defense or non-wartime production this is where some company's throughout America traditionally will do very well within taxable earned income. These are factors within any and all well developed, and socially moral nations of establishment of a disciplined government, country, and the people. This is a vital aspect of the public, private businesses, and government working together to solve a problem with a productive solution.

In the United States, and with certain valued members of the United Nations the issues of certain G-7, and or G-8 (c/o G-20) economic summits on trade, and business agreements are occasionally vital to maintain most disciplines within economic, and social stability. These are more so a factor of an immediate foreign and U.S. economic levels of valued agreements. The format between the different countries, and governmental resources of discipline are important so that the U.S. government, international issues of business, and the diversified citizens (contrary to war time issues) therefore can have a balanced agreement of economic discipline of trust between the different national governments. Considering this global economic issue, the laws in America consist of executive, legislative, and judicial established government duties that give local citizen business owners a lawful opportunity to compete with international business concerns "Constitutionally". Contrary to this fact lately various companies have been relocating their manufacturing facilities outside of the United States leaving people unemployed, and with economic stress on various communities. Company's like Whirlpool Corporation, and Maytag Corporation moving to Mexico, and others like Amoco Oil (now BP Co.) headquartered in Loudon, England. Then with concern, the RJ Reynolds Tobacco Co has had discussions about moving, and opening a manufacturing plant in Japan. This therefore is within the format of losing government tax revenue. Upon this fact the local, state, and federal government systems of relevant duties for most all factors of good, and bad foreign relations becomes the subjects that are, and can be observed with proper evaluations, and even possible corrections.

The (43rd) President of the United States George Bush, and his governed agenda being slightly different from the (42nd) President Bill Clinton, and considerably these times of the first decade of 2000 have fared different, but similar to the tuff times during the

Vietnam War. Following the years after the United States fought the Vietnam War the issues (c/o the Watergate hearings) of President Richard Nixon, and the American citizens went through various good and bad foreign relation issues. These conditional foreign, and domestic conflicts especially from the Watergate hearings with opinions, and legal support forced President Nixon to resign. Observing France, Great Britain, and more so the United States, American corporations including the citizens earned money in a productive manufacturing environment, and market, but other government issues such as the Watergate scandal, and the "Energy & Oil Embargo Crisis" made things very complex. These become the American issues apart from foreign relations that are vitally important upon even how it applied to places such as Canada, and Mexico with the observation of certain tropical islands with industry, and government concerns. Apart from the years of the 1960s, and the 1970's the issues of good, and bad foreign investments has changed with certain laws, and legislature not properly being enforced. These issues where abusively destructive when they suffered issues of U.S. Constitutional law, and law enforcement procedures being abused which lead to the Iraq war during the late 1990s up until 2000, and upon the consideration of 2010 having an economic repercussion.

When we as American's observe investments, and the American liquidity of public, private businesses, and most households during the first decade of 2000 some matters consisted of critical indicators of these financially troubled times. This is valid within the late 2008s economy consisting of financial markets with values of strict, or tight spending limits (c/o some lending) upon resourceful taxable earnings. The stock market exchanges daily closing prices have been some of the worse volatile trading days in American history. This has consisted of trading days where the Dow Jones average has seen more 400 points to more than 700 point "losses" within individual trading days. These days of market transactions have outnumbered the 100 point, to 200 point "gains" within trading days that are considered as economic corrections in most stock exchanges in the United States during these early years of 2000. In more detailed additions this resembles the investment trading activity of the Tokyo, Japan "Nikkei" average issues of the 1980s which was an unstable or complex issue of a volatile trading market. This future within trading of today during 2008, and the coming years hopefully will endure less volatility, and stable business growth numbers from most publicly traded companies. These two "market comparisons, and nations" are totally different as it applies to government, but they have become similar in the relevance of volatile stock market trading activity which one nation seems to trade, and exchange stock's like the other.

Within the fact of observing more stable trading (c/o less volatility) in the American financial markets of long-term American investments, and business operations, a stable market has slightly been threatened. An assortment of company's offered for investment opportunities on most logical stock trading markets in America have suspended or cut their dividend pay tremendously, and this means that they are holding more liquidity to operate thru tuff financial times. American corporations have a good valued record of paying investor dividends at a lawful rate better than most foreign companies, and investments. Another strategy is that a majority of American companies are buying back their own stock to manage the control of their company to survive in a dangerous time for publicly traded American companies.

All of the economic times, and issues of struggle in the American markets of business, and government have also severely hurt the American tax collected dollars from citizens, and even certain local resources of government. The American society of people, and businesses cannot help foreign people in any way without the vital help of necessity, and duty that its own country, and the people as citizens whom deserve it first, and foremost! These U.S. citizens must be served with opportunities, and discipline within their priorities of productive duties! This is even more so considered within the fact that the inventory of residential, and commercial facilities that are for sale (due to foreclosures); are a troubling subject. Also in these troubled conditions various new facilities for sale have lingered unoccupied at record historical rates during the first decade of 2000. These equity, and asset liquidity issues failed from the good, and more so bad decisions of Fannie Mae, Freddie Mac, upon which more so includes the people, and certain businesses as mortgage lenders. Some of the sadder business people, and owners instigated these un-level conditions of a business economic market, with concerned decisions that lacked most all professional disciplines. This is slightly considered for people, and some businesses (c/o mortgage lending) receiving diversified loans with long-term commitments that suffered various conflicts, and could not compensate these business agreements. Even the extent of judicial negligence to reward fraud without the best possible solutions of "Due Process of the Law" has instigated failure in other American businesses, and markets. An enormous concept of manipulation throughout marketable businesses was part of a more vital need for the scenario of "Due Process of Law" solutions.

Considering these factors of failures in a good, and more so bad capacity, all government officials, and business professionals are not perfect. This becomes relevant because of the "ethic codes" for all licensed, and some non-licensed professionals which have a responsible concern to apply, and except this lawful understanding of conduct. The fact of this is similar to imply that their professional commission is based on the fact's that doing less than your best is lawfully, and conditionally forbidden. This occasionally is not considered right by some foreign people, and young Americans whom are considering how important it is to value sacrifices in most productive American businesses. Therefore when it comes to lawyers, doctors, engineers, accountants, and other professionals, the vast amount of common people deserve the best possible services. This means it's not just for the wealthy or complacent surroundings of rich people that these become important codes of ethics for businesses, government, and all levels of professionalism to apply. These American ethical standards (c/o American government value's) keeps most all businesses, professional duties, and the people lawfully governed, and served properly, and productively.

American values of strong professional organizations of all kinds where part of the establishment of the American Codes of Ethics with not so much the decisions of most good, and bad foreign relation issues. Codes of law, and ethical standards exist in other countries other than the United States, but these are factual disciplines that the American society has valued with the U.S. Constitutional laws, and even how the Civil Rights Act, and certain established cultures of nationality have resources of people to work together productively. When the people such as in America work together, this has become the balance of technology improving, the laws improving, the economy improving, and other values of intellectual rights that are considered as respectful endeavors of improvement have progress. Some would consider this as part of the best solutions for most all advice, and consent in the American society. Therefore the American society that we live in has ups, and downs that are opinionated to value the right progress, and not the wrong.

CHAPTER FIVE

INFLATION, TAXES & THE
AMERICAN POPULATION

The American population of people (an est. 300,000,000), and how it applies to business, and government consist of vital, and conflicting issues of inflation including the relevant support of government tax dollars. Inflation along with the evaluated tax dollar input (collections), and output (managing, and spending) of money has been a vital discipline in the American society for century's. This is applied financially within what has been maintained through the format of increasing cost with large, and "new projects or maintenance within government infrastructures". Although at this time the American issue of a vast amount of infrastructure's are in need of renovated upgrades. This vitally includes the government duties of budget spending, and cost disciplines. These are the tax dollar concerns for certain population expansions, and a vast amount of other things such as assets to manage government duties with liquidity.

The U.S. population as it applies to inflation also vitally includes such benefits as Social Security, and other government benefit measures. These are disciplines that require government officials to observe, invest wisely, and consider responsible decision making. A vital factor, and format of this tax economic, and finance issue of reality is the formal consideration of controlling inflation without losing important disciplines to serve the citizens. Considering this the United States governed system of all executive, legislative, and judicial powers of duty within officers is a vital part especially when it effect's businesses with bankruptcy issues, or the need of a considered bailout. Therefore the American population has many important subjects that are effected by inflation, and the limitation of tax dollars.

Understanding the different, and complex factors in the American system of government, and it's social values which are important, the use and concern of discipline within these value's are applicable with inflation, and taxes. They are also factual to understand, and cope with subjects that apply to the importance of the control within manageable, and effective budgets with inflation. This applies with government observing business products, the rate of currency, and certain issues of success that are found on different balance sheets in government, and business. Within the format of the price tags at retail level stores most items from diversified American corporations, and businesses have price control issues with products, and services that are vital for what earns people a taxable income. This usually applies to the improved conditions of certain products, and services as times go on with productivity in the American society.

The operating capacity of all tax dollar generating businesses in the American society must value these issues of inflation with lawful consideration of the United States Anti-Trust laws to maintain governed business responsibilities legally. This is where Anti-Trust laws apply to the prices businesses charge, and any lawful inflation without conflicts to other businesses. Also understanding the law's that oversee the good, and bad mergers, buyouts, and specifically government bailouts due to inflation, has caused a tuff time to the housing mortgage market, and even certain farms with agriculture concerns.

Considering the years of 2008, 2009, 2010, and within future years various parts of America has established an over built real estate market with housing, and commercial properties that is the total opposite of normal inflation. These market issues of uncontrollable inflation also effected vast amounts of American people purchasing house's "observing" that the cost of some average home's for a family went from $100,000.00 to more than $425,000.00. Following this economic trend the same market of houses then went back down to $100,000.00 or less between the years of 2000, and 2008 with some being auctioned off for around $20,000.00. Some of these conflicting mortgage issues where due to people suffering an economic diversion of losses including their responsibilities to sub-prime mortgages sustained on foreclosed real estate. Therefore the inflation factor was out of control along with corporate / business mergers, and the "supply and demand" of various products including real estate properties being constructed with the consideration of future mortgages.

If you compare houses, and gas for automobiles the issues of inventory, sales, and inflation has caused these economic factors to be vitally important business, and personal matters. These are subject matters that must be controlled within most all diversified businesses, and various government operations. Within the format of controlling businesses that sales house's such as by real estate companies, and bank mortgage business divisions in 2007, there were 2.2 million foreclosure filings with 265,968 properties repossessed with foreclosure notices. Between 2006, and 2008 12 million homeowners lost extensive equity from moving in, and out of houses that they bought. Most of these "homes, and or commercial" facility purchases consist of conflicting calculations of inflated cost issues, and sub-prime mortgage concerns. Understanding the 100 million people buying gasoline on a daily or weekly base they were starting to get less gas for each dollar they spend. This continued to push people, and businesses into a position of having less (money and assets) to do all the important things that require a vast amount of driving to different places. This observation was a factor within the people, and their time to adjust economic values with budget concerns, or in case not to be able to pay their mortgages, and other vital issues of debt with increasing inflation.

Considering various factors of inflation, government, and businesses which had enormous duties to keep all things fair or logical within market values of financial security, these economic equations that inflate a products or services cost exist with certain levels of business, and product disciplines. This from time to time becomes an anti-trust or patent law issue at the state, and federal government level. Then therefore this can be considered within the U.S. Department of Justice's Anti-Trust, and Patent Product Division's legal process of procedures which the patent may cost a company a logical amount of money for the rights to use, and own it. Usually products can be developed throughout the company similar to the Coca Cola Company developing a similar "Coca Cola bottles and can" design very similar to the previous one, and taking 10,000 design hours to agree to this patent. The internet browser was another patent dispute which may have inflated the price of these computer programs.

Observing another issue of liquidity, and inflation as it applied to the cost of gas for automobiles, this issue was another expense that went from $1.80 to over $4.75 per gallon between 1991 to the years of 2007, and 2008. This also effected a vast amount of trucking companies, and various drivers that distribute a vast amount of products delivered to various businesses. Considering this conflicting rise in the cost of a vital product such as gas, or diesel fuel the employee's, and business owners had to pay more which take away from their earnings. During 2008 the price of gas has been lowered from the $4.75 per gallon price to an estimated $2.30 (+) throughout most regions of the United States. This is a problem all over America with the weakness in the dollar, and not just effecting the cost of oil, and gas.

When the American society of people including the importance of taxes which had inflated the price of gas, and other products in various parts of America, this caused a majority of the people to need some kind of economic bailout, and government assistance. This was the 2007 decision, and considered need for the U.S. government to establish appropriations for a stimulus package. Then due to the additional rise in unemployment rates, the American people observed financial trouble within an economic recession which was declared by a vast amount of the population. In appropriate addition some of these issues of gas prices, and some housing prices with property taxes where priced out of control. A legal study with various concerns about certain company's products could have been part of certain U.S. Anti-Trust legal proceedings before this unlawful inflation caused an enormous amount of harm.

Making public, and private businesses work properly, and productively during these economic times of needed bailouts within the years of the 2000 to 2009 time frame was consolidated with various personal bankruptcies. Most personal bankruptcies hold appropriate levels of confidentiality, and then businesses have different responsibilities that occasionally require lawful disclosers. Observing the issues of Bernard Madoff whom provided fraudulent investments, and manipulated billions of dollars from certain taxpaying citizens this caused other businesses, organizations, and other taxable concerns to suffer. This was a lack of discipline by the U.S. Securities and Exchange Commission (c/o the chairman's Harvey Pitt, William Donaldson, and Christopher Cox) that severely missed proper disclosers, and important details too late. The factor of these laws that are part of the United States Constitutional disciplines, and detailed government regulative duties are the appropriate consideration of enforcing, and retrieving truthful business financial records. This was discovered in the Bernard Madoff scandal, and a few others which coasted certain investors "dearly" apart from these acts of abusive "Constitutional power" or greed! When it comes to the tax dollars of the people, and government with issues of greed, and or conflicting subjects that occur, these factors become important to understand lawfully before it cerate's a budget misappropriated concern that's severely out of control. Observing these conditional issues of the state, and federal governments managed money disciplines of how inflation apart from even bankruptcy is financially evaluated, this is credited for the future, and certain issues within the concept of developing markets. Therefore, and with financial leverage the society of America becomes a part of economic budgets, and logical financial planning.

All small, and large businesses, and corporations of America including organizations of a charitable capacity with facilities that these resources of people of America may own, have disciplines to manage money, and their resources of committed organizational cause's. Inflation effects all types of businesses, and non-profit organization groups that all recognize taxable earnings, and occasionally the non-taxable issues of income. The Bernard Madoff scandal manipulated, and basically stole money from individuals, and non-profit organizations before he was convicted, and sent to prison for 150 years. Then these people which include small, and large business owners suffered from this recent conflict with severe problems within inflation as well to recover losses.

Every educated American that passes the (6th) sixth grade, and hopefully the high school graduation level of educated knowledge has observed the format of good, and bad issues within inflation. Example's can be observed within the good to build roads, parks, and comfortable structures including community settings, but it is slightly disastrous to have to pay high increases in gas over a vary shot amount of inflationary time. This was an oil industry practice in the Middle East associated with the "Organization of the Petroleum Exporting Countries" (OPEC) which some oil price conditions went from $8.00 a barrel to $30.00 a barrel in a day. The factor of gas gouging in American (c/o international affairs) became a legal format of issues throughout different parts of the United States to stabilize the legal format of illegal fuel price concerns. These issues are seen in other various products from soda pop, candy, and newspapers, to cars, clothes, houses, and thousands of other products like food, soap, and cigarettes. This means with or without the good or bad of inflation with likes, and dislikes of international, and more so U.S. domestic business including government issues these factors consist of managing certain values that are economic evaluated parts of logical price adjustments during a vast amount of the time. Also even good decision making throughout the American society of productive, and responsible business becomes applicable in a logical, and lawfully considered process.

Considering the automotive industry, and businesses such as good engineering firms with government contracts that have been productive with taxable earnings, these certain businesses in America are due for restructuring. The number of Ford Motor Company, and General Motors Corporation manufacturing plants that are closing (c/o some temporarily) have increased between 1998, and 2008. It is vital to remember that this barely makes any vehicles a whole lot cheaper considering the next years coming of new automobile products. These issue's vitally includes the operating liquidity of dealership's that consist of the sales of these products being an important revenue earning, and expense factor. Even more so the manufacturing of cars or any other manufactured products will not easily get any less expensive to manufacture, sale, or manage. These are business facts considering the massive corporations that already have a concerned responsibility for the large, and or extended conditions of their inventory.

The General Electrical Corporation, Boeing Corporation, Raytheon Corporation, and General Mills Incorporated are businesses that also work thru the important mass production, and manufacturing of products that includes this inflationary factual means of cost. Observing, and understanding these businesses, they pay taxes for small items in cost, the very large items in cost, and property taxes. In addition all other logical tax issues are appropriately considered in these massive corporations with products and services of the American society. Therefore the management of taxable product supply, and demand is considered different upon appropriating "warehouse and or storage issues", which is vital to the managing of inventory.

Bowing Corporation, General Electric Corporation, and Raython Corporation have a tendency to have complex inventory (which offsets inflation) because they will take orders for larger ticket items, and then start production. Considering these companies, and businesses consist of contractors from certain businesses the United States government usually has a logic to evaluate these diversified businesses which apply inflation when logical. This is a valued difference within individual state government facilities observing their duties for the people, and consumers which also consist of the quality of work that is excepted as professionals with relevant disciplines. Then the importance of government contractors that manage the concept of economics, and inflation has been observed for the important issues that effect's all products for the people, and the agenda of the American society, and the system of government.

When a person, and more so an official of a corporation, and certain engineering firms that "do work and understand" productive duties for utility companies, and government the issue of inflation exist for products such as electrical transformers with large amounts of wiring, cable, and other technical production parts. General Electric Corporation, Westinghouse Corporation, and a few others manufacture, and sales these large, and important components for electrical engineering projects, which include certain public utility and equipment business projected cost issues. This vitally includes projected earnings, and issues of inflation that are considered for raw materials, and appropriate management duties. These are large ticket items for vital projects that usually have a big cost within demand such as with large hydraulic pumps for mechanical engineering projects, and water process operations. A vital fact besides professional's, goes along the concerns of some of these projects that are not done, and the cost of aged or obsolete infrastructures will include the loss of life, and expensive asset damage. This becomes the subject of innocent citizens being harmed by things they cannot control from certain business monopoly's, or misguided government budget ambitions. These taxable business procedures have complex, but logical taxes most times, and with evaluation factors become's relevant after 90% to 100% of the project, or in a quarterly or annual tax filing format. Considering these issues of complex engineering projects, this also becomes a big part of the American economy's "GDP and occasionally GNP", which includes the American system of government tax revenue.

Inflation has been severely complex along with the 9-11 Report of Terrorist attacks on the airline industry, and other businesses in the United States. The airline company's where some of the first businesses after the terrorist attacks of September 11, 2001 in America to receive government assistance that has similarities to a fractional bailout. Even though these companies have good insurance on most all of their assets, certain contingencies are appropriate when government has a responsibility in the matter. United Airlines Corporation, and American Airline Corporation were hurt slightly bad by the fatal loss of people, and how this destroyed (c/o financial damages) their high priced inventory of 4 commercial airplanes. This became an economic conflict, and struggle for these large corporate business operations. Contrary to this problem of terrorism these businesses had to still be lawfully competitive corporate citizens with logical prices. Both of these companies earned, and managed American taxable income with thousands of employees throughout the United States, and certain parts of the world. Then decisions came from the United States government to take observation of this wrongful act, and consider the things that become important to help these taxpaying business constituents of the American society to be valued as relevant to survive.

Immediately after the September 11, 2001 terrorist attacks the American society of people, and businesses suffered, and observed inflation that became economically severe. The industries within businesses that where effected the most was transportation with a severe reduction of car sales, airplane travel, hotels, and even a complex market within gas, and oil product sales. These conflicting income earning issues are causing good businesses, and companies to reorganize. This being one of the fastest inflation growing times in the history of America, the United States government within the George Bush presidential administration had to take control of things, because an expensive war was the next step to protect the American society. This was also the agreed concern by most other's such as the U.S. legislative, and judicial members of the American system of government. Considering "now" a war had to be declared the factors of the economy, and certain business decisions of the recent past laid the groundwork for a recession, and hopefully not a future depression.

American oil companies have been some of the first businesses to find profitable business operations with increased pressure from a vast amount of American people with good, and mostly bad opinions during the first decade of 2000. Besides hurricanes, and maintaining business operations without oil spills for years, certain oil company's like ExxonMobil Corporation, ConocoPhillips Corporation, and a few others provided strong earnings, and valued tax revenue for the American system of government. A good lawful example with an issue of criminal negligence was when the Exxon (Corp) Valdez oil supply tanker ship on March 24, 1989 caused a massive oil spill in Alaska. Considering this, most oil company's history of being a good taxpaying corporate citizen was part of their business liability to pay, and clean up the contaminated waters caused in this Alaskan Bay disaster. This considerably is another discipline of government, and the courts supported by tax dollars to insure that Exxon Corporation cleaned up the 20 million gallons of oil that they had spilled into the Alaskan Bay.

To protect the liquidity assets of the environment, and even good levels of integrity from the business activity of Exxon it was recognized that they understood the enforced concern, and agreed to help restore, and resolve this problem within the negligence from the liable companies disaster. Exxon's various legal matters including certain law suits observing the U.S. government assessments of damage range from $250 million dollars to certain expense consideration's of over $4.5 billion dollars. During the last 80 years, and through various times these are the factors to support contingent liabilities for the businesses with operational duties including economic, and financial conditions of business survival. Most good American businesses, and corporations plan, and manage their budget expenses for these contingent liability accidents upon damage to the waterway, and natures sea life. These are the business operating conditions that are applicable to the relevance of tax dollar circulations throughout society. Also this compensates the resource of the United States governments valued duties concerning the American society of business, and even more so people.

The American liquidity as it applies to commodities within fish, oil, and even water apart from other types of commodities are vital to protect within the natural conditions upon which they exist. These are responsible values for the well being of all of these commodities, and the people that live, and survive from these natural resources apart from oil business concerns. This also creates the different values of profits including wealth, and or survival from these commodities, and other things that come together in business, and most livable factors of society. Although oil is one of the most complex commodities to create liquidity in a business environment of tax generated dollars, this is part of one of America's strongest markets with tax revenue. Profitable, and taxable earnings from the diversified concentration of food group commodities is just as profitable if pursued properly. Markets providing revenue for the American tax dollars are to lawfully be used to maintain, and supervise these important resources by the lawful observation of consolidated government, and business processes. This vitally includes all the American citizens, human life, and the lives of certain animals to not be destroyed in the overall industrial business processes of society. These are critical parts of most values that keep the American population of people living, safe, and productive including how water, and food items like fish are important for survival, business, and the environment.

The population of America is around more than 300,000,000 (million) people as of the year 2000, and the course of the new decades to come. Within this consideration of hundreds of millions of people a large percentage of the citizen population is responsible for paying taxes on the money they earn as income. Children, and only a few including some senior citizens don't pay taxes due to not having a job that earns them a taxable wage, and or a complex or relevant retirement, but they are supported as important citizens by law. This is considered the prosperity of the general welfare of the people supporting this logical fact as much as possible. Considering these governed facts, and the percentages of the employed or disabled population of American's, a vital consideration also exist when healthcare benefits, and Social Security is applied to the most needed pharmaceutical products, and medical services. Observing the estimated 300,000,000 plus American's almost none have escaped the necessity of this healthcare, and pharmaceutical issues of inflation.

American pharmaceutical companies are another complex, but disciplined business market of small, and large tax generated corporate business constituents, and professional activities. Inflation that effects the American society is most all the time evaluated in the pharmaceutical company's of the United States with medications that are produced, and sold to the general public. The cost of medication has always been slightly complex considering that most of these products require a prescription from a doctor of internal medicine. Understanding most healthcare, and medical procedure disciplines all internal medicine procedures, and prescribed medications sold in America must have approval by the Food and Drug Administration of the United States government. This becomes a process that requires certain testing procedures, evaluations, clinical trials, and even certain scientific, and patient / citizen testimony's. This is a format of liquidity used to consolidate the safe, and appropriate use of a prescribed medicine.

The process of clinical trials are conducted to evaluate chemical product health concerns that can be severely harmful if medications are not used, or prescribed properly. In most concerns if a medication is important for a sick person, the relevant treatment may have issues if a vital need is professionally or appropriately applicable. This becomes fairly expensive within the factual procedures of the doctors providing diagnosed symptoms of the patient. Over time this seems to be an inflationary process within time, and with the commitment of professionals, and products that becomes applicable to the discipline within the tax dollar generating revenue process of small, and large healthcare businesses. Considering this process a vast amount of the population of people have a required understanding of this considered healthcare need that applies to medicine.

The American economy has been valued with the concept of tax dollars generated by pharmaceutical companies. This healthcare sector of American businesses during these times of an economic recession have diversified market corrections, and a few other businesses in some healthcare sectors which have did good, and managed themselves slightly well. Within consideration of the drug making pharmaceutical companies in America I believe the recent times of economic issued conflicts where predicted just as a vast amount of contingent up's, and down's normally effect the sale of medicine. Not many if any pharmaceutical company's throughout America suffered economic or vital harm from the September 11, 2001 attacks, or the 2005 Hurricane Katrina. In retrospect the pharmaceutical company's throughout America ended up increasing their sales of medicine following these sad events of American history. These slightly complex events, and subjects are far from bailout, or bankruptcy issues of facts that are the consideration of law suits, and the liability's of government that occasionally becomes a manageable practice. This also includes the legal consideration of facts, and scientific principals with internal medicine that pharmaceutical company's appropriate with ethical standards, and conduct argumentatively in most court proceedings. Therefore government procedures, issues of inflation, and the concentration of people, and other professional facts are "a taxable evaluation upon inflation" that lawfully must be considered properly.

As inflation and taxes are considered with healthcare, one vital problem of this business sector has been hospitals that were forced to close. Although the rate of hospitals that have closed lately is a small percentage, these are usually vary large hospitals with a vast amount of people effected in certain metropolitan communities. This is dependent on these facilities which the business obligation's is occasionally "simple" apart from cost consisting of payments upon rendered medical services. Then the vast amount of citizen / patient's that pay for their medical services keep the hospital, and society productively working together. The American establishment of hospital's during the 1990's, thru 2005 have seen some conflicting issues of social change, and business matters that keep certain hospitals from earning a taxable profit. They vaguely collect the proper cost of services rendered, which occasionally includes issues of private or government insurance enterprise programs like Medicade, and or Medicare.

The concept of a hospital is a vitally resourceful place compared to any other business that spends or receives money for the services that they provide. Occasionally some hospitals where dependent of county government funds which had been helpful before tax revenue finances decreased with other economic problems, and this was conflicting with various county government budget item's which were cut out. Uninsured people, and illegal immigrants have taken a large part of this evaluation to bad levels upon which the hospital dose not refuse anyone service in America. Contrary to this logical discipline a vast amount of immigrants don't have a social security number which is applicable to the American government process of payment for services. Sadly this includes a group of people in Chicago, Illinois that were caught selling illegal drivers licenses, Social Security cards, and other conflicting items of false identification. Previous to this law enforcement crackdown two (2) major hospitals throughout the Chicago metropolitan area closed, upon which some of these fraudulent identification items were used. This is where lawful supply, demand, and management that is applicable to the laws of America have found certain severe problems.

Observing the overall gross domestic product, and the American economy of businesses such as with Merck & Company, Eli Lilly & Company, Johnson & Johnson Company, and a few others this appropriates enormous tax dollars generating revenue for the American society, and government. These companies, and the extent of a vast amount of profession's in America considering no matter how complex the products, and services may be, the U.S. Anti-Trust factor of inflationary prices must be relevant within negotiated responsibility. Occasionally this takes some taxable scientific products, and services to the revised level of research, and development for valuable issues of study with the most important increase of disciplines within liability. The American society that consist of values for all rich, or poor citizens which is applicable to government statues that apply to the general welfare to maintain balance within price limitations, and lawful resources are a distinct concept, and consolidation of inflation. Large public, and some private corporations, or professional firms including some morally educated foundations that value this consideration of research, and development to achieve urban social values of efficiency are slightly active, and formatted occasionally with this progress.

The urban population with inflation, and taxes is a center point of issues that provide the people, and the American economy lawful similarities. Considering most taxable product's, and service's the enormous Gross National Product (GNP) can consist of millions of items from the lowest of prices, to the highest priced items, including the conditions of finance to own, and use them properly. These issues of GNP are important to control, and observe inflation, and even more so the concept of the U.S. Gross Domestic Product (GDP) rates that mean American manufacturing, and sales are achieving certain business quotas, and doing their part. This supply on demand value of purchase issues, and or agreements is part of the lawfully considered free markets, and the disciplines of competitive responsibilities of most managed businesses.

Within the American values of disciplines outlining inflation, and taxes which are applicable to healthcare, engineering, and other subjects like manufacturing are the business values of America, and the concern that exist in some other countries, but laws, and legislature in the United States must be enforced to keep this process lawfully effective. These are factors that determine how a monopoly of products (c/o corporate issues) that may include valued services "effect" the hundreds of millions of people in the United States, and the important disciplines of occupations, and professions. This becomes the concept of taxes within the American circulation of money that is based on the money and the many concerns of vital revenue. These monetary values of income earnings, and the increase or decline of the American dollar, pursues the effective issue of rates that apply to people, banking, business, government, and other livable values of society. Therefore taxable long term money deposits, and investments (c/o some short term issues) are established for the complex values of considered public, private business, and even logical, and lawful government tax revenue. Then our American concept of rapid, and occasionally considered business government bailouts can be eliminated to its resource of productive small, and large business earnings, and positive government tax revenue. This can conditionally be helpful to most all American's.

CHAPTER SIX

BANKRUPTCIES, MORTGAGES
& LIQUIDITY IN AMERICA

The bankruptcies, economic bailouts, a mortgage lending crisis, and the liquidity problems of American business earnings during the 1st decade of 2000 has caused business, and government tax revenue problems. These disastrous economic, and financial conditions from small, large, and or various corporate businesses is a tremendous setback for the American society within what is considered a recession. This vitally includes the liquidity of government tax revenue to support the American system of government which controls the regulated liabilities of bankruptcies, mortgage banking, and other important issues. These factor's of government, personal, and business revenue has also affected the good, and more so lately bad conditions of residential, and commercial mortgages with households effected the worse. These problems where accumulated from the many conflicts of corporate, and government fraud with some bad foreign relation matters, and a lack of the American system of small businesses to expand as they did two decades ago during the 1980s.

Considering the tax revenue problems of various local governments, the corporations that consist of small, and large businesses, and locations including the people have endured a certain amount of these complex issues within economic problems. This is a repetitious factor that requires clear observation by all business management constituents, and government officials. American businesses including some issues of government has not prevented certain losses of liquidity, and bankruptcy concerning the good, bad, and legally hard working issues that exist in the diversified valued markets of America, and its system of government regulation. This is slightly similar to how nobody in Corporate America, and the American system of government did not prevent the "death of people", and "business losses" from the (9-11 Report) September 11, 2001 terrorist attacks. Also this includes the economic decisions that apply to tax revenue in most all individual cities, towns, and state governments throughout the United States with the changing conditions of business owners, corporations, and operational components of government.

The format, and issues of taxable earnings in most businesses are relevant to the liquidity that is loss, or established in a conditional amount of American businesses. This is also factored in transactions of money from business revenue which creates liquidity for business, and government revenue including assets, and services to be helpful, and expand. This is vital within most long term lawful progress observing the conditions of government appreciated tax revenue. Understanding what the better businesses do with the consolidation of markets is relevant to a concentration of this taxable economic level of prosperity which consist of the vast amount of productive small, and large businesses providing a long-term commitment to the American society. Then the circulation of money within government issues, and the diversified markets of businesses can maintain stable growth with government services for the people, and assets of the American society, and the system of all livable standards.

Observing the sad issue of bankruptcy in businesses, and even in the banking sectors of America the citizens, and or clients which includes various bank employees suffered traumatic losses.

Indymac Bank that mostly had bank business operations in California was forced into filing bankruptcy during July of 2008. This type of bankruptcy with "lose of bank business control" means that the Federal Deposit Insurance Corporation (FDIC) had to take control of the bank to insure the funds of the bank customers, and their deposits. All accounts for depositors at Indymac Bank were secured to the maximum of $100,000.00 dollars is the good, and then inflationary bad relevant liability factors from the FDIC. Any accounts exceeding $100,000.00 belonging to these bank customers loss the equity concern of their additional uninsured money that they had managed, and saved at this bank. A few months later some people had been saved economically when the United States Congress, and the President George Bush administration increased the FDIC account insured limits to $250,000.00 which they passed into law with great speed to help these traumatic losses. This law that was voted in, and passed was discussed extensively by the United States Treasury Secretary Henry Paulson, the Federal Reserve Bank Chairman Ben Bernanke, and more so the Executive Director of the FDIC Sheila Bair.

Another bailout issue was the "Troubled Asset Relief Program" (TARP). The TARP program also consisted of additional U.S. Federal Reserve lending facility expansion's that became the relevant factors of more than $700 billion dollars being appropriated to support more so big businesses. Considering these factors the U.S. government's effort to help the financial industry, and possibly various other businesses that have been financially hurt, became the equation of thought to save job's, and or certain massive businesses. This period of time within economic matters during 2008 consisted of banking institutions, and other businesses which found a vital need to layoff American employees. Considering these "troubled asset relief" issues, and the government duties within official's, a vast amount of hard work was committed to this concern that is required to prevent a recession. This was considered a problem that could lead to a depression, and therefore every professional business, and the resource's of corporations has to work within a certain discipline to productively reorganize. Upon this fact of reorganizing business, and personal assets this vitally includes the effort to achieve progress within the increase of asset liquidity. This business turn around, and restructuring of liquidity effort with liabilities is vitally important for these conflicting economic times during late 2007, 2008, and the future.

When the United States government TARP program appropriates $700 billion dollars to bailout American public, and private businesses this is slightly different from the 1929 economy, and a vast amount of other conflicts within these optimistic, but conflicting years in America. This discipline of appropriated money mostly as loans is a hopeful consideration that the existing control of most businesses will change in certain productive ways. One of the first things that occurred during these massive bailouts was that the U.S. government took over a temporary controlling stake of American International Group (AIG) with an $85 billion dollar purchase of securities in the company. As one person would logically understand apart from AIG's $85 billion government bailout, there was slightly more than $615 billion dollars of government bailout funded money advanced with lending requirements to other corporate businesses, and banks. The CEO of AIG Robert Willumstad was asked to step down, and resign by the U.S. Treasury Secretary Mr. Paulson, and he was to be replaced by Edward Liddy; formerly a top executive at the Allstate Insurance Company.

The American International Group sense 2001, and the 9-11 Report of terrorist attacks has consolidated various suffering with many complicated losses, and high clam adjustments. Years later with additional economics this qualified AIG for a TARP investment of $85 billion dollars by the United States government. This included another complex consideration with AIG observing the vast amount of foreign insurance related businesses that they own, and have insurance agreements with considering different business, and social valued issues throughout the world. These worldwide insurance, and some brokerage business factors including agreements will more than likely be closely evaluated, and considered upon restricting any fraudulent factors, to be supported by various U.S. government appropriations, or certain invested money. Then observing the 2008 U.S. government TARP bailout package (c/o most financial institutions and large businesses) these matters have vital restrictions. These restrictions, and the evaluated level of conditions hopefully will provide great potential for compliance to the United States Constitution. Therefore most governed laws, and equitable liquidity will apply aggressive guidance, and advancements within this 2009, 2010, and future economic U.S. restructuring process.

AIG, and Indymac Bank (c/o 2008) both are under the business, and American government control to be reorganized within careful merger, or restructuring conditions for their managed assets, transaction agreements, and business operating duties. What can be understood from this is the fact that AIG, Indymac Bank, and a few others did not survive in a business capacity, or legal operating format, and this has left them, and others in a critical state of business existence. Whether the cause of failure is negligence, non-productive work, or the importantly observed repercussions from this time of war (c/o Iraq & the 9-11 Report) and other international factors, the establishment of the United States government will more than likely keep these businesses, and asset issues working closer to the U.S. discipline of laws. These issues of considered law decisions within facts are also vital with the process procedures of the (state & federal) American system of government. AIG Incorporated has been considered a different financial conflict due to the many large corporations, and professional firms that they have insured agreements with. Therefore, they will have specific guild-line's from most all the "Executive, Legislative, and Judicial" members of most levels of the state governments, and more so the U.S. federal government.

Understanding the United States federal government over the last 100 to 200 years, when they (c/o government) pay for something or buy something, you can hold relevant that they will work to get the right parts, and everything else in the right way concerning whatever it is they have paid for. These become some of the valued issues of interesting comparison within a few companies that the United States government has observed as contractors. This also includes others with the understanding of not having to provide a bailout to their businesses. Concerning this fact it is important to the laws that the state, or U.S. federal government cannot buy people, or assets that are not for sale except eminent domains, or assets of probable cause, and concern.

Some of the interesting businesses besides AIG, and Indymac Bank included also a possibility within the Lehman Brothers Investment Bank Company that have similar financial market concerns, but they are different upon business establishment outlines. The Chrysler Corporation, and even the LTV Corporation was a few of those companies that had problems in these economic matters. Then besides Chrysler Corporation needing, and asking for a bailout during the 1970s, they were fighting, and litigating this issue between the individual state, and U.S. federal courts including with certain business creditors. An additional conflict is observed that we must remember that some of the first large American company's in financial trouble (c/o the 2000 decade) where the ones closely involved or effected by the 9-11 Report of terrorist attacks, but other bad business issues, and Anti-Trust law violations lingered. On September 11, 2001 AIG, and certain airline company's where effected in a negative way. Before that in the 1990's various U.S. Defense contractors were affected in severe ways. Now the U.S. government has (temporarily) purchased or more so pursued an investment in AIG, and various other corporations to help the stability of their business liquidity. During 2009 it has become conflicting with certain U.S. Defense contractors that were sold to foreign businesses, and individuals. Therefore the U.S. government has only been able to provide minimal national security regulation after foreign control of these "conflicting" levels of ownership in these American / International companies.

Today within the times during 2009, and 2010 the U.S. government owns almost a controlling 80% stake of AIG Inc., and its stock trading concerns. This is similar to U.S. Treasury & Savings Bond guidelines, and agreements upon which doesn't easily consist of corporate shareowner voting rights, but more so enforceable agreements from government. Upon this being something that the U.S. government bought, they will be watching with certain involvement until termed agreements are settled. Also the FDIC is controlling former business banking establishments like Indymac Bank until the United States government will lawfully agree on a buyer to own, operate, and restructure the bank efficiently. Considering this their customer and client deposits, and assets are closely observed, and evaluated until a later date. These considerations are included within merger approved concerns that can lawfully apply, and even eliminate high risk in government spending, and liquidity advancements. Conclusively this becomes dangerous to American private business issues that are similar in other communist countries. In some of those communist concerns the government owned businesses are not all that friendly of a neighborly constituent.

Now in retrospect Lehman Brothers was a large investment bank for about the last 30 years approaching 2007 that had close ownership conditions before filing bankruptcy with their major shareholder American Express Corporation. Bear Sterns was a large investment bank that was over 90 years old, and both of these investment bank businesses are far from a government bailout. Contrary to certain factors, now the business operation of Bear Stearns vaguely exist with any kind of business operation, and this becomes the loss of another corporate business, and resource of tax dollar liquidity revenue. Actually, during 2009 Bank of America received a financial bailout package that consisted of more than $40 billion dollars, and then the CEO Kenneth Lewis, and Bank of America found more trouble with using government bailout money in a newly considered corporate buyout. In less than 2 months after receiving TARP bailout money, Bank of America established an agreement to buyout Merrill Lynch & Company in the range of $3 billion dollars. In addition during 2008 Bank of America made an agreement to buyout Countrywide Bank for a price of $4 billion dollars. Understanding Countrywide Bank, they had lost $24 billion dollars in value before they filed bankruptcy during 2009. These issues of business liquidity are conflicting factors between the United States government, and the American private sectors of business.

To understand during 2009 how bad it has been with other financial brokerage firms Lehman Brothers Holdings Inc. received a $29 billion dollar bailout package form the U.S. federal government, and still months later they had to file bankruptcy. One logic of how the American system of government has liquidity is that a firm such as Merrill Lynch paid $7 billion dollars in taxes during the 2008 fiscal year. Considering the fact that Merrill Lynch had received help from the U.S. government, and TARP funding this seems to describe that the United States government was paying the bill's, and taxes for Merrill Lynch. Observing this the U.S. government has valued consideration on when a business may qualify for a bailout, upon which this conflicting consideration is determined within how responsible or important the business is to American's. Lehman Brothers Holdings Inc., and Merrill Lynch managed a vast amount of American investment financial transactions, upon which these financial brokers are nothing without very productive American businesses that make good on all things in business including income earnings, and GDP rates. Therefore various companies end up in the bankruptcy courts under the state laws, and the procedures of the U.S. Federal Bankruptcy Court system with certain government enforcement, and the narrow option of creditors.

When, and whatever the consideration is within relevant decisions for a business or a corporation to file bankruptcy, there was, or is usually "something", or a vast amount of important issues that should have been corrected ahead of time. Bear Stearns Investment Bank, and Lehman Brothers Investment Bank where businesses in the financial banking industry that suffered from bad decisions, and their asset liquidity flow "which" had became totally written off its balance sheets of value. This was similar to some other American businesses, and corporations throughout society. Then it's important to remember that diversified investments are different from certain levels of business investments to increase disciplines within customer base, manufacturing disciplines, or production business matters that are to create, and manage additional revenue. Contrary to this diversified economic effect one or two sectors of investments, and more so the industry of residential mortgages became one of the largest American economic elements.

During 2006, and 2007 a vast amount of American company's were finding their Securities and Exchange market investment concerns consisting of transactions being shifted more so towards foreign companies, and American debt. This was one of America's most critical problems within the duration of these economic diverse times. American small, and large investment dollars are vitally important to the Corporate American format of equity, and revenue. When more of these American dollars are going to foreign companies instead of American companies, and the people observe there is a lot of financial hurt, this occasionally includes the best citizen / investor opinions at most corporate annual shareholders meetings. These are issues that might have produced something good from businesspeople, and the American people of most professions, and occupations in the United States that honestly can provide good insight with spear money for investments.

Throughout the United States, our American society consist of vast amounts of small, and large investors that pour investment dollars into the diversified companies that offer investment opportunities within the financial market stock exchanges. A valued condition of liquidity growth for American corporations is established from the multi-millions of small investors that take chances, and risk with their valued savings, and investment dollars. When these issues of American business are considered for the various large investors in a business, these people as investors have lawful similarities to small investors because of the percentage point loss or gain effects for the underwritten company. This mostly consist of the fact within all the good, and bad investments that are invested in certain individual company's of choice. This also includes how investors have regular values of job security, and income earning conditions that provides advancements to a well managed better life for American people most times with good decisions.

Every small or large business, or any concept of employment in America believes in the format of future progress, and or more so successful earnings of income. This means that the concentration of earning's, and then extra income can be used as appropriate investment dollars. Considering this the small, and large tax revenue conditions for the government is also created, and valued within these issues of income earnings, and future investment dollars for potential expansion. Contrary to the fact this is a valid consideration of working or workable commitments upon which it is vital to remember that there are U.S. Anti-Trust laws with other vital laws which are established so small businesses can prosper, and even sometimes with logical competition. Other corporate law's, and rules applicable to all investors require equally enforced disciplines by the U.S. Securities and Exchange Commission (SEC) that protects all small, and or large investors, and their investment dollars from illegal conflict. Therefore it is vital to protect the honorable integrity of these American people as investors in a lawful, and productive process to insure the values of prosperity within sacrifices that applies to the U.S. Constitution.

Observing lawful protection issues Constitutionally the SEC of the U.S. government is the legal enforcement agency for complaints, and occasional lawsuits that government observes to keep company's, the investors, and their money lawfully safe, and productive. This is the process to observe financial matters, and the laws on a leveled condition of opportunity for all businesses, and investors. When the American society, and government becomes too important or complacent to prosecute crime in reference of the small investor, or business owner whom may not be a millionaire, or better, then we as American's are losing vital interest in these hard working markets, and constituents. This was the relevant problem with the former U.S. Attorney General Alberto Gonzales whom was from Texas, and seem to be complacent when vital legal issues required hard work. Also just as bad was the Indiana U.S. District Attorney David Capp that allowed white collar, and satellite crimes to destroy hundreds of millions of dollars belonging to Indiana and American small investors, and businesses. These destructive issues also included various issues of violent crime. Vitally in addition, this included certain businesses, and department stores like Montgomery Ward's Corp., Service Merchandise, and other business conflicts, and people throughout "Indiana, Illinois" and other states. Considering this, and a host of other people that considered certain opportunities of this capacity, the decades following 1990 has proven very disastrous economically for millions of Americans "young and old".

Just as an employee dose a good job working from an entry level position, and job, then over the years this makes that business a productively better place, and or operating facility or environment within format. Some small investors with corporate investments do the same for certain other companies. This consideration of facts dose not exclude the large investor, but also the determination of others at corporate shareholders meetings. This also can consist of information that is fair, and lawful within facts of awareness that become valued. These important values include subjects within the progress of an annual business review that are not to be ignored, or "disrupted illegally" which logical investors can offer productive opinions of value. Between the board members, the company's, and certain investors as it applies to growing, and prosperous businesses including certain companies this becomes an asset within constituency. Then it is vitally important for most all American investors, and the future of all involved to manage these investment liquidity issues. These are the factors of American productive small investors that create high levels of prosperity in most small expanding American markets, and various communities. Therefore with all people working productively together contrary to any good, and bad opinionated agreements this becomes the possible advancement of public, private businesses, and certain values of government.

The lawful format of issues that produce government tax revenue for the equation of American communities is relatively important within the productive capacity of the business, and the liquidity of all small, and some large business operations. When the American small and large communities understand, and work together in a productive evaluation of cash flow liquidity the public, private businesses are usually helpful to all people involved. This even applies with the U.S. Anti-Trust laws so that new companies or expanding small companies are not disrupted by illegal conflict from larger businesses or companies that may not be making the same effort. Considering these vital issues of city, town, county, state, or federal governed matters, the local (rich or poor) people from a young age to the older age's of capacity within citizenship can value the American concept of prosperity.

Understanding the concept, and hard work to recover from bankruptcy, and or government financial bailouts the lawfully true values of decision making, and hard work are management issues that apply. Some clear examples of businesses becoming productive out of bankruptcy, and other complex financial times can be observed within the Chrysler Corporation, and the General Electric Corporation. Also this more so could be observed within the government sponsored enterprise of Fannie Mae (the Federal National Mortgage Association) that was founded, and established in 1938 as a government owned enterprise that has endured some very complex up's, and down's financially.

Considering less American people as employed citizens work for Fannie Mae then the Chrysler Corporation, General Electric Corporation, Goldman Sachs Inc., and even Bank of America including a vast amount of other businesses, Fannie Mae has been involved or invested with mortgage, and mortgage lending issues in most every part of America. This, and observing the United States government, certain funded disciplines where consistently applied, and appropriated or sponsored for Fannie Mae stock, and or bond values which intervenes with government bank rates. These government levels of support did not make Fannie Mae an outrageously high earning government enterprise comparing other business operations, but during certain years it gave them, and some others that financial opportunity to do so with discipline.

Between 1980, and 1990 Fannie Mae achieved some of their best annual earnings with doing business in the financial markets, and the "mortgage lending markets" of the United States. Understanding this consideration, and comparison of Fannie Mae, and a business such as Bank of America, and some other companies, Fannie Mae was established to maintain the federal government's lowest overhead rate of employment to dispense their government disciplines of mortgage business operating duties. Bank of American as a large commercial bank has more cost factors, and branch locations then Fannie Mae has employees (1,200 to 1,300 branch locations) considering both may have presents in all individual states in America. Therefore the factor of restructuring a business is to earn profits from the sale of products like at Chrysler, and or General Electric (c/o vehicles, light bulbs, or transformers: compared to real estate) including the help of commercial banks, most issues are not just the disciplines of government. Then these businesses, and banks must do productive evaluations for most conditions of financing business transactions which has comparable concerns to all good decisions including various state, and federal government appropriate values, and discretion. This is vital for businesses managing the larger projected cost, and product demand sales with their tens of thousands or more employees. Upon this understanding within financial investments, and market resources this is relevant as it applies to most all diversified American businesses.

The observation of underwritten stock investments between Fannie Mae, Bank of America, Chrysler Corporation, and General Electric Corporation are severely diversified. This is a fact due to tax revenue factors with massive employees, and liquidity. This is relevant to the businesses so that established operational disciplines within product, and service duties may consist of valued progress. When these public companies provide a public offering of stock ownership to the investors of America's stock exchanges concerning the investment bank stock underwriting process, the price values become a serious financial, and economic concept of business. This includes the fluctuating "owners upon satisfying investors" with good work that seems to consist of a level of security. Considering a vast amount of the business earning profits that are taxable belongs to the company, people working for these issues of productive outcomes of progressive work, and commitments which are valued from their duties. Then therefore they should be rewarded appropriately.

During the 1960s (c/o government conflicts and business) Fannie Mae was taken private as a government enterprise entity that had an offering to purchase stock. This is also one of the factors that started the "Mortgage Backed Securities markets", and therefore business with some investors, and government has similarities within opportunities of investments. Observing this, the outline of the business, and the control of its future which includes the opinions of banking issues has these vital similarities that must be considered properly. Therefore one business does not easily take the other core business into a bankruptcy environment, especially with the concept, and market conditions within questionable "Mortgage Backed Securities"!

Considering the term "Mortgage Backed Securities" these are investments established from Mortgage Backed Certificates that can cause economic default of a banking business process of leading into bankruptcy if management is not careful with decision making. These Mortgage Backed Certificate's, and Securities which come from the United States government enterprise (Fannie Mae or Freddie Mac) is where sometimes banks issue certificates backed by Conventional Mortgages. The Fannie Mae or Freddie Mac mortgage investment securities are packaged as certificates, and put together in a procedure, and process of the selling of the securities to large institutional investors for long term liquidity growth, and hopeful investment cash profits. Within years of business the growth of mortgage backed certificates, including the secondary mortgage market in which they are traded has helped keep mortgage money available for home financing. As American's pay off their mortgages these securities earn money, but during 2005 thru 2010 the bank's, and mortgage companies have endured their worse years of payment collections in U.S. history. The logic, and consideration of this format of transactions includes the failure, and bankruptcy of some of the largest American investment banks that held, purchased, and sold these mortgage backed securities.

When tens of thousands of American household foreclosures occurred during early 2007 this severely affected the Mortgage Backed Securities market, and the economy in various regions of America. The fault within this high rate of household foreclosures was diversified within questionable homeowners with expensive mortgages to pay, and banking officials providing these complex, and diversified resources of loans. Also various other conflicts occurred such as business bankruptcies form business owners that did not always make the best decision including some international business conflicts of interest. Some would understand this problem has went back further then 1999, and the year 2000 to accumulate an economic recession, or worse. These transactions, and securities where leveraged on investment assets from a vast amount of diversified companies, and this has destroyed a percentage of the financial markets, and the economy apart from other types of businesses.

When a person or an American investor of concern understands how the mortgage market's has effected American citizens, this includes concerns similar to the Chrysler Corporation, and General Electric Corporation during 1981 that suffered, and then recovered. Upon this considered timing, America is now (c/o 2008) in a quite different financial crisis then years before. Understanding the American citizen's as investor's, and their commitment of employment or business earnings (c/o liquidity) with investment dollars, a business or government that is caught in a financial bind, this forces the other businesses, and citizens to restructure. If these businesses, and people have not planned a proper budget with contingent restraint liabilities, or they don't recognize this problem in time, certain assets are threatened. Most of these asset concerns consist of earnings (including Investment Assets Leveraged on Mortgage Backed Securities) which will be destroyed, this then caused people conflicts. Understanding individual conflicts various issues made every day problems worse, and worse which instigated more suffering economically. The liquidity of this business process in most banks, and investment bank business procedures are a format of asset leverage supported by most good, and certain bad investments. This also includes ownership of mortgage back securities which became a losing factor to society, and most tax revenue concerns

When the Chrysler Corporation has found themselves in a financial crisis that may require a slow down rate of production, car dealers earn less money, and certain automobile company's (c/o Chrysler and others) order less raw materials including steel from company's similar to U.S. Steel Corporation. Considering these facts the "steel corporation" then also makes less money. Then, it's observed by most all people including most state, and the federal government evaluations of annual tax revenue collected dollars which they have also loss value with, "the observation" of their conditional resource of liquidity which was in vital question. Observing this good, and more so bad issue of business, and government tax revenue from year to year, this becomes a local, and national problem. Chrysler Corporation, and the state of Michigan observed this economic cycle many times that included other state government revenue issues where Chrysler manufacturing facilities had to restructure certain plant operating facilities. This makes these businesses, and their smaller subcontractors or business constituents suffer from a loss of work, and a loss in their quarterly, and annual business revenue.

Operating cost, and earnings is not without too many conditions of indifference, but this is the management observation that all businesses large, and or small must keep strict discipline to prosper. These become the important facts of consideration when all business, and government consist of limited liquidity that must be managed property. General Electrical Corporation, and companies like Westinghouse observing the consumer electrical products that they manufacture, and sale suffered some of these same market slow down issues. These good, and bad issues of sales in a slow market consist of when residential, and commercial "building and construction" products are important to various regional, and production markets. Certain markets such as the new construction sector's of business which are occasionally reduced or have questionable need to buy these products is part of this "occasional slowdown" in market process conditions. This need within products vitally has market values within "decision making", considering the supply, and demand fluctuations of these products that most time consist of construction services. Along with supply, and demand the values of cost of production with issues to earn a profit is part of the vital management factor. Therefore the observation to prevent bankruptcy, and problems within business liquidity planning including good budget decision making consist of skills that are used not to allow bad effects that cause economic defaults.

Default's within the format of American business, and employment tax revenue has been severe, but this has affected the American people as consumers even harder. During the 1990s, and approaching the years of 2000 the credit markets of the

United States became much more active to consumers. As the 2005 and 2008 years approached this issue of credit spending with businesses (c/o internet services) including the concept of lending thru bank rates, this became an offered issue of spending that was not controlled properly in many ways. Due to the expanded use of credit cards with internet consumers buying newspaper prescriptions, various conditions within certain newspaper company's seem to join the source of this liquidity economic problem. This included newspaper company's such as the Chicago Sun-Times, the Star Tribune of Minneapolis, and a few others that found themselves filing for bankruptcy, and having problems keeping entry, and staff level employees was factored from a certain loss of liquidity, and readers. Considering the lack of American people to buy newspapers these changing markets (c/o some internet use) with bankruptcies consisted of a vast amount of their customers that began suffering credit delinquency problems. Observing this increasing economic problem in the American society it also means a level of liquidity could not be quickly restructured with the economic problems of others.

The issue of controlling credit spending was also partly affected when the good, and more so bad of corporate, and business mergers would change the name, management, and interest payment rates against loan customers. At the Chicago Sun-Times Company the bankruptcy consisted of liquidity, and business credit managing problems which became so bad that this newspaper company was sold with a low buyout price of $5 million dollars in cash, and $20 million dollars in liability. The City of Chicago suffered also with the indifference of various conditions of violent crime that compiled a loss of people, and committed customers within a readership capacity. Understanding this, the arbitration of internet subscriptions where still considered an advantage, contrary to the ratio of computer, and non-computer users, but more so computer users apart from criminals is the better equation for the newspaper business issue. Upon this concern the lawful long-term economic resource of people, and businesses still had a long way to go.

Considering this problem within consumer lenders, and loan customers that also had responsibilities to secure employment earnings, or income status the concept of liquidity for business, and the people became slightly loss. Therefore a change of interest rates, and the lack of monthly payment increase's destroyed a normal format of paying off creditable lending agreements of all kinds.

Credit delinquency's by vast amounts of citizen's has become an unorganized problem that includes tax issues, and certain court proceedings to settle financial disputes. A vast amount of American people filing bankruptcy, or living near bankruptcy conditions has factored economic conditions for small, or large businesses, and individuals that depend on a logical format of payments, and or as income. The delinquent issues of credit payments, and income earning wages becomes part of a subject that most of these people must apply budget planning within their daily decisions. This is where certain people involved in certain conditional factors suffered when a bad business concern had issued harmful additional cost to consumers. The majority of the time these consumer price issues can be illegal, and this includes the U.S. Anti-Trust law factors if other businesses cause financial or manipulative conflicts that are vital to the format of applicable liabilities. Also this includes other subjects that becomes complex to fight, and or argue within the courts. Therefore at the same time it occasionally becomes conflicting to be a productive employee, or employer at profitable, and or productive rates. Most productive and supportive employers would allow an employee to take a Leave-Of-Absence, but sometimes they even have conflicting concerns. Considering good management in retrospect to certain conflicts, and precautions these things of importance are not impossible to achieve.

The rate of lawful prosperity is vitally important whether a person or business with credit delinquency, or credit advancement problems cannot maintain the best format of these business transactions at profit earning rates. Considering the person or business with these difficulties the issue of bank savings is just as important to achieve with any type of retirement or future adjustments of cost, and contingencies in life. Bank saving's, and managing of personal funds has not been a good mix for people when their credit payments are delinquent, and upon this consideration bad credit has been declared. Most personal funds and more so some assets such as houses, and even apartment buildings have suffered potential credit losses and foreclosures as they are put into receivership. This is occasionally due to the local economy concerns, and all other governments with losses of tax revenue. Considering this loss of tax revenue the government then needs more liquidity, and cash assets to operate. High property taxes, and other conflicting issues has cost people their conditional values of ownership that occasionally they depend on for credit, and income earning supportive disciplines. Therefore some of the worse problems as it applies to their skill, or ability to manage these assets may require legal procedures, or a severe restructuring of all their personal, and business activities.

During 2005, thru 2010 businesses and people's personal property have endured the conflicting, and consolidated process of being put in receivership. The definition (c/o the Receiver) of Receivership is a person appointed by a court for the purpose of preserving property of the debtor pending an action against him / her, or applying the property in satisfaction of certain creditor's claims, whenever there is danger that, in the absence of such appointment the property will be lost, removed, injured, or damaged. This is a lawful process but the personal assets, and funds lately in these matters have been subjected to bad public, private, and occasional manipulation causing damages throughout an expense driven time. Therefore delinquent overall managing issues occur especially with some young people, and occasionally the elderly that may lack some wisdom or that don't manage as well as some other people. Upon this issue considering how someone that may become absent or disturbed from part of a conflict within a home or a business, the courts have laws that can prevail with lawful work, and valued considerations.

The rate of Americans with bad credit ratings, and or conflicting opinions has hit all time historical depression levels (with recession talk) for people during 2006, 2007, and 2008 not being able to achieve economic prosperity. Considering most American citizens can't pay the full price of cash for various large cost items such as within new vehicles, houses, or a college education the format of budget planning is vital. Also the consideration of any bailout within restructuring must secure the liquidity within the managing process, and most lawful agreements. Managing credit, and even cash within the same relevance as a holding company in the American society is a personal, and business value of decisions. These issues of financial observation should not be taken for granted. When this format, and consideration of value is a loss within proper decisions, these problems can be considered similar to being insecure, or reckless within spending money with no values of good business decision making. These are factual issues, and reasons why during 2008 and 2009 the United States Congress will not easily bailout any businesses that have not made the long-term proper effort or valued success. Over the hundreds of years observing our American history financially, bailing out businesses that fall into bankruptcy is therefore not the normal duty within the system of government in America.

Observing these issues of bailouts, and credit business concerns, this consolidation of business has consisted of complex factors, and occasionally issues against American born citizens. Whether this is done within a financial crime capacity, or a level of disastrous financial negligence, it's bad, and it is an issue that should be considered in the courts if no resolution is properly considered. The business owners of America, and the consideration of good, and bad foreign relations where credit issues are involved has taken a vast amount of American communities in a complex financial direction. It has clearly seem that within the consideration of American gas station owners that have now been taken over by people from the Middle East, a large concentration of American citizens are losing opportunities. Upon these recent conflicts that have occurred, American citizens educated to be productive people in business are not using all their skills due to a lack of opportunities.

Another vital factor of losses within American values of income earnings, and tax revenue also includes the born in America citizens that barely exist when tax filing documents are due in April every year. The format, and duty of American citizens having opportunities of employment, and or business ownership with a responsible logic in the American tax filing process is vitally important. Considering this the concept of American government should have concern that local, and national businesses prosper along with taxpaying employees, and business disciplines that must be pursued with logical liquidity. Observing the millions of people that do, or do not file taxes; in retrospect all top level businesses, and corporations take this duty of tax payable involvement with the highest concern of corporate commitment. This even includes any charitable contributions that some corporations provide to other American constituents, and this also comes from reliable individuals with smaller contributions that are tax deductible. Therefore the American system of small business owners should be valued by the American people to increase their resources of U.S. government liabilities as it applies to expanding a business in the environment of business prosperity, and logical liquidity. This helps the discipline within maintaining community values apart from international conflicts of interest.

The increase of international conflicts as it applies to business, and issues of employment including American tax revenue is based on the values that Americans have established the lawful, and U.S. Constitutions concept of understanding, and sometimes without due process of law. This has occasionally eroded with good, and bad government, and social valued decisions during the last hundred or more years. A relevant factor in this concern is how we keep government operating to support the state, and federal Constitutional laws, which includes the people's rights of liberty. In addition, Americans have a tax duty, and logic to protect, and defend their values as citizens of the United States, and all individual state governments. Considering these issues of liberty, and tax duties a citizen can observe certain bankruptcies, government bailouts, and all importantly conditioned court rendered decisions, and issues. This is even vital to issues of relevance which can be addressed to most lawfully concerned American citizens, and not with diversion to bad foreign dictators which caution may apply. Within all these issues, and values the American people can, and should maintain fair composites of tax dollars in our formal circulation of rights, liberties, and the pursuit of a productively good life.

CHAPTER SEVEN

THE LIQUIDITY OF AMERICAN GOVERNMENT

The liquidity of the American system of government with matured disciplines, and duties is applicable at all levels of official government business, and it's resources to apply financial support within lawful appropriations. Liquidity is a vital financial issue within all cities, towns, counties, and the United States federal government. Over the last two (2) decades various foreign government's such as China, Japan, the United Kingdom, Brazil, and a few others have increased their social, and business concerns of liquidity from U.S. government security investments of Treasury debt. This is partly due to the reasons that the resources of the individual states, and the United States federal governed laws has a duty to collect taxes, manage and purchase assets, and oversee this access of government expense money. These issues of discipline have been the formal concept of government, public and private business concerns of American liquidity factors for hundreds of years.

Sense the 1930s certain Federal Deposit Insurance Corporation (FDIC) liquidity measures are most times Backed By The Full Faith And Credit Of The United States Government when applicable to all types of American commerce banking. A clear understanding of business, and government "Liquidity" is the characteristic of a security or commodity with enough units outstanding to allow large transactions without a substantial drop in price, or value. Considering this is factored as cash holdings, a stock or commodity within the progress of business, and personal earnings including a great many shares outstanding, this therefore consist of productive liquidity upon which good management is still found to be inevitable.

The American system of government liquidity is valued on cash holdings that are mostly established from tax revenue. Also state, and federal grants, and municipal bonds including appropriations are part of this liquidity concern for local, or prosperous lower levels of government which is different for the business sectors of investments, and earnings. Observing certain levels of liquidity, "institutional investors" are inclined to seek out liquid investments (c/o even municipal bonds) so that their trading activity will not influence various (stock & bond) market trading price issues. These factors also include the ability of an individual, government, or a company to convert assets into cash, or cash equivalents without significant loss. Understanding cash holding, and investments that have the cash equivalents of liquidity apart from corporations that exist in all levels of government these are issues of vital importance. Then the sectors, and budget values of government must be managed, and properly expanded for future years of American prosperity.

Investments in money market funds, and listed stocks are much more liquid then investments in real estate, but in retrospect there is disciplined faith for instance as in the U.S. government funds for regular monthly payments such as for Social Security, and annual tax refunds. Having a good amount of liquidity means being able to meet maturing obligations promptly, earn trade discounts, benefit from good credit rating, take advantage of market opportunities, and apply discipline with strong revenue such as within collected tax dollars. During the 1929 Great Depression a vast amount of these American benefits did not exist as it applies to liquidity today. Therefore a depression following the years of the 2000 millennium issues of today will have some of the 2008 social details, and different future effects from 1929. This is similar, but with different concerned factors of a worse economy if everything around liquidity assets are not controlled properly. The content of these assets become even more so important as it applies to foreign businesses with investments that send more investment earnings to other countries. This transaction process of U.S. assets disrupts the American money circulations, especially if American investors are held in severe conflict.

One of the reliable issues to observe, and understand within the concept of liquidity from the American system of government is the purchase offers, and agreements of government securities within municipal bonds, and U.S. Savings Bonds. Also for long term, and short term investments the United States government offers U.S. Treasury Bills, U.S. Treasury Notes, and U.S. Treasury Bonds which includes other asset management issues of government value. A sad factor in the system of financial markets is that these types of secured government investments have been side tracked for international, and domestic greed during the early 1990s. Two of the largest foreign investors of U.S. Treasury Securities (c/o 2009) is China (c/o over $800 billion), and Japan (c/o over $700 billion) which means they earn a big, or secure investment return just like a vast amount of other foreign business, and government investor's. Other levels of security within U.S. investment's was substituted on occasion's for certain foreign investments which also lead to bad "international investments in America helping international terrorism" with fast money to certain (Middle East) enemy countries. Upon correcting this level of American negligence (c/o a kindness for a weakness), is how the value of these assets of liquidity are sold, and managed for maturity which is thru U.S. government short term, and long term market offerings. Considering this the money generates additional investments, and or operating liquidity which is helpful tax collected revenue upon how these can be important accumulated local, state, and federal government dollar's. Then these businesses that can do good, and are considered for the more valued condition of taxable government revenue will, or can be used to benefit, and employ other citizens apart from government layoffs.

Within a logical concern to understand the defined factors of "Treasury Investments" of interest earning opportunities, these issues consist of a strong liquidity base for the U.S. government. Contrary to the differences of business, and government, these government investment agreements are provided, and Backed by the Full Faith Credit of the United States government. These Treasury Securities of investment holdings are largely held (c/o trillions of dollars) with observation by the United States Federal Reserve Bank, but this is investment debt from the U.S. Department of Treasury. One of three security debt obligations consist of these outlined factors; is the U.S. Treasury Bills that are short term securities with maturities of one year or less which are issued at a discount from "Face Value".

The U.S. Treasury Department auctions off these investment assets of 91-day, and 182-day Treasury Bills that take place weekly, and the yields are watched closely in the money markets for signs of interest rate trends. Many floating-rate loans, and variable-rate mortgages have interest rates tied to these bills. The U.S. Treasury Department also auctions off 52-week bills once every four weeks. At times it also issues very short-term Cash Management Bills, Tax Anticipation Bills, and Treasury certificates of indebtedness. Treasury bills are issued in minimum denominations of $10,000.00, with $5,000.00 increments above $10,000.00 (except for cash management bills, which are sold in minimum $10 million dollar blocks) for personal, business, and government investors. Individual investors who do not submit a "Competitive Bid" are sold bills at the average price of the winning competitive bids. Treasury bills are the primary instruments used by the Federal Reserve Bank in its regulation of Money Supply through "Open Market Operations".

Observing a second set of government debt obligation securities within separate title's such as U.S. Treasury Bonds; these investments are outlined as long-term debt instruments with maturity of 10 years, or longer issues in minimum denomination of $1,000.00. The third issue of government securities within this logical format is the U.S. Treasury Notes which are intermediate securities with maturities of 1 to 10 years. Denominations of U.S. Treasury Notes range from $1,000.00 to $1,000,000.00 or more. The notes are sold by cash subscription, in exchange for outstanding or maturing government issues, or at auction. Within this consideration of low end investments that are more so debt obligations the American society with cities, and towns observes "Municipal Bonds" as a part of this format of government liquidity. Municipal bonds are debt obligations issued by the state or more so the local municipal entity. The funds raised may support a government's general financial needs, or may be spent on a special project such as a housing development, or a sewer treatment plant. Municipal bonds must be approved by some electoral body such as a legislature or by the voters in the jurisdiction. For the most part, the bondholder dose not have to pay federal taxes on the interest, and usually does not have to pay state or local taxes if the bond was issued in the state of his or her residence. This also applies to 20 to 25 other bond issues that appropriate similar government needs, and disciplines.

Within the concept of another government secured format of liquidity with investment high grade levels of condition are the government securities that where established in the termed issues of U.S. Saving's Bond's. The defined investment of U.S. Savings Bonds are a United States government bond issued in Face Value denominations ranging from $50.00 to $10,000.00. Issued at a discount, these bonds are rendered at face value at the date of maturity. From 1979, the government issued Series E bonds. Starting in 1980 Series EE and HH bonds were issued. Series EE bonds range from $50.00 to $10,000.00; Series HH bonds, range $500 to $10,000.00. Both earn interest for ten years, though the U.S. Congress often extends that date. Series EE bonds, if held to their maturity, pay 85% of the average yields on five-year availability only through an exchange of at least $500.00 in Series E or EE bonds considering that they pay a fixed annual 7.5% rate *(c/o 1990) in two semiannual payments.

The interest from savings bonds is exempt from state and local taxes, and no federal tax is due until the bonds are redeemed. Thus, bondholders wanting to defer the tax liability on their maturing Series EE bonds can exchange them for Series HH bonds. Earning interest on money in this government capacity of liquidity, and investment values has from time to time made productive levels of benefit for the citizens, businesses, and corporations that purchase them until maturity. Also the U.S. government has a need to maintain revenue for its many duties, and assets which these where part of the progress that slipped from the purchase of U.S. Savings Bonds, and therefore some cities, and states have suffered, which is a vital concern. Otherwise a format of traditional long-term investments in these bond's have loss appeal, but this is similar to the 2008 loss of revenue support within most factors of the American economy. Understanding this a vast amount of bondholders where important to the help within the increased levels of liquidity for the American system of business, and government economic stability.

The consideration of good, and bad foreign relations, and investments has caused a certain amount of harm to the liquidity of American government, and certain businesses that are government contractors including some global business operations. This part of the American tax dollar revenue, and the economic structure of certain cities, and towns keeps a money circulation that rewards the future of America if things are done right. A known format of people working together has been lost to foreign competition in a unproductive capacity that is the vital factor for businesses in a city, or town to maintain strong revenue. This vitally includes the tax base that supports that local government's resource of liquidity. Considering this, more local businesses have opportunities of earning money from government, and this includes the people in the most lawful, and productive economic way's. Sometimes this is observed as the "majority, and minority" factor of nationalities, but another fact consist of how the educated people are able to invest, and manage money wisely without crime in a domestic or international capacity. Truly this becomes important for all people considering government provides a fair tax rate. This therefore appropriates logical economic growth, and liquidity within a format of confidence in the future of the people that make up the local American citizens of society.

Upon the format of the 1940s, and 1950s the concept, and purchase of U.S. Savings Bonds accumulated additional government revenue to build highways, and other government structures. Observing that this is borrowed money or debt from the people (c/o American citizens) it provides enormous economic, and financial leverage for the U.S. government to get vital, and important things done. Between 1941 and 1945 some of the first years of offering the sale of U.S. Savings Bonds the United States government sold $54 billion dollars worth of these bonds. Considering a vast amount of corporations that offer corporate bonds, this is a steady format of interest rate barring investment concerns similar to some government, and even corporate bond issues. The Internal Revenue Service helps the collections, and regulative disciplines that these bond agreements are applicable under the law to be disclosed, or filed thru with the normal tax documented procedures, and process factors. Although tax payment advantages apply when anyone purchases, or invests in these government securities of valued liquidity, the rules must be considered in a logical, and lawful capacity. These issues of public, private, and government concerns of working to maintain valuable levels of economic liquidity, and investments are not overwhelmingly complex, but like anything of responsibility, these sacrifices have to be pursued, and honored.

Understanding various sacrifices, and providing honor to the U.S. Constitutional rights of the citizens, the U.S. government is appropriated the duty from time to time to give citizens, and businesses the lawfully logical help they need. During the Great Depression (1929) when 1,000s (thousands) of banks closed, and other businesses endured very complex problems the U.S. government pursued the duties of passing certain helpful laws, and followed up by enforcing those laws as quickly as possible. Today during the first decade within the years of 2000 the U.S. government has similar problems where the asset liquidity of government funds are being used to fight a war in Iraq, and Afghanistan. This severely involves the law enforcement and defense on terrorist matters against American citizens, and certain valued assets, but a lack of enforced U.S. Constitutional laws has lingered making citizens vulnerable. These diversified issues can be observed when people from other countries such as Japan (1941), Iraq and the Middle East (1990 & 2001) have brought negative conflicting ideas to the American society during their migration. Even more so this includes how business crisis such as the first decade of 2000 consisting of a financial mortgage, and bank business operating crisis became a disaster that negatively affected America. The Energy Oil Embargo of 1973 also negatively affected America with similar concerns that the U.S. government worked to resolve with enormous frustration. This therefore is a format of the U.S. government that protects it's liquidity to pursue appropriations for the general welfare, and prosperity concerning the domestic tranquility of American citizens, businesses, and assets.

The liquidity within certain state, and federal government funded engineering, architecture, and construction projects has been an issue within cost estimated overruns. When a project has a cost it is important that budgets are maintained until the full completion of the project. Between Indiana, Massachusetts, Illinois, and a few other states, a certain amount of cost overruns have existed on large library projects, and numerous highway projects. Considerably a format of government liquidity has been paid out when other projects like water retention levees, and drainage projects where not considered or completed. Another observation is government engineering and construction projects had more detailed importance for roadways and highways when sub-grade sewers, and storm water control systems where needed more so. This is vital when a vast amount of "flood damage cost escalated" from obsolete sewers including a vast amount of storm water systems that need repairs, or "new project considerations" thru government.

Outside of government contracts this has occurred frequently in certain Hollywood (California) movie entertainment filming productions, but that is factored more in the private sector of business, and movie making detailed considerations of a market. A vast amount of movies never earn a profit from the money that is spent to make the film, and this discrepancy caused harmful liquidity values to the banks and others upon becoming a loss to overall production, and liquidity advancements. This occasionally is an additional severe cost of local, state, and federal funds (c/o private business) that could have been appropriated better with good planning, and management. Good management applies in entertainment because every year a big film making company or an independent film producer may come up with the biggest seller of the year. This generates enormous profits which is valued on all accomplishments that must be held effective. Upon these factors the profitable earnings will exceed the cost of making a good movie or entertainment production project. These relevant cost appropriations also include other government assets, and therefore they would help eliminate the suffering of people's homes, assets, and even their lives if conditions change in a negative capacity. Considering this, and the movie productions that are done all over the United States, and other parts of the world, the American values of Constitutional law, and management apply. Then the American format of business disciplines is complete for a logical amount of time.

The format, and liquidity within the American system of government as it applies to health care, education, utility infrastructures, and other subjects are vitally important to keep excessive cost in complete order. Within the concept of the lowest to highest format of government, excessive fines are bad, and most times are ruled or pursued as Unconstitutional. Understanding this in the American society certain expensive projects have important relevance just like certain values of "research, and development" that will benefit most all citizens. Contrary to this relevance the evaluation of the right projects is the vital issues of tax dollar liabilities of an appropriate factor. A few vital examples during the 1990s and 2000s are "Stem Cell research" that is one of these important considerations that has to be put into a legal, and legislative format for governed, and more so professional medical use. Stem cell development apart from television production, and other issues helps strengthen a humans vital internal organs with conditional hormone growth, and development of organs to survive better. This hormone development process is important when these organs that are ill in a person, or that are factored as "irregular" from proper growth, and survival has potential that can be reconstructed productively. Therefore these importantly considered health care issues of excessive cost applies to all proper decisions, and the decisions of other market sectors of governed consideration.

The observation of a second excessive cost evaluation concern is "Storm Water sewers", and drainage systems within older cities with obsolete drainage infrastructures. This vitally includes the drainage systems with river water infrastructure details that are another vital consideration for government tax dollar spending. Some other things go as far as the need to regulate the use of commercial satellites, and the concept of internet computer systems that are applicable to the U.S. Federal Communications Commission (FCC) regulative duties within the input and output of information issues of concern. This being an advanced time of hopeful normal living with new scientific principal matters, includes good, and bad technology. Considering this technology in the American society means we have to get most all of these factors of advanced technology operating or processing with lawful conditions accurately applied, and without harm or instigated conflicts to innocent citizens. It has seem relatively so that a vast amount of American citizens are victimized by these issues that apply to infrastructure concerns, some scientific principals, and the deceptive part of information technology from the arbitration of certain internet activities.

The public, private, and government participation of working together is an important logic that keeps government liquidity, and most small and or large businesses including most normal citizens productive in their day by day duties. Observing the arbitration of good, and bad research that appropriates certain products for the American general public, these conditions have important legislative concerns so that the uses are lawfully right, and not destructive to other citizens in an Unconstitutional format. Some new factors of technology have cost citizens additional money, especially during a time when a financial recession is keeping the people, and the economy from issuing the best levels of American prosperity.

A valid example of an American recession that is taping a near depression is the concept of problems within the American Automobile Industry of 2008, and what is being considered as American troubled asset relief issues to strengthen liquidity. The "American Automobile Industry" consist of the issues of where the 3 largest automobile companies have loss an enormous amount of money within quarterly, and annual earnings. This includes their relationships with the good, and badly troubled banks during 2008 to finance their vehicle products with service agreements. These publicly held companies within Ford, General Motors, and Chrysler are all suffering financial problems to the extent that they need TARP bailout or loan considerations from the U.S. federal government. During the last months of the year 2008 this effort by the major American auto company's of the United States has consisted of them asking for $25 billion dollars out of a $700 billion dollar bailout government plan for certain financial companies. Considering these three corporations that would split at least $25 billion dollars, it was something that the U.S. Congress would not except easily, but there was concern for them to survive. A formal concept of logic explains that this effort by the automobile companies is not over easily as well until they achieve a more improved economic future, and outlook.

Now that a very bad recession has caused harm to numerous businesses, and corporations including the American auto manufactures, they have returned back and forth to testify, and bargain with the United States Congress on lending them money with approved agreements to financially restructure. From these bad economic times this commitment will consist of large sacrifices. This effort, and process has not been received with easy acceptance by the U.S. government, and citizens. Ford, General Motors, and Chrysler have now had to change a few things to ask the U.S. Congress, and the executive office of the President Barack Obama for the U.S. appropriated approval of $15 billion dollars in bailout money that they intended to pay back in time. This TARP lending issue to the automobile companies is considered important to retool manufacturing facilities to make cars that apply to newly established U.S. EPA and U.S. Energy proposed standards as it even applies to battery operated cars. Also this effort is to try to reduce the amount of foreign oil that America depends on!

Considering this effort, this includes the discipline that has brought the United Auto Workers Union (UAW of America), and the management of these American automobile manufacturing companies together in a valid, and needed way. Truly my opinion, like some others is that the Barack Obama Presidential administration has already applied too much bailout money to big corporations, and businesses without a vast amount of smaller businesses benefiting that have similar problems. Also in addition the results must be a format of all people working together to achieve some goal to save the company, and operate a productive business. These are some of only way's that the liquidity of these businesses will improve, and that is by producing a high level of employees working together, "not" just against each other as they have done occasionally for years which occasionally cause harm to America. This format of working together vitally includes without any loss of discipline to restructure their market share. Then their levels of production cost, and the overall business operation is among corporation's that consist of appropriate liquidity values of liability.

Understanding the separation of powers, and business in an American format of concern from the United States government, and the people working together is a powerful tool of social value within the applied effort of all branch's of American government, and these values must be taken serious. Contrary to perceptional failures with good products, and some business planning throughout the American automobile industry lately, certain financial market businesses with the executive, legislative, and judicial branch of government will all have a powerful role to play. The important role of government in these matters is to keep the American society out of an economic recession with certain businesses maintaining equality.

Considering the various CEO's of Ford Motor Co. Alan Mulally, the CEO General Motors Rick Wagoner, the CEO of Chrysler Robert Nardelli, and Ron Gettelfinger of the UAW their job of needing to be heavily involved in the U.S. government bailout concerns is complex with careful consideration of the future. It was even more important that they all come together for a common agreement, and goal. The vast amount of American cash liquidity that the U.S. federal government is using is an indicator that business revenue, and the American issue of employment is losing ground. This management, and labor issue is vitally important to recover without a loss of faith in government. Considering these facts the U.S. government, and others in industry including social conflicts can be the blame of isolated problems upon which can result to an increase in crime. Therefore a lot of changes will be required, and some issues will more than likely go back to the older ways of doing some things that work properly, including the decisions to depend on the right advancements of technology.

The separation of powers that the American system of government consist of has the resources to correct the problems of the major economic recession of 2005 to 2015. Considering this time period of 10 years the concept of government will change a number of times in the future while the solutions of these problems are hopefully being corrected. A new U.S. President such as Barack Obama the first black American President is only a slight consideration of answers to correct this liquidity crisis that America is faced with. Within a strong example the American society is observing that weeks before President-Elect Obama's inauguration Chrysler Corporation is planning to close all 35 of their North American manufacturing plants for one month to save money. This indicator cannot continue to get worse considering they have an estimated 36,000 employees.

Observing the factors of the Chrysler, Ford, and General Motors resource of businesses, a certain value of consideration is the labor workers within the United Auto Workers Union. For years labor unions have served some good purposes to the people that are members, and their families. Considering this I have recognized that if unions ask, and or demand more than necessary from these companies management, they will eliminate the logical factors of the business. These issues are critical in businesses which have established their place of employment, and this then destroys important facts within business liquidity values. Basically no matter how big, or how much a business is worth, there is a limit to everything within logical money, time, and effort. I believe some people involved have forgotten other people apart from labor unions that must earn a more detailed wage, and be productive as well considering the company's management officials with important duties. Therefore when labor union wages continue to go up, "but no cars are being sold" to earn the company "money" this becomes a very serious problem for all including government that must evaluate the many things, and people that will be effected.

These liquidity factors of public, private businesses and government in America become the relevant long-term concept of disciplines of tax revenue for productive living. Considering these American values that consist of managed tax revenue by American states, and the United States federal government these formal factors of liquidity are the responsibility of all people, and business working together. When all the good, and bad of business, and government keep this lawful format together in its diversified nature everyone from the young to the old are valued with meaningful assets, and opportunities. Within this worldwide concern of liquidity that is valued in other international business, and government concerns, it is relevant that the United States continue, and more so improve their work duties. These are the valued issues of managed asset liquidity, and then our American prosperity is, or becomes factually good, productive, or better.

CHAPTER EIGHT

FEDERAL FUNDS FROM TAXES &
THE U.S. INFRASTRUCTURES

As American tax dollars are considered, the format of federal funds, and the federal funds rates including tax dollars are a vital American government resource. These tax dollars besides waged salaries are spent on a variation of United States government infrastructure projects, and even within the vital resource of banking regulatory matters of the United States that consist of management concerns of asset liquidity. The duty of the United States government consist of values to protect citizens, and liquidity growth throughout the American society which is extensively from citizens, and more so the productive commitment of small, and large businesses. This becomes the bi-partisan level of sovereignty that the United States Constitution, all levels of government, and the American people's society was established on. Considering this format, the process of all taxable income earnings creates large conditions of liquidity within federal funds, and government asset's such as vital infrastructure projects.

The issues of the U.S. Federal Reserve Bank funds, and Federal Reserve Bank rate values consist of conventional lending with rates such as within prime rate lending, and most discount lending rate issues. Within these business, and more so banking issues this process is to benefit the American society in a long-term concept of financial and economic disciplines including most conditions of financial solitude. Understanding the United States Federal Reserve Bank, and the format of the Chairman Ben Bernanke (c/o 2009) raising, or lowering these bank interest rates, this is a money lending, and managing issue for bank institutions. Considering this resource of bank duties including the bank depositors, this provides cash liquidity savings, and finance resources of discipline throughout the American banking system which includes the stability of liquidity in various businesses.

The diversified (c/o commerce) federal bank fund managing concerns in the United States is from the federal governments banking procedures within the state, and more so federal governments way of regulating vital American assets of liquidity. This is applicable within all individual state government issues that the state executive and legislative officials observe with agreeable procedures to pursue formal banking decisions. Then this format of the state, and federal governments banking regulatory conditions are valued regionally (c/o jurisdictions) as it is applied occasionally from the court's, and the U.S. Federal Reserve Bank, and government. Upon these factors of regional banking procedure's, and the concept of banking laws these factors then can be reviewed just as it applies for the diversified concentration of citizens, government matters, and businesses. Considering these issues of asset liquidity, the money is approved, and managed by the U.S. governments Treasury Department, and other sectored departments of government as occasional loans, and or appropriations to build government dams, levees, highways, bridges, and or certain facilities. Some of these bank disciplines is part of prime lending considerations that applies to the best or most disciplined bank business clients, and customers, "which" is factored as "Prime Rate" lending. The Discount Rate of lending is for member banks, and banks that do business at the U.S. Federal Reserve Bank Discount window.

Understanding the funding and process of U.S. government funded projects considering this may also consist of research, and development of these levels of liquidity which are financially approved congressionally as helpful, safe, and lawful to the citizens. These are federal funds that even help businesses with these regulatory issues that includes factors of government discipline. The funding of these U.S. government projects is the distinctive way the American Restoration and Recovery Act, and other similar bill's before where passed by the U.S. Congress with the support of the president. Considering this, it is also important to remember salaries, and retirement pensions of all logical, and diversified government employees are a valuable part of this process. Then both government, and business is funded properly "which has some similarities" to all types of other businesses besides government contractors. Therefore all government money is considered for the input, and or the output of government cash liquidity that is subject to the highest possible condition of managing duties.

The highest bank managing discipline in the United States is at the U.S. Federal Reserve Bank. If we review definitions from the financial resources of the U.S. Federal Reserve; Federal Funds has three conditions, and the first is that funds are deposited by a commercial bank at the U.S. Federal Reserve central bank locations, including funds in excess of bank reserve requirements. Banks may lend federal funds to each other on an overnight basis at the federal funds rate. Member banks also transfer funds among themselves on behalf of customers on a same-day basis by debiting, and crediting the balances (c/o the Fed Wire) in the various reserve banks. Another condition of federal funds is money used by the Federal Reserve to pay for its purchases of government securities. Then federal funds are used to settle transactions where there is no "Float, or Uncollected funds".

Observing the U.S. Federal Reserve bank system we must find it logical to understand the definitions of federal funds rates. Our American concept of this, "Federal Funds Rates" is the interest rate change by banks with excess cash reserves at a Federal Reserve district bank to the banks needing overnight loans to meet cash liquidity reserve requirements. Alan Greespan, and the present U.S. Federal Reserve Chairman Ben Bernanke have been active in adjusting the Federal Funds Rates with coordination, but the recent 2008, and 2009 American economy may take more than banking rates to recover. American people and businesses have to be advancing their savings, and checking deposits as well. Apart from 2007 a vast amount of businesses got worse with over 150 banks during 2010 closing, or restructuring with new owners buying some of these troubled banks. Also during 2010 other types of business bankruptcies have hit historical rates, and therefore adjusting bank rates was far from the only solution. The federal funds rate is also the most sensitive indicator of the direction of interest rates, sense it is set daily by the market, unlike the "Prime Rate", and the "Discount Rate" which are periodically changed by the banks, and by the U.S. Federal Reserve Board, respectively.

These sensitive indicator's within rate structures are vital to small expanding businesses establishing prime rate lending, and with business bankruptcy filing increasing, the Prime Rate "advantage" is slightly obsolete until business improvements are established, or they are properly adjusted. Considering the fund issues, "lending is established with "Prime Rate" defined as an interest rate banks charge to their most creditworthy customers. The rate is determined by the market forces effecting a bank's cost of funds, and the rates that borrowers will accept. The prime rate tends to become standard across the banking industry when a major bank moves its prime rate up or down. The rate is a key interest rate, sense loans to less-creditworthy customers are often tied to the prime rate. Considering this, Blue chip company's may borrow at a prime rate, and a less-well-established small business may borrow from the same bank at a prime plus discretion of around 2%, or 12%. Although the major bank prime rate is the definitive "best rate" reference point, many banks, particularly those in outlying regions, have a two-tier system, whereby smaller companies of top credit standing may borrow at an even lower rate.

Upon these factors there is relevance within the "Discount Rate" that consist of interest at a percentage rate that the U.S. Federal Reserve charges member banks for loans, using government securities or "Eligible Paper" as collateral. This provides a floor on interest rates, since banks set their loan rates at a notch above the discount rate. Then upon other matters of the interest rate issue this is used in determining the "Present Value" of future cash flows which also occasionally applies to a certain capitalization rate issue. Observing 2008, and 2009 various banking establishments filed for bankruptcy, even after building new facilities upon which they could not even hold the equity in their businesses, and pay this Discount Rated lending fee commitment. Therefore the evaluation of the Present Value within future cash flow had diminished due to various cliental problems such as the economy, and even the cost of flood damage repairs. Inadvertently the hardest hit States (c/o banking and housing market issues) where Nevada, Arizona, Michigan, Indiana, California, and Florida upon which the majority of most of these states consist of senior citizens, and immigrants. Considering these economic troubles various senior citizens are supporting most economic resources upon which their younger relatives are having a tuff time not finding adequate employment.

Within the format and considered issues lately in certain corporate American business structures the "Discount Window" of the U.S. Federal Reserve besides "Prime Lending" has played other complex roles. Considering the U.S. Federal Reserve discount window is where banks go to borrow money at discount rates, doing business at this extent with the "U.S. Federal government, and the Federal Reserve Bank becomes a privilege, and "not" a right. These factual disciplines vitally include banks that are discouraged from using the privilege except when they are short of cash liquidity reserves, and not just bank (c/o corporate) holding assets. From the years of 1995 to 2001 up until 2008 a vast amount of businesses losing revenue, and American dollars being sent to foreign countries, their banking establishments have caused a severely weak dollar currency rate, and eliminated additional liquidity in American banks. Therefore it is vital that the money circulation in the United States improve to appropriate liquidity to control debt, money supply's, and a comparable overall tax revenue base.

As a business understands prime lending when it applies to corporations that have established a business relationship with the U.S. Federal Reserve Bank Discount Window the first version of prime lending was a unit that came into existence with American Telephone and Telegraph Corporation (AT&T). This consisted of the AT&T underwriting stock in late 1983 becoming active in treading with prime lending, as AT&T was understanding divesture. Some investors may have reorganized the issue of how this prime lending rate (c/o a discount window rate privilege) issue with certain corporations like General Electric (c/o GE Finance & GE Capital) Corporation, General Motors (c/o *GMAC) Corp. and even Chrysler (c/o Chrysler Acceptance) Corporation, Ford Motor Company and others exist in this relevant concept of lending. All these corporations became "also" bank holding or finance (unit) companies to sell their large ticket items. This becomes a slightly productive process without certain banks, and then they manage their business operations (c/o the sale of inventory) with banking matters of which include some investment dollars to increase, and stabilized liquidity.

There is an observation of very severe differences between banking procedures, and the engineering and construction of United States government funded infrastructure projects, but for over 100 years these values of government have consisted of a vital logic within coming together. In 2009 to apply help for the economy, and vital upgrades to the infrastructure the President Obama administration and the Congress passed the American Restoration and Recovery Act. The effort within the American

Restoration and Recovery Act appropriated $800 billion dollars for American infrastructure projects. Understanding the consideration of all the diversified geographical settings of the United States of America the government has been good about building certain parts of the infrastructure that is helpful. Occasionally the long-term maintenance of infrastructure issues may suffer some ups, and downs, but this is similar to the applicable disciplinary process of quality work for any project. The lack of quality work within engineering, and construction which has consisted of certain very expensive accidents over the last few decades could disproportion some of the $800 billion dollars that the American Restoration and Recovery Act will, and has applied. This more than likely will not happen out of control, but the U.S. government needs to apply this money to most rightfully important projects, and not the wrong ones.

The level, and rate of employed American people, and government working at productive rates to maintain their regional infrastructures is usually a good size number, but during 2010 the number of unemployed people reached some of the highest levels in U.S. history. The consideration of people with professions, occupations, and opportunities to benefit from government liquidity, and money appropriated for various infrastructure concerns will not easily influence the Federal Funds rates. Observing the good working skills from various workers is a vital part of these tax dollar funded projects (c/o duties) being done at good rates of efficiency, this is vital only with them, and other American's creating new businesses is how the U.S. economy will improve with logical spending.

A good rate of work done on needed infrastructure projects during the years of 1995 to 2005 has been important, but even more so "vital" is the consideration that these concerned projects have certain detail's that were missed or ignored that has caused the American people of certain regions to suffer. Throughout the Northern parts of Indiana, and Illinois where hundreds of millions of dollars have been spent on new highways considering there has been additional cost factors, this has caused government liquidity problems. Contrary to these federal funds, and the cash liquidity that is applied to these projects, upon which there is "conflicting" subjects, but this is of severe importance as it applies to factors around most American assets. These new or existing asset highways occasionally make sense, but even more so the important fact is that the highways as it applies to the resident's, and businesses surrounding them must have a productive drainage system from the rain, melting snow, and or storm water that is to be properly managed. This also may apply to other important issues of the region.

Upon the completion of certain highways (c/o 2002 to 2008) each year in certain parts of Indiana the concept of flooding got worse causing people that live near these highways, and certain rivers massive problems. These flood problems become very expensive with additional cost that had to be observed considerably. This factor of inconvenient cost, and liquidity may one day exceed the cost of building the regional highway due to flooded house's, and businesses who's asset's were damaged. Within these obligated government tax dollar projects, and most all professional engineering duties that apply, it is vital that the determination of good, and bad operating conditions must be evaluated, and corrected with proper revisions.

State and federal appropriations of government money is the important concept of liquidity that some infrastructure projects receive upon the relevance that they should not consist of excessive cost within other things such as residential, and commercial damages. During the first decade of 2000 each time we defeat the financial purpose of doing very expensive projects, a loss of liquidity is strongly possible when project components don't work right. These are revisions as in their best possible designs, and calculated solutions as completed projects that are approved in this professional and government level of progress, but the highest level of complete efficiency is vital. It has been recognized in Kansas, Pennsylvania, Iowa, Indiana, Illinois, and a few other places besides the a-ray of problems in California consisting of sliding mud, and earthquakes. This vitally includes the concept of hurricane's in Louisiana, including other near-by southern States such as Florida, and Texas.

Each time various states have been declared by the U.S. President or a State Governor as a "Disaster Area", or they are placed in a "State of Emergency" a valuable resource of government liquidity becomes important. Some acts of nature are unavoidable, but some conditions of bad weather can be dealt with in a responsible way. Federal funds rates are then considered as an asset to use in a protective way. These issue's of American public, private business liquidity within issues of architecture, engineering, and construction becomes the process to appropriate an infrastructure solution. If things professionally are not done right this can potentially cause damages, and this becomes the need to be corrected, and revised possibly in some insurance, and professional capacity to help victims, and or survivors. Considering a rate of fatalities is "low to even none" some people become ill, and therefore these infrastructure damage issues that appropriate renovation projects are pursued at conflicting levels of "personal ability, and production".

When the U.S. Federal Reserve Bank observes financial issues in certain markets the vast amount of government, public, and or private business duties are vital to most American assets, and people. After various private real estate projects expanded during the 1990s throughout the 2000s these overbuilt facility markets caused various contractors hardships in receiving payments within profitable earnings. The concept of government contracts consisted of different business, and market equation concerns. Considering the increase of bankruptcy filings with public, private business sectored engineering, and construction contractors this also consisted of discretionary government projects which still had considerable difficulties. Considering this process of liquidity quotes, and estimates that could not be profitable, the rate of lending money, which was important became another discipline that became just as important. Then within all government projects these became the most secured appropriations of earning logical money as taxable earnings. These become vital issues for tax dollar procedures, and uses to be productively workable in the American society. The engineering and construction of American infrastructure projects funded by government helps protect the liquidity of most all people, and assets of certain regions. One of the only other conditions of engineering, and certain detailed construction duties that may have a steady flow of vital "professional, and occupational" duties of work is valued within the public utility company sectors of the United States. Contrary to public utility upgrades the United States government, and all other systems of American government should be slightly observant, and productively ahead of all others in upgrades of infrastructures that enter-phase with utilities. These projects are usually managed in a Constitutional law level of consistency by the U.S. Department's of Energy, Interior, and Transportation considering a level of support from individual state governments. In addition it is even important to understand the extent that corporate businesses may endure in a management capacity. These concerned factors are recognized in the automobile, and steel manufacturing business sectors that subjectively may slow down due to economic issues, and demand which requires "continued progress that is vital".

Theoretically infrastructures, government, and public utilities are a sure factor of business observed procedures, and planning for involved solutions. Over all a vast majority of public utility infrastructures are closely relevant to most government projects, and then this becomes vital with water, wastewater, telecommunication, electricity, and natural gas systems to the general public. After all the people of the general public pay for the utility's in their home's, and businesses. Another similar issue of concerned fact is that government pays the cost for its separate jurisdiction of utilities as well. Therefore even the continued maintenance, and upgrades of these utilities and infrastructure's becomes part of the different business revenue, and tax revenue of most American regions. From this slightly complex lending and "appropriations process of government money" and work duties as it applies to the U.S. Federal Reserve, and or certain government department appropriations, this therefore goes along the value that the people, and citizens have a logical right to good service.

The concentration, and duties within the U.S. Federal Reserve Bank has been around over 85 years (c/o 1913) with modifications by the President, and the U.S. Congress. Observing the courts have a role to enforce the laws that apply at, and from the U.S. Federal Reserve Bank they have two out of four consistent duties that help infrastructure projects in the American society. After President Woodrow Wilson and the U.S. Congress established this U.S. government banking process and facility; one applicable duty (c/o the U.S. Federal Reserve Bank) was conducting the nation's monetary policy by inflicting the monetary, and credit conditions into the U.S. economy in pursuit of maximum employment, stable prices, and moderate long-term interest rates. A second (2nd) U.S. Federal Reserve Bank duty out of the four other major duties was providing financial services to depository institutions. These depository institutions, and the United States government including foreign official institutions became slightly relevant upon providing a major role in operating the "nation's payment system". Although these check payments are endured from the U.S. Department's of Transportation, Energy, and others more like the U.S. Department of Treasury these concerning issues are also applicable to the U.S. Federal Reserve Bank standards. The payment liquidity factor has lawful, and logical obligations that must be preformed, and satisfied. Considering this foundation of government providing liquidity, and payment to different firms, and corporations to improve the infrastructure these business transactions with disciplines become issues that consist of an applicable format to get things done productively.

During the late 1990s thru 2006 a highway tunnel infrastructure project was funded, and built in Boston, Massachusetts that consisted of a proposed engineering and construction cost to the government for the project at $2.6 billion dollars. At completion of the project 6 years later in Boston the consultant engineer / construction contractor for the Massachusetts Transit Authority had increased the cost of this highway tunnel project to $14.8 billion dollars with cost overruns. Even as an addition to the Central Library of Indianapolis, Indiana started with an estimated appropriated cost of $23 million dollars, and then escalated to over $150 million dollars this issue of "asset liquidity conflicts" is a problem in the format of most government budgets. Contrary to any cost factors of logic for the completion of these engineering, and construction projects, they must be done or completed to 100% operating capacity. The government appropriations for these project's has been a serious concept of cash liquidity for the State of Massachusetts, and as it applies to the indifference of Indiana, Illinois with massive projects lately, and the U. S. federal government. This is occasionally similar to a problem within U.S. Anti-Trust laws of controlling the cost of something that normal citizen's have been hurt by which includes issues such as in the mortgage, and credit markets that is not easily tolerable. These conflicting factors have seriously hurt the nation's payment system in reference to the U.S. Federal Reserve Bank system of standards within their government banking provisional duties to evaluate liquidity.

Observing the need for certain state highway, and waterway projects it becomes an important consideration to be an engineering consultant of good cost estimating, and productive work creditability. Contrary to disciplines of the Boston project, a different set of issues occurred within the State of Minnesota where in August of 2007 the I-35 bridge collapse was tremendous due to overloaded heavy equipment on the bridge. This issue of negligence occurred during construction upgrades, and this tragedy also vitally consisted of a loss of lives, and additional asset contingent liability cost. This format of liquidity has resources of good, and some bad activities upon decision making, and upon any conflicts considering this is a format of American "Engineering and Government" occasional failures. Observing the high levels of perfection that a vast amount of American engineering and construction projects consist of, this becomes the format of liquidity that is sadly insured, but relevant to the improved effort that must be applied carefully. Even more so the caution, and discipline within these conditions of heavy machinery, and labor with the cost of were citizens, and worker's can also be victimized is most times considered.

Damages that are observed with sad levels of awareness during the 1990s, and the years of 2000 have increased in various industries including government to a point that the American society has went backwards in logical work skills, and ethics. The consideration of infrastructure projects has always been an American value of awareness that during construction of certain projects "serious accidents can happen", but the enormous amount of occasional negligence is a contingent liability factor that can't be ignored. These liability factors have devalued certain occupations, professions, and the concept of tax revenue dollars from businesses. The fatal Minnesota bridge collapse of 2007 was a severe problem which created attention on other up grades of bridge's around the country. This becomes a sad, but slightly progressive way to consider a vast amount of bridge engineering, and construction projects. This was not a great way to evaluate the important load strength, and life capacity upon the renovation of a bridge, but the American system of government followed suit. Considering other issues of negligence with contingent liabilities, a vast amount of fatal manufacturing explosions did not influence manufactures to upgrade for the worse like these bridge projects, but the concern should be logically observant. In all good, and bad infrastructure, and other projects a certain amount of these concerns caused a slow down within manufacturing businesses and other issues as well the concept of being able to expand with productive revenue earnings.

The loss of different resource's of business revenue means that the U.S. government, and federal funds will not expand as it did with better economic numbers form businesses providing tax revenue. One of the major factors is that with accidents were people are injured, and the industrial facility's that includes equipment is damaged, the government is providing a larger output of financial tax contributed clams within the format of disability cost, and unemployment calms. The concept of Social Security Disability funding is important, but a capable person as a citizen of America within earning a logical wage holds better tax, and wage factors to issue productive social outcomes. During December of 2008 a record amount of unemployment clams hit more than 570,000 American people needing jobs. This increased the unemployment financial benefits that the state, and federal government guarantees most qualified unemployed workers which had to be activated. This concept of economic difficulties within most businesses that have lost the ability to pay a certain amount of employees have arrived at the consideration that the U.S. economy is part of the severe problem. Upon this slow down in the U.S. economy it has forced businesses also to have concern that there may be a serious need for a government bailout due to some industry factors. These industry factors, and certain issues have existed during the late years of 2008 going into 2010 as it applies to most large businesses upon also occasionally effecting the smaller businesses as well. Most of these bailout factors consist of the ignored cost within the good, and bad changing times, and technology including the subjects within bad decisions made by Corporate America, and some small businesses. Within the logical concept of business, and government bailouts as it applies to American tax dollars this issue will more than likely be an adjustment due to the limitations of the United States government.

The limitations of the United States government, and the format of how American government duties are appropriated becomes indifferent form establishing private businesses that consist of the enterprise earning factors of one person, and or a family. On other occasions a certain amount of people as American proprietors, and beneficiaries is recognized with valued concerns of discipline. The good, and bad of international business is observed, and considered occasionally as well, and this offsets the numbers of American business factors concerning some issues of business competition. These concerned numbers of people in the American society of earning money, and working with certain professions, and occupations is a factor of individual business, and employment duties to manage relevant products, and or services productively. Considering this fact the state, and federal government more so recognizes, and occasionally commends the best, and good within efforts of businesses with no unlawful, and or bad activities. These businesses usually can pursue, or have produced good results within evaluated or projected earnings, and certain social issues that have provided support within the potential of future progress that is valuable in society. This also means that all small, and large businesses have economic factors of progress from product or service business factors with logical limitations. Although businesses may make adjustments if the money is in proper budget form, and or appropriated properly thru these duties considering this requires the right planning. Then this becomes the logical format of consistent values with the best logical business decision making possible.

When we have understanding of U.S. federal funds as it applies to the limitations of government money from the cities, towns, counties, states, and the federal governments procurement of funding the concept of business disciplines is valuable. These disciplines consist of acquisitions, wages, and other commitments to things such as retirement funds upon which these are budget expenses that become vitally important. All levels of government in America consist of these important budget commitment's, and duties because of the people that work for government productively is part of a bench mark to settle financial transactions from the Treasure to appropriate employment wages, investments, and retirements. This becomes important even thru the formal concept of government vendors or contractors, considering which there is logical commitments.

It is a fact that it takes trillions of dollars to operate the U.S. federal government with all branches of government that have an evaluated equation of relevance. Considering this, all other lower governments consist of "the equation of trillions of dollars of separate issues throughout the thousands or more of conditional government budgets" that small, and large local governments have within their logical establishment's. These government constituents have a duty, and value to be responsible for conducting their many aspects of government procurements, and duties. Observing this, the purchases, and payments of anything in government most time becomes a productive resource of liquidity leveraged on products, or a services liability.

The procurements, and asset liquidity of American government has been the life of a well developed American society in all regions of the United States. Upon this observation of social developments in America the duties within managing state, and federal funds including tax rate issues that apply to the concept of all government infrastructures is relevant within the liabilities of stable growth of asset liquidity. Considering there are 50 state governments, and capitals where the governor's of each state works along with other state government employees every year, there are assets in government that are needed, and certain assets that are not being observed which becomes obsolete. Actually every time technology changes certain other products become more, and more obsolete. When America thinks of crime against these assets of government with certain criminals including a diversion of business, a resource of people won't worry right away where the money is coming from, or going concerning a factor of spending. In Washington D.C. spending is closely monitored in most aspects, but in the city of Gary where the average city government employee will make $25,000.00 a year a diversion to spending became evident. This was done by a city director of the Gary Urban Enterprise Association (GUEA) whom took destructive advantage of government liquidity assets.

The former Director - Jojuana Meeks with a salary of over $60,000.00 a year became a severe problem of financial disaster with various conditions of evidence. During her employment as director she embezzled $1.2 million dollars on items that are far from any need of government, and most logical issues of any business contractors. This especially includes city government issues as it applies to the renovation of abandon houses, and the infrastructure applicable to urban revitalization. Observing Jojuana Meeks, and a few others the city of Gary government, and its citizens had to live with vast amounts of revitalization problems. A severe amount of these problems were incomplete revitalization projects, and due to others the sewers all over the city where sinking in dangerously for motorist. Considering there was other people involved, and the misappropriations of large amounts of GUEA money was ruined, these funds have not been easy to recover, and or be replaced. Considering this problem of embezzlement the city of Gary, Indiana government changed with additional severe problems. These problems vitally included the financial operations of local and regional government justice consisting of conflicting concerns to city employees losing vital jobs. Considering this restructuring with subcontractors hired for trash collection, these duties of the city government therefore was causing the citizens conflicting levels of grief. This therefore is a factor that only took clear advantage of the American system of city government in Gary, Indiana and how this may, and dose occur in other places, and ways that cause damages to the tax revenue liquidity, and expenses of government.

When you compare what happen at the Gary Urban Enterprise Association that was established to renovate or demolish abandoned houses, the government and people have a loss of valued support. Then the good, and more so bad of urban development or revitalization went in all kinds of bad directions that provide no agreements of good services to society.

Considering these financial issues of liquidity, and liability facts if you can understand some of Americas other smallest towns, the entire budget may not be more than $1 to $2 million dollars with the consideration that some don't even have a bank. Within some economic cost of living issues of awareness some small town banks may not ever have over $250,000.00 dollars of cash in the vault at one time unless it's a private bank business with long term established equity assets within its ownership capacity.

The small town or city mayor may earn about $35,000.00 to $45,000.00 a year, compared to some that may have a salary over $100,000.00 a year in larger cities. Observing the town or city population they may not have more than 1,000 men, woman, and children altogether. This may include the local schools that may reside in neighboring cities, or towns where the budgets are smaller, and these cost of living standards exist with vital importance. Observing this indifference upon all American values of government, these cities, and towns are connected, and are "constitutionally" established. Then they are governed by the "American State Government values", which usually have geographical similarities. This means that it requires less money to manage these smaller towns, but they still pay income taxes including the disciplined awareness of taxes for the U.S. federal government. Therefore the factors of waste or embezzlement at the expense of more than $1.2 million dollars observing any small or mid-size city or town this becomes a big percentage problem for most any city or town issues of a budget. These problems within expenditures of government money from appropriated budgets are therefore vital to maintain the governed order of economic discipline.

The format of financial expenditures that are within the appropriated budgets of government fund's are usually voted on by a council of legislative members. These legislative councils usually consist of (town, cities, counties, states, and federal) elective government officials. Considering this formal process that has been established with amendments over the decades these government duties are factored by the needs of the citizens, and their officials to solve a vast amount of problems. These procedures are done as a duty to protect the integrity of citizens as taxpayers with the enforceable laws that government has established. Recently during 1990, and the first decade of 2000 these enforceable laws have been part of the good and bad issues of technology, and ethical standards of where the legislature seems to be slightly behind. This is the formal concept of technology that during the 1990s, and 2000 which have slightly outpaced most state and federal legislative branches of the American system of government, corrections are part of most logical changing times. One other vital and important factor is that the judiciary has a logical, and lawfully aggressive duty to acknowledge, and enforce the old and new laws with all issues of evaluation. Some issues I have understood apply to when some court's, and even occasionally some executive office holders ignore, and deprive the citizens of justice, and this has been a severe problem for most people as Americans that try to pursue a commitment of hard work, and sacrifices. These factors of managing government funds just like managing the American infrastructure will be issues for now, and the future generations to come.

CHAPTER NINE

THE CIRCUMFERENCE OF TAX DOLLARS & GOVERNMENT ENTERPRISE

Considering the past history, and the future years (c/o the 2000 millennium) and days of life in America that consist of a money circulation including the vital factor of taxes, an outline of government enterprises become important during various good, and bad economic times in America. This observed outline of government facts are even more so vital within the circumference of revenue from taxpaying citizens, businesses, and others of a lawful financial capacity. It is relevant to observe this financial and economic cycle of tax dollars as it changes hands, and how it is spent and transferred within most business transactions concerning all levels of government to maintain or establish the format of a workable government enterprise with budgets. During the early 1900s this also consisted of the U.S. government's commitment within World War I & II, and those years of war time economic, and production values. Therefore the input and output of government money in the United States is valued with the same taxation of appreciation within the American values of hopeful future ambitions.

During the 1920s, and the 1930s the ambition of prosperous determination in the American society was tested with the un-enterprise factored lessons from the Great Depression, and the United States government which found reason for certain newly considered government enterprises. Some people observed these times in America as the days of the industrial revolution. This means that within most conditions of business, industry, and certain markets within the American system of government our nation found a duty to keep the American people, businesses, and government operating with logical conditions of cash flow including asset, and social values of protection. From these depression years of bailout restructuring the United States government, and the Congress strongly established the Federal Deposit Insurance Corporation (FDIC), and the Securities & Exchange Commission (SEC) to regulate the control of banking, and investment legal activity. Also during that time in the 1930s to support a secondary mortgage market, such government enterprises as the Government National Mortgage Association (Ginnie Mae), and the Federal National Mortgage Association (Fannie Mae) where established to support the Federal Housing Administration (FHA), and the people with mortgage economic problems. Due to the fact that an enormous amount of citizens with money saved, and money invested was important, vital issues had to be observed. Considerably this consisted of whom suffered complete losses from those times into economic total hardships. Conditionally they were victimized with unevaluated conditions of the time, and subject matter. These issues became reasons for a few of the newly supportive government sponsored enterprises, and agencies to control financial discipline with newly established laws.

It is relevant to say that the U.S. government, and the people had found a severe lack of economic security, and this recovery would take tremendous effort with other values that required various levels of coordinated corrections to improve economic resources. This included also most valued resources of investment brokerage business operations that where held valuable to the growth of longer or more expanding corporate business in America. These important resources becomes the logic of how American's had to work together without racial turmoil, and respect each other to maintain quality workmanship, and expanded business equity, and liquidity. A resourceful concept within hundreds of thousands of commercial and residential facilities with business ownership values, and various business properties became threatened without these government enterprise liquidity levels of support, and legal disciplines. Following these conflicting market, and government factors, bankruptcy for many businesses became inevitable, but some survived with more needing to do better! This vitally included subjects of land and real estate mortgage being different from the Depression of 1929 that became very complex within ownership due to the loss of financial earnings. Therefore this was a downward overall market factor with most economic values of opportunities.

Considering America during the 1930s certain times of economic hardships in the United States which included business, and the bad social conditions of family life with children needing education, and housing the U.S. Federal Housing Administration (c/o domestic welfare) was established by the U.S. President, and the Congress. This was vitally done to manage certain values upon having a home, and way of life consisting of livable standards. During the times of President Herbert Hoover, and the U.S. Congress of 1932 the American system of government established a government enterprise (c/o legal disciplines) called the Reconstruction Finance Corporation. This Reconstruction Finance Corporation was commissioned with responsibility to loan money to "bank establishments" and other firms that where threatened by bankruptcy as a level of long term work within business, and government planning. These factors of work were followed by the National Monetary Commission, and the Federal Reserve Bank established in 1913. This concept of tax dollar supported resources observed apartment developments, housing developments, nursing home's, and medical institutions for the sick and or elderly, which includes even some college dorm room living establishments for college students. These and other establishments to keep people from living on most city streets, or within dangerous camp grounds during the 1920s, and 1930s became a vital asset that intervened with certain corporate or private business groups, and professionals.

As tax dollars have been used within various factual issues of survival, certain people in the American society could put themselves back into the prosperous format of earnings, and spending money. This process of public, private business and government working together produced good results in the American economy. These issues and subjects are the details of what produces the American economy's money circulation of economic budgets, and resourceful financial expenses for adjustments within the cost of living. Upon this factor, and format of conditions the United States Securities and Exchange (Act) and Commission was established to be part of certain government enterprises, corporate businesses, and the meaningful logic to enforce a variation of financial laws that apply. Considering this the people, and their assets were a factor within these established concerns to support these complex values of important liabilities within the business of mass production items, and tax evaluated transactions.

The value of tax dollars, and a productive concept within the American format of a money circulation between the 1940s, the 1950s, 1960s, and 1970s has valued some similar concerns of resource. Most good and bad opinions have lingered, but some government enterprises with a good format to balance spending requirements have certain budget concerns to keep the enterprise active within government, and business conditions of activity. These budget and enterprise values have supported issues of healthcare, and the National Aeronautics Space Administration (NASA) which consist of space exploration including travel. Also this includes the importance of oceanic evaluations, and studies within the National Oceanic Atmospheric Administration (NOAA) upon protecting people, and their assets from predicted hurricanes, and other tropical, and conflicting hazards. This is the process within research that turns into storm weather conditions of a lawfully observed conflict of protective process concerns which is vitally helpful to meteorology, and the regions they serve. All these factors occasionally apply to some disciplinary resource of various hazardous warning activities, diversified defense issues, and the National Security of the United States. Now during the years of 2000 an exhausted or exchanged resource of financial earning's, and social values of security where effecting businesses, and social values upon which are safe, and effective to endure most bad weather conditions that apply.

Observing the determination of America to progress, various assets, and people of value have suffered damage to the extent that survival had become very complex. These problems have lately been a conditional part of the transition of America during a time of war. The conflicts of the Iraq & Afghanistan war that the United States is engaged in (c/o the 2000's) is the format of government tax dollars for the solder's fighting to protect the lawful life style that American citizens Constitutionally value within safety, and prosperity. Our American society has consistently improved technology within the capacity of (NASA & NOAA) protecting, and defending America from danger, and enemy's including how the U.S. strategically fights war's. Therefore within the changing times, and decades within the circumference of tax dollar spending, and the concentration of budget evaluations, this offers America hopeful prosperity for the things we need, and want lawfully within livable, and logical resources.

As the people, government, and the American society offers provisions of a taxable capacity, certain needs are met within appropriate roadways, highways, airports, and even shipping harbors to manage vital factors of productive living. With a vast amount of Americans working to build, and maintain these govern assets, the concept of income earning wages, and taxes are part of the input, and output cycle of productive resources within financial, and economic provisions. During 2008 only 20% of the businesses, and wage income tax collections are applied to the U.S. federal budget for these types of projects. Observing Northern Indiana, and Illinois these factors of government spending procurements became slightly unbalanced. These issues of bad coordination occurred when drainage systems where needed, but they (c/o government) then expanded a highway system including establishments like the Midway Airport of Illinois, and the Chicago / Gary Airport of Gary, Indiana. It became a factual problem concerning some airports which could not produce much revenue, which lead to an evaluation of what would be a working problem within the overall economic income need of solutions. Some airports do earn money well, but renovation up-grades (c/o regional economy's) is an item valued as important within "U.S. Federal Aviation standards" and other industry business standards. In addition this is vital with the right business, and government decisions including a lawful money circulation with a commitment that becomes resourcefully necessary.

The concept of flooding continued too damage vast amounts of people's homes, and businesses upon which this therefore cost citizens additional money; if they survived. There was very few to any fatalities in Indiana, and Illinois, but some people still have not recovered various assets. Within these factors of government economic, and financial decisions concerning the objections within strong or weak factors of liquidity, these factual resources had subjective values of importance. This is practical within the prosperous needs of the American people and society, but the other side of certain government fund's require the logic of managing these issues of asset liquidity. All levels of government including the consistent and power separated executive, legislative, and judicial branches of American government will severely require these factors in the future. Considering this, the 50 plus state governments, and all cities and towns including the U.S. federal government, can maintain financial budgets for the resources which apply with the most important government duties.

Ginnie Mae, Freddie Mac, and Fannie Mae during 2008 have become government sponsored enterprise issues of mortgage, and credit lending liquidity cash concerns. Other government sponsored enterprise issues are factored within certain duties that consist of details to maintain or improve government support. Observing the format of support the United States federal government money becomes applicable to Sallie Mae for college educational funding as it applies within grants. With some conditional commitments certain resources of college student loans become applicable from the Sallie Mae format of an enterprise. These student loans and grants now suffered with a conditional concern of liquidity problems. To some extent a vast amount of American college students are finding themselves returning home, and or re-evaluating how to continue their college studies within education. Within these valued issues of consideration that apply to the circumference, and circulation of money, these became assets that these young Americans could not get various financial ends to meet. Also as it applies to assets, and even inventory within government sponsored enterprise values, these issues are more so applied to business partnerships, and this is, or was a relevant factor for the management of overall liquidity in the American economy.

An expansion of houses, and commercial facilities that were financed, and constructed between the years of 1990, and 2005 is an indicated subjective factor that included most all types of productive business financial considerations of responsibility. Observing the years 2007 thru 2010 the United States has the probable concern that with the (GNP c/o GDP) rates of all products, and services except houses is how will market's recover? Also, will American businesses, and the economy appropriate an equation of financial support to banking establishments from the people to compensate the expanded supply of mortgages, and new housing within inventory? Constructing an access of houses, and commercial buildings as inventory is financially different then manufacturing cars which also consist of a supply and demand inventory concern. Due to economic issues of the foreign, and United States domestic markets with most amounts of large priced inventory this has become a very complex long term issue to determine certain quick results.

The property within residential, and commercial facilities is the American domestic land values of public, or private revenue concerns which are applicable to the American state government, and U.S. federal tax dollar circumference values of society. Therefore Ginnie Mae, Fannie Mae, and other government factors upon business resource securities in America exceeded "bad economic levels of support, and investment returns" for these important equation's that should have been considered. From these equations of accountable issues of housing, and other products like cars, this consisted of long-termed payments (c/o certain delinquencies) concerning most supply, and demand obligations. These things are valuable as it applies to the people as employees productively working, and this maintains the tax revenue circumference of dollars, and productive business levels of opportunities if done right.

So far within the recession of 2008 with certain factors of supply and demand from a vast amount of products within the American money supply and circulation, this is complex with large retail store's liquidating their inventory, and business assets. This has been a large loss "financially" to the American economy which is applicable to people working, but some real estate is questionable because it will be around for years to come. Circuit City Corp which had, and consisted of a consumer electronics retail store chain of locations is eliminating over 540 stores throughout the United States during the years of 2008, and 2009. All employees, and their jobs have been eliminated upon the concept of "finding, and considerably needing" new jobs within the factors of employment concerns throughout a very complex American economy. Some federal government officials throughout the American system of government are "considering" hundreds of billions of dollars in economic stimulus check's. From 1995 to 2007 the American society has lost more than 10 to 15 major department (corporate) store chains which has eliminated tens of thousands of jobs, and this is a critical format, and loss of a money circulation.

The format of economic stimulus payments to taxpaying citizens is from the former President George Bush, and now U.S. President Barack Obama administration's agenda with some debatable members of the U.S. Congress. These efforts by the executive and legislative branch of the U.S. government are noble, but this is not the same as the U.S. Constitutions prosperity of productive taxable business revenue. Between government in America, and the private or public sector of business, more people living off government programs; means that the economy and its U.S. money circulation has taken a large loss! This therefore provides a money circulation to an enormous amount of Americans, but the issue of government liquidity, and the Gross National Product rates of businesses suffered in how the American people (c/o the Gross Domestic Product) are part of a severe discretion for a productive economic business cycle.

Most productive business, and economic processes that consist of an annual cycle of products, services, and business issues that people depend on with savings, and investments are the issues that keep financial bailouts, and or bankruptcies at very low rates. Keeping all bankruptcies, and the considered American business bailouts at low rates can appropriate the factors of a stable economy where people can prosper without stressful financial conflicts of interest. Within the people of America these issues of savings with most banking establishments are a vital part of managing money that is part of the obligated circumference of interest rate earnings on money within most bank accounts. These vital account factors from most any bank in America is part of the backbone of maintaining, or establishing any kind of wealth, and future financial decisions that may include long term planning.

Understanding the values of large or small conditions of wealth in America means that all logical obligations can be lawfully maintained with appropriate sacrifices. Observing this, certain values consist of the basic definition of good "liquidity" whether from a citizen's personal finances, or the consideration of a large or productively operated small business issue. Considering this concentration of liquidity a money circulation is valued with liability factors that apply to prosperous growth. The banking establishments within liability and their circulation of money, and asset management conditions have been restructured to occasionally not apply prosperous banking opportunities to customers. This concentration of banks harshly applied charges for customers to pay fees in retrospect to appropriating good levels of interest on money because of the extent of the American societies negative economic conditions.

Upon the issue of banking establishments within 2007 and 2008 some banks are charging a cost for every detail that certain customers try to pursue in some format of most bank business, and personal decision matters. This becomes income to offset most of their traumatic losses from delinquent loans. Also this sadly includes the rate of banking establishments that lacked the business effort, and decisions to overcome these different times of financial, and economic resource's. Theoretically this has been vital to realize that it was not just the problem of certain or most banking establishment facility operations, but there have been many complex issues that created these overall financial, and economic times of business insecurity. Therefore the difference between the 1929 problems of the American economy is that a vast amount of banks went out of business with the concept of people losing their savings, access of employment, certain businesses, and taxable revenue within earnings. During the late decade years of 2000 the accumulated fact of businesses upon which their employees are suffering, the banking industry is slightly observing some tuff decisions. Contrary to this business crisis some laws have been enforced, and considered, which therefore a vast amount of banks (c/o some other laws) are achieving the value to stay open for business.

The American banking industry has overcome problems that gave awareness to the bank owners, some businesses, and employees that are surviving an economic depression or recession to consist of every detail, but also to maintain a basic outline of valid customers. Considering this awareness within the American people as customers, and clients to the diversified factor of banks, vast amounts of people are making economic decisions to adjust to the negative economy. This is relevant, but not so easy to absorb with certain bills to pay, and family issue concern's that requires financial help. Paying bills that consisted of the over expanded American credit markets, and businesses (c/o good and bad foreign and domestic economics) that includes the laws of the United States is vitally a new resource of detailed issues of future legislative consideration. Personal bankruptcies, is another partial, and complex subject in these factors, but this legal process is not free to all people. Therefore within this consideration of facts the restructured conditions of financial matters is the validity within changes to personal or business income earnings, and taxes that become a working factor of close evaluations. To recover from bankruptcy is occasionally a long term process with legal proceedings that may take month's or year's. Our American society studies these lessons from the Great Depression, and other years of financial disproportion, and therefore a vast amount of people took caution, and tried to plan accordingly.

When some people go from $60,000.00 or $70,000.00 dollars a year of income, and then must adjust to $15,000.00 to $20,000.00 dollars of annual income or less there is losses within the circulated use of money to survive. The years within taxable earnings is applicable to the individual state, and U.S. federal government's relevant benefit values from the commitment of programs in government. This commitment is factually important for the logic of citizens, and government working together. Some of these problems include the expanded subjects, and factors of crime that cause a vast amount of people to be found in a negative, and or different living, and earning category. Within issues of being near bankruptcy, any factors of severe "crime, or negligence financially or fatally" becomes a critical concern to these social issues to restructure most all livable standards. Bank robberies, and "Investment Banking crimes" are diversified including fraud, and even embezzlement from public, private businesses, and government funds which have been harmful to the vast amount of all age's of American's. This has contributed to the late years of the 2000 to 2010 decade with various economic issues of a social, and economic crisis. People young, and to the very old aged of American citizens have been left with almost nothing financially in some of these conditional conflicts.

The details about government tax dollars that are appropriated to the people, and even now to businesses as financial, and or economic bailouts are considered government decisions of priority which consist of important financial evaluations, and duties. These are factors that apply to the U.S. Constitutions concept of "business or the disciplines of the general welfare". Some would more so consider it corporate welfare. The words, and values that promotes the "General Welfare" from the United States Constitution has expanded to some of Americas most diversified resource's of people, company's, and occasionally to other different countries. Individual's, and corporations suffering from a logical concept of income earnings that basically gives them the statue as a welfare recipient (c/o corporate welfare) has hit most parts of America during 2009. Considering this logic of global business issues these factors go along with the financial problems that occurred with Enron Corporation, Zenith Corporation, and a few others. This vitally even includes the Alan Standford Company issue of prosecution that sent hundreds of millions of dollars to foreign country's for discretionary business dealings, and development without lawful (SEC) investment disciplines which suffered losses. These were losses that their investors did not completely understand, and they only created a large hole in an American money circulation that included tax revenue issues, and SEC violations of law. This is a negative business discrepancy of sacrifices, and hard work upon theoretically not being a new issue.

A vast amount of this government rescue money circulation is factored from the American governments system of asset managed liquidity. The United States government has entitled its legislative version as the Troubled Asset Relief Program (TARP) to offset the current economic crisis in America. This rescue "grant and loan" money becomes one of the great or more so interesting factors about "Promoting The General Welfare" from the U.S. Constitutional establishment of the American system of government. Contrary to the concern of the General Welfare which looks like a hand out within "money" issues with a more productive public, private business sector was more "so" important within a vital or well to do developed American society. When manageable duties are applied to help the economic prosperity of individuals, families, and certain businesses or corporation's the term promoting the general welfare leaves no one out. Considering these diversified budget concerns, this is lawfully part of the governments close review, and evaluation to understand the lawful nature of certain problems that require valued solutions.

The concentration of individual's, or small and large businesses in almost every part of America can be victimized with vulnerable economic, and financial hardships as the General Welfare factor, and this is the consideration of better performing businesses, and corporations. Also most local or state governments have valued levels of involved duties. Observing the general welfare the need to maintain a strong format of duties that is applicable to the Constitution of the United States, this consist of most established or considered laws, and legislature with the American people working to resolve these problems. Victims as a corporation, and the vulnerability of good, and more so bad issues has cause problems into the future within stable or expanding business markets, and opportunities. These lawful business values within corporate welfare, and even the discrete financial, and fatal damages of events such as the September 11, 2001 terror attacks can cause business, and society overall harm, and suffering. Upon this consideration of facts this became the long term conflicts which have lead to certain factors within the struggles against poverty.

Following the 9-11 Report of terror attacks billions of dollars from foreign investors (c/o new citizenship issue) living "partly" in the United States pulled large percentages of money out of American corporation's as market investments. These investment dollars within the format of investment banking, and most business concerns severely affected a vast amount of corporations, and people in America. Another important issue of relevance or potential future business includes vital government tax revenue issue's that has become threatened within most discretionary or contingent liability values. This means security of all kinds including insurance for most assets that people own have a questionable level of long-term stability. Over the decades of the 1950s to the 1980s distinctively after World War II, and most conditional fighting in the Vietnam War, most American corporations, investors, businesses, and even some labor unions became productive from these American times of national support. Therefore within these changing times there is a balance within how most all American business, and individual tax revenue matters will be maintained for the general public of American taxpayers.

The American observation, and debatable issue's of taxable revenue becomes an important concern within the values of logic that American people have appreciation for, and with most issues after taxes are settled. This is the consolidation of when they are settled with all itemized filing requirements, and then those taxes are considered properly paid in full. Tax dollars within the liquidity, and circulation of government funded matters, and certain enterprise factors are most time recognized, and important throughout this overall tax dollar circulation process. This means the circumference of money is active due to the American taxpayer helping government, and other diversified people as Americans. Therefore the relevance of the American system of government has observed certain values, and citizen duties of rewarding appropriate deeds which becomes an appropriate deductible tax item process opportunity. Immediately within the logical values of people working properly together, this governed process with personal and business considerations for most concerns is of good logic for the American society unless they are pursing crimes against the citizens of the United States.

When foreign people from the Middle East, and other conflicting countries as close as even Mexico gain control of vast amounts of American businesses, and corporations American tax itemized condition's where distorted. During the years 1995 to 2002 the American tax payers over the last 5 decades have observed a descent, and "Constitutional loss" of American social, and governed values. This is the fact within military veterans, and or issues that include the American people, and families that depend on businesses that are acceptable to the U.S. Constitution. In addition even more so this combination of American (c/o international issues) must be acceptable to the support of the United States Department of Defense resource's of America. These become patriotic rules of ethics that must be considered with appropriate opinions, but more respectfully by the rules of most American laws. These are vital issues of "National and Local Security" that valued American's have worked together in various "conflicts, and resolved problems" with the help of government. This is the subject of assets that where, or may have been replaced with losses within the sovereign factors of prosperity that sometimes becomes a conflict of bad foreign (c/o some domestic) relations.

Understanding the levels of sovereignty within the prosperity of young people throughout the American society, some people have observed various honorable issues of defending the struggles of war, and worded values to restructure failing American businesses. This vitally included people even more so becoming fatally loss to the unhopeful values of occasional unlawful guidance. Considering this, the leadership of American government, and corporations have seem to lose control from most vital living standards of business, and issues of employment to a foreign control within currency, and opportunities. Therefore this capacity within lack of proper, and productive leadership was leaving us as a majority of productive American's within being the worse concept of American domestic welfare.

Within taking up the vital business, and issues of the United States government tax revenue values that have obtained considerable foreign control of American businesses illegally (c/o some legally) this is the corporate, and small business problem starting in the 2000 millennium. The concept of American businesses, and even the financial markets that prosper from a vast amount of investment dollar resources has loss logical United States Constitutional values for the greed of rationale insecurity. The thousand's of corporations, and then other small and large business operations that consist of American citizens with values including government concerns are being victimized by this factor of conflicts in American business. Revenue within business, and government issues of operating standards with tax strategies, and planning has provided issues of understanding that the 2000 economic, and financial crisis is pondered with various conditions of good, and bad technological advancements. Some values of technology are important, but these good, and bad issues of capacity must be regulated properly, and restructured to lawfully appropriate good business, and tax revenue issues within opportunities. Then this is not just to interrupt these American business operating establishments, but occasionally this is a format of crime, and various conditions of negligence within oversight technology that harms the American society. These factors within America that includes the issues that occurred with companies like Amoco Oil Corporation (now British Petroleum), and even the discretion of the Enron Corporation have taken international business to certain levels of severe conflict.

Observing these corporations there was hundreds of billions of dollars of assets, and potential earnings that were at stake. Then the legal discipline of the United States Constitutions integrity became a bargaining priced factor for global resources of money. Considering there was hundreds of other corporations, and individuals like Bernard Ebbers, Alan Stanford, and even Ken Lay that were involved in complex (c/o various unlawful) investment or business concerns, this devastated the American society before these three or more individuals, and or companies dissolved. Then these American issues where valued with severe economic conflict upon the good of recovering from long-term bad justice that must be corrected. Upon these factors of business discretionary issues within businesspeople with a lone few American businesses which had logical values below their human feet to hold solid ground, these businesses only looked like a variation of good decisions were made. Observing good business disciplines, some businesses only tried to support the money circulation part, and not the vital parts of business to be productive with logical expansion. This has been a losing equation in American business sense the early 1990s, and therefore very few American businesses have expanded during the 1990s throughout 2010. Concerning these subjects of an American money circulation, this included resources with productive values of liquidity, tax disciplines, inventory effectiveness, and asset holdings.

The by-laws of most all established American corporations are consistently parallel legally to the American resource of Constitutional laws. This vitally includes certain individual states, and the United States federal laws that apply to the American society. Understanding, and observing this formal value of American business a valid example is how vast amounts of corporations are registered in the State of Delaware concerning their business Articles of Incorporation. These Articles of Incorporation or a "State Declared Corporation" are some of the vital factors of an American business that produces a relevant money circulation of income earnings with tax revenue values increasing the money circulation. A vast amount of American corporations have their home offices in Delaware to appropriate a taxable advantage. The state government of Delaware appropriates a state law allowing companies to incorporate in Delaware "even" if they do much of their business in other places. Also Delaware makes it easier, and less expensive to incorporate a business than most other "American State" governments. Considering these factors of corporate by-laws that are established including their Articles of Incorporation the cost of maintaining a corporation can be held low. Inadvertently this becomes a different level of state government business issues apart from Texas with oil industry concerns, and Michigan with automobile industry concerns making other states, and industries look more diverse within taxable industry values. Therefore the corporate, and or business sacrifice values of hard work can be beneficial in a long-term resource of discipline with good revenue.

Discipline's, and the resource of corporate revenue are values occasionally within the securities and exchange market investments of government sponsored enterprise offerings. During the years of 2005 to 2009 even in the State of Delaware, "corporations" in the United States Bankruptcy courts occasionally has consist of record amounts of negative corporate revenue issues of liquidity. Upon this understanding they have been overloaded with these due process of law, and court proceedings during this first decade of 2000. This corporate discretion including certain government securities, and corporate earnings with investment bank conditions is pushing large businesses into total, or high percentage factors of business liquidation proceedings. These issues of massive bankruptcies, and business liquidations are activating decrease revenue factors upon corporate bill payment obligations. Therefore this also means the money circulation has weakened in vast amounts of American corporations as it applies also to the currency values of the dollar.

Inflation as it applies to bankrupt businesses is a diversion on the currency value of the American dollar. The cost of manufacturing, sales, and other controlled cost issues of products is one part devised into the business plan to receive a non-inflated or inflated price. Also the issue to compensate (c/o invested time, people, and money) inflation occasionally becomes a vast amount of time the improved conditions to various business overhead values. This is the process where the business must spend less money operating the entire business, more so then earning a positive cash flow with their products, and additional services. These are the factors of business that they will spend money on in all provisions of the operating capacity of business. Therefore the business must earn more money, then the business spends on a "day by day", quarter by quarter, and annual business operating condition. Considering these business factors in America, and even in other places throughout the world, it has been a problem when business operating expense values (c/o cash money or currency) are used with no control of responsible discipline. Then corrections become vital, and relevant with good managing skills.

CHAPTER TEN

GOVERNMENT BAILOUTS &
ITS TAXABLE EFFECT

The American private corporations, certain small, and large businesses including more so a vast amount of "public corporations" that have received U.S. government "Troubled Asset Relief Program" (TARP) bailout money also have taxable responsibilities. Although no "tax" exist on the billions of dollars that businesses borrowed from the U.S. federal government bailout funds, these businesses must continue to be some of the elite taxpayers of commitment in America. Understanding the United States government, and bailout money that is provided thru the "Troubled Asset Relief Program" this was established during 2008 to rescue financially troubled people, and "more so big businesses". Considerably this TARP is "an intense big money corporate welfare program" that the United States Treasury Department, the Federal Reserve Bank, and the Federal Deposit Insurance Corporation have had to closely review. This also includes the duties of review, and evaluation of the United States Congress, and the President. Upon these issues of conflict the word "welfare" really does not eliminate hardly any citizens because a vast amount of citizens (c/o the rich or poor) within

American people are suffering, and pursuing a way to recover from an economic recession. For hundreds of years the general welfare seems to apply to the poor people of America whom have right's also, and then this conflict seems defamatory within large wealthy business bailouts.

This formal condition of tax dollar resources also includes the United States government within bailing out smaller local bankrupt (city or town) government systems of the American society. During the years of 2008 thru 2010 the taxable effect that most large corporate tax filing, and payment duties have consisted of had factual considerations of importance. These valued considerations were upon weather the business will survive in a bad economy? This issue of business survival applies to certain small cities, and even at the state level that have loss severe tax revenue, and liquidity with certain elements becoming important. These factual issues of an element are established from the loss of business owners, and business with certain foreign business conflicts. This included these conflicts of how a corporation does not go completely out of business within the factors of various economic details without logical compliance of the laws. Various cities and towns have less economic hardships when the largest businesses have a readjusted level of accumulated tax payments for government tax revenue including more opportunities of workable income.

These logical factor's, and occasional tax details with bailout money that consist of business property, amounts of inventory, and or sales of products sometimes consist of special services. Then these are the taxable earning subjects that the individual states, and the United States federal government have to evaluate from time to time within the fairness of taxation. During this economic recession before 2009, and 2010 this includes smaller new businesses just starting to operate, which has accumulated new challenges within business. Another vital factor during the first decade of 2000 is the severe anti-competitive issues of American business where international people in business have come from certain enemy countries, and control certain markets in various ways. Therefore what has happen is that changes have occurred in the American communities of business with advantages that only look good, but have not sustained an easy format of long-term commitments that include taxable income.

Every employed American person, and business has a responsibility to the obligations of most to all logical concentrations of taxable earnings. The concentration of large or productively small businesses with taxable earnings during the 1960s, 1970s, and 1980s consisted of certain employee benefits that helped other small business professionals. These decades before the 1990s also had vast amounts of business values that consisted of good healthcare benefit's that large amounts of American people depended on. This is the format of where small doctor's offices, dentist offices, funeral homes, drug stores, franchise businesses, and other diversified businesses prospered with these helpful disciplines. Even the concentration of barber shops, and beauty salon's consist of taxable earned income resources of discipline which may not earn the same annually. Therefore their estimated taxable income consisted of negative adjustable tax rate factors.

As vast amounts of Americans have observed gas stations, and auto repair service centers with good and more so bad issues, these businesses have become more diversified within sales of items other then gas, and oil products. This issue and concern increases a taxable liability within businesses, but also occasionally causes a unlawfully congested market for product goods. With the format of logical business disciplines this has seem to be an American loss with unlawful monopolized conditions at the expense of taxpayers contrary to a business with questionable tax responsibilities. Therefore, upon where large businesses within the oil industry compensated tax revenues, other marketable industries had local business concerns that where similar. This consisted of the good business opportunities for Americans which became the taxable resource of businesses, and franchise dealers that consisted of a conflicting future. This was due to a massive increase in foreign connected ownership of business with some national security concerns. The bulk of business operations in the United States will continue being actively observant with citizens to overcome the economic prosperity that needs to be corrected during the first decades of 2000.

Within the hundreds of years that American people have established business, and socially productive organizations, and corporations there has also been a the logic for tax revenue from most all corporations, businesses, and individuals that has established a format of tax filing process procedures. These vital procedure's, and taxable activity concerns appropriate themselves (c/o Citizen Rights) with the best advantages by law. It becomes complex with no earnings, and therefore none or very few taxes can be reported. This is the logic upon which certain factors of employment or business ownership have lacked within discipline of certain benefits, and various resource levels of earnings, and liquidity. Considerably, this also means occasionally being homeless or just starting a business with absolutely "nothing", filing taxes may be differed, or severely impossible. The concept of businesses in America especially with the facts of growing from a "small business with a tax filing and process" of procedures plays a part within the concentration of future years of business expansion, and success. Considering certain businesses that are seeking American government bailout loans, and money there is hardly no issues of these businesses expanding. Contrary to this fact the automobile company's within General Motors Corp, and Chrysler Corp wanted to use bailout money to expand manufacturing facilities to build, and comply with new EPA legal standards for cars.

The larger, and more active a business is with certain people that held valued investment (interest) within the business they pursue with different or new procedures, it is normal that they have more complex or outlined details within their concept of taxes. These taxable issues consist of a larger list of items, deductions, and "sometimes" diversified income. This became temporary, or even a long-term issue within their taxes that most times will consist of U.S. government requirements within their tax filing procedures. Within the duties of the Internal Revenue Service (IRS) of the United States government they offer this formal process with government approved documented IRS forms. Occasionally changes with logical revisions, and updates on a year by year base are approved by certain members of the Congress, and the U.S. Department of Treasury which are then published by the IRS. Considering these American facts of society from time to time certain levels of expertise within accounting, and taxes which becomes an important fact of logic, this especially applies to government bailout loans that are appropriately considered.

Managing income or funding has always required a careful evaluation process for tax preparations, and or payments including the money that may consist of long-term commitments. During the financial crisis of 2007 and 2008 these business, and or organizational items, and commitments of tax considerations for government revenue are becoming more complex. This is due to the vast amounts of prosecuted fraud cases, and the lack of earned income to file on taxes, or certain issues of conflict. The vast amount of fraud legal cases in the American banking industry during the first decade of 2000 has given taxpaying employee's a complex understanding of paying taxes, and various tax laws. All government employees (c/o the others) that pay income taxes, the American society still has a consistent flow of tax revenue. They also have a need within the increase of steady taxpaying businesses, and other economic, and financial resources that are lawfully consistent within format of the same progress. This progress in a well governed society is the resource that provides advancement of prosperous living that also includes an educated resource of opportunities, and workers.

The American worker's in numerous businesses apart from undocumented illegal alien workers has cost the income tax revenue input tax factor great harm with expenses, and damages. These problems exceeded most command values of business liquidity within the output of tax dollars to the American society when business has damages, and or slows down within sales of production items. Foreign people that don't completely understand the American language is one of the factors causing damage's at a criminal, and negligent capacity. The production, and sale of small and or large cost items is vital apart from banking as it applies to generating tax revenue, and a societies money circulation. Upon this observation, factual concerns also consist of government disciplines that are vitally followed by the U.S. government within bailout money to supplement the loss of income in most issues of society. This process of money being appropriated during 2008 to American citizens, and businesses helps with certain taxable income or wage items of support. Therefore considering rare appropriations of federal government money this condition of industry, and markets must improve with the future quality of American businesses.

Considering American income tax rates won't change "without a lawful government process" just like the minimum wage rate law of American workers with these rates, and issues this becomes applicable to the American economy. In retrospect these taxable values are part of what partly makes a good business valuable to the American society. Observing this, all other business issues are just as important if not more so to small businesses with comparison to massive business operations like at General Electric Corporation, and Ford Motor Company which still has their local values of work applicable to their day by day business operations. The ratio is about 50:1 or more within businesses like Ford Motor Company, and General Electric Corporation that will cause an effect to several smaller businesses, and contractors due to the 2007 and 2008 hard times of most bigger business concerns. The large investment bank businesses of Bear Stearns, and Lehman Brothers has been financially hit bad. This also includes a vast amount of commercial turmoil, this equates to overall economic problems that must be given certain prosperous solution's.

Considering most all diversified corporations share certain command resources of business within American industry standards, and tax revenue that is fractional to increase earnings, a vitally important part of business, and some personal matters must be clearly understood. Observing this array of business concern's, and their diversified industry of disciplines certain activity such as training workers, and managing all other business aspects including some tax filing matters became a joking matter that hurt the future. This includes during the decade of the 1990s where most all American corporations looked good until certain concerns became a legal issue of resources. This was factual until certain banks, and other corporate earning report's looked better than their true existence. Upon this concern vital problems occurred which included the American society of business consisting of more manipulation, and certain levels of fraud that pushed down the truth in earnings.

Another conflict occurred when more corporations started considering bankruptcy upon which caused a large consideration of government to provide business bailouts to support business, and the taxpaying employees. Other tax revenue generating businesses like Enron Corporation, and WorldCom Corporation including a few others are a basic deterrent that started the 2000 recession with vibration's of business bailouts. These two corporations accumulated very large, and expensive business operations of wealth from mostly financial market transactions. They also lacked true or original products, and therefore the difference is that the American values of honest production (c/o GDP rate's) was set at the lowest levels of progress. This means that only slightly did they have good product rates, and therefore with manipulated fraud they existed as very bad businesses.

Within the format of most good, and then some occasionally bad or complex corporate tax generating businesses with strong, and steady growth, a concentration of productive management eliminates most questionable needs for a government financial bailout. During the 1990s leading into "the 2007 American

Economic Recession" certain businesses that followed a validity of greed without logical products, and services took certain banking establishments into complex financial levels. Considering this, certain businesses, and banks could not achieve, or lawfully compensate long term discipline with their logical business resources. This means even their respect for the laws of the United States Constitution where not applicable to the secured long-term values for investment banks, and even investors that suffered due to their most important discipline's; "which is true business that maintains progress". These are important issues to observe upon which manageable logic applies. Most truly productive businesses lawfully exist from the hardworking discipline of the business operations with people that provide good values. Therefore within most of their outlined business plans, and procedures this is how people, and assets are managed which will more than likely keep a business from bankruptcy contrary to questionable bailouts.

Considering the facts within the best or most logical small and large businesses that have been considered for government financial bailout money, this "has and will" consist of a past, and future concern for government required disciplines that fully apply. The vast amount of corporations that received billions of dollars of financial bailout money, they also have been recognized for the loan, and tax payments that they made during the pass. In retrospect this now includes these adjustable fluctuations of money from private banking, and the U.S. federal government. Within this taxable business process the individual states, and the United States federal government appropriately observes the losses of tax revenue as well the jobs that various employees may lose as taxpaying citizens. Corporations with these factual levels of financial distress are effected with the hard-work of restructuring, and sacrifices by these conditions. Upon these business duties within how they must review the past, and present issues to evaluate solutions, this more so applies importantly to these new government requirements, and their future in business. Therefore these requirements, and liabilities that have appropriated taxable federal funds to help their corporate conditions including some small businesses, should consist of improved American values that are considered with relevance.

During this 2007 and 2008 economic recession of the United States, certain agreements between the government, and corporations have consisted of stimulus money lending matters. Observing money lending matters of applicable disciplines of liability, this is provided by government to pursue a responsible format of business, and social funded activities. Other businesses that don't have a strong chance or opportunity of earning a good profit from future business operations may have a risk factor that is too great to logically participate. This is factual for companies that have went out of business. Most of these diversified businesses, and citizens will depend on commercial bank lending upon which a vast amount of the banking establishments have received helpful support within government bailout money. Similar to local bank lending the taxes that a bank pays from their business of managing money or assets within lending is different from other businesses.

The requirements of lending from the U.S. federal government can sometimes consist of different low interest rate factors, but the U.S. Federal Reserve Bank, and the legislative duties of the U.S. Congress apply. The courts and the judiciary also most times are prepared to be "Constitutionally" fair, but aggressive to the various factors of agreements. This is where termed agreements are important, and lawful to receive certain large sums of U.S. government funded money with tax filing issue requirements. Some issues are tax exempt, but not all factors of income, and relevant transfers of money are included as tax exemptions on funded accounts, and procedures. These tax issues with stimulus government funds, and certain tax filing procedures includes exemptions, deductions, and the format of earned income. This is the factually required concern by all small, large, and major businesses as it applies to the American economy to return to productive business operating balance sheets.

As businesses in America grow, and prosper with certain non-profit organizations including all financial reporting requirements with tax exemptions, this becomes subjects of accounting with long-term economic disciplines. The format, and consideration of IRS requirements, and other government issues that apply to the tax exemptions of money management accounting often are applicable to business, and government having social factors in common. These issues of tax-exempt funds upon observation of spending are clearly within different excessive spending resource's that occasionally almost leads to fraud. This capacity of fraud is vital to observe when you consider the manageable use of government, and some corporate funds. The fraud occurs when the higher levels of people in management even as it applies to government officials don't value personal, or professional disciplines within their business, or as it applies to "citizens and government" duties. Within the concept of businesses, and organizations including church, and non-profit establishments with tax exempt funds, and funded collections these are considered factual to donations, and are managed in different bank accounts for long amounts of time. A vast amount of corporations make certain large donations, and occasionally like small businesses that make donations with tax exemptions, these funded issues are of a management duty, and responsibility of valid concern.

Upon the millions of different issues of accounting, and fund management values the concept of home owners, retired people, entrepreneurs, securities investors, military personnel, clergy, fisheries, and farmers, there is accountable issues of resource. This included complex sales people that from time to time are part of the American tax conditional effect of economic values. Within this array of American constituents a maximum resource of tax benefits becomes the issue of American tax dollar values that appropriate most relevant concerns of an educated, and determined society to be well governed, and productive. This is valued within the diversified concept of taxpaying citizens, and how they work to file, and or pay taxes which applies to beneficial living standards "applied" by the government. Also this applies to, and from the people lawfully thru mostly the authorities of legislature. Even as technology changes, and markets are developed with the formal resource of fair, and lawful tax procedures this is the goal that the states, and the U.S. federal government value for the people, and society. Considering government officials live, and pay taxes at the same applicable legal standards as others, the U.S. Constitutional value of "We The People" is applicable to all American's.

Our American standard's of taxes as it applies to bailouts or bankruptcy has various good detail for the employed people of America. Observing that bankruptcy, or the need of a government bailout is not good in most ways, these factors considering the fairness to reorganize business (c/o personnel) is a very important social aspect when terrorism, and bank fraud was the deterrent. These are issues that effect our American society which consist of very few productive opinions that may apply. This is important when people occasionally have issues to redress the government to compensate certain unlawful contractions against American liquidity assets. This vitally includes when business owners need time to understand certain levels of fault or even realize if a crime was committed that affected their business. In retrospect most productive small businesses, and occasionally large corporations will recognize vast amounts of things when they start to look like crime, or an issue that will disturb business negatively. These levels of business awareness keep's thousands of businesses operating with productive factors including keeping thousands of businesses in America with taxable income, and profitable earnings. Upon this observation even the American system of government has not been perfect, and therefore corrections are inevitable.

The fact that hundreds of businesses out of thousands of other corporate businesses in America during 2008 and 2009 have fallen on severe hard times with some going out of business, this is not just because of taxes that can't be paid, and the economy "only". New business arbitration, legal disciplines within National Security, and the best business decision making including wasteful spending is relevant to be improved in these issues of the changing times lawfully in America. These are the most vital problems that where established or created during the 2000 American economic crisis. It's important to observe that even though the American economy is in bad shape during this time there is a vast amount of corporations that are doing fairly good. These corporations that are doing slightly good are companies like U.S. Steel Corporation, Exxon-Mobil Corporation, Ely Lilly "Pharmaceutical" Company, Johnson and Johnson Corporation, and others like General Mills Food Corporation, and Kellogg Company. These corporations with their employed workers do recognize the financial hard times, and this is relevant even more so within their personal lives as homeowners when they occasionally suffer from high property taxes, and even sales taxes.

The property tax issue throughout certain parts of America is affecting residential, and commercial property owners at levels that may require government redress. Observing this from the beginning of 2009 the depressed housing market in America consisted of *1.5, or 2 out every 10 mostly new houses that were occupied is a critical number of new houses unsold. Upon this issued fact leaves an enormous level of inventory (c/o 8 out of 10) within houses that are unprofitable within timely sales. This rate of inventory is much too high in most regions of America, which includes the taxes a business must pay on this inventory of real estate. Following this expansion of new construction, certain construction contractor businesses, vendors, certain developers, and realtors including other businesses suffered severely with various bankruptcies. Considering this conflict of financially bad times, "no property taxes or occupant rent collections" are becoming helpful to the owners liquidity assets. Other unhelpful conditions are discretionary budgets that applies to properties losing value that are vital factors of these bad economic times. Therefore these bad decisions that only looked good was a disaster from the effort of investments into these small, and large regional properties that could not be sold in a timely manner.

An overbuilt housing, and commercial building market such as this during 2009 leaves too much despair for short-term economic resources. This vitally includes property with facilities that certain corporations had constructed like at Enron Corporation, and then commercial real estate had to be seized by federal authorities, and auctioned off for sale. Considering the bad economic atmosphere in America during this time very few expanding businesses had a use for these exclusive facilities of real estate. Therefore the diversified issues within the credit markets, and the stability within job security has caused people to lose equity in their homes upon which also includes moving from place to place. This was common during the Great Depression which consisted of some living conditions that became even worse.

Most all the good, and occasionally some of the bad within large or small businesses within America have property they own, and therefore the property tax is a valued debate within observation, and long term commitment issues. Some considered bailouts could have possibly been prevented with lower property taxes, and better management issues from government. Within valued issues this format of property taxes have been a serious rate percentage dispute upon considered laws because of so many conflicting losses such as bank bailout issues, and business bankruptcy concerns in most American regions. From time to time certain government officials have raised what tax they can too cover the losses of people, and local business tax revenue. Automobile corporate new car dealerships have been part of this struggle sense the September 11, 2001 terrorist attacks. These business properties are becoming vacant in vast amounts of places around the United States. The equation on both sides especially including the "higher" property tax rate duties is observed, and considered financially unfair due to the good, and bad issues of earned income, and other regional economic losses or conflicts.

Observing the millions of people that are employed or sufficiently retired with good or logical income, certain change's from government, and some inflationary conditions are vital for them to understand these disciplines of economics. Companies that receive the U.S. government (TARP) funding bailout money are businesses that strictly must watch inflation, and any additional excessive cost, upon which they may have throughout the entire business process, and operating disciplines. Therefore, and considering these relevant factors of long-term commitments, cost and purchases within the managing of bank accounts, and money concerning this lending process becomes an issue. This becomes more stressful with reorganizing proper appropriations as retired citizens. This means there are values of importance within the U.S. government TARP program that must be used with appropriate business procedures that are considered productively cost effective. Before normal issues of home ownership, and stability with certain commitments of economic restructuring are achieved, these "lending" and "money management" factors of important values must consist of overall improvements. These are some of the valid conditions of stress factors that must be eliminated upon all economic concerns, and more so business long-term restructuring.

Understanding, and observing the residential, and commercial property ownership issues of the American society is a factor of taxes, projected or possible income, and U.S. Constitutional commitments to the service they provide people, and the American society. This understanding during the middle to late years of 2000 has consisted of apartment and housing facility owners being foreclosed on, and then most times their tenets must find other places to live, or run their businesses applicable to commercial property. These property foreclosures are partly due to taxes, and the economic hardships of management duties with these times of an economic recession within the American condition of businesses. Between apartments, condominiums, and houses the concept of paying rent has benefited more people than the ownership, and equity a family receives from owning a house. Observing this, a vast amount of people are losing the equity from home ownership that occurs after less than 5 to 10 years, and then the property is foreclosed. Some people and families may earn more equity within staying in the right apartment or living arranged condition's, and then follow the best decisions before the purchase of a family home, and or household with additional assets. The U.S. government's solution is only fractional due to how long it would take for these thousands or more families (c/o some businesses) if ever to retain the equity that they invested, sacrificed, and then lost.

Equity in business property, and even homeownership property values has been one of Americans most valued issues of liability, and resource besides the people that manage the livable, and workable standards of these places. The issue of government bailouts of commercial real estate is closely contingent on banks, mortgage companies, and the owner. This is conflicting as it applies to these valuable factors in America that are slightly the observed concern with certain factors of productive business, and the security to pay all responsible obligated resource's. Certain businesses within the automobile industry in America such as Ford Motor Company, General Motors Corporation, and Chrysler Corporation have accumulated losses within regional business dealerships that had to reorganize, and or be eliminated from certain business locations. The foreign car companies have only suffered slight problems because their plant operations in the United States is not as large, and extensive as most American automobile companies, and their extensive ways of production in other companies. Understanding this problem, it distinctively is considered by the individual proprietors of a car franchise dealership upon which lately has suffered personal business losses from their sponsored corporate constituents. This is the format of equity within the facilities, utilities, taxes, and the staffed employees upon which the business is not earning a profit by the sale of vehicles to compensate the owners, and their establishment. Within this format of business evaluation factors of appropriate operating standards, a vast amount of other businesses are suffering similar problems. Considering not many retail stores or franchise dealers are being considered for government bailouts these tax generating businesses have credit, and cash issues that are part of their business equity. Therefore between credit, cash, and the valued resources of equity, the American society of individuals, public and private business including local government all have issued concerns for the future of bailouts, taxes, and the present or future American economy.

CHAPTER ELEVEN

TAX DOLLARS, EDUCATION & LIABILITIES OF AMERICA

American tax dollars, education, and liabilities of the United States, and all systems of government have a vast amount of disciplines, and subjects in common. Considering the state and federal government tax appropriations for education in America, the liability of valued importance is to educate children with an applicable commitment. This is important to every state, and local taxable governed duty as it applies to all lawful responsibilities. Teaching with logical funding at this capacity is the fact of providing an education to all grade school children, and secondary students in America. Also this includes certain opportunities to all American people; old and especially the young when this level of ambition is the continuation of education that consist of academics, scholastics, occupations, and professional opportunities. Then progress can be lawfully factual (c/o legal requirements) throughout all populated areas from the smallest American state governments, to the largest populated state governments. These requirement's therefore then support certain remote areas of diverse geographical conditions of concern.

Understanding educational resource factors of the state and federal government that spends, and appropriates substantial amounts of tax dollar funds to maintain the liability values of education, "this applies" to teachers, other staff members, materials, equipment, food, and certain programs. Within these issues to educate children from kindergarten to high school levels, and the format of adult studies at colleges and universities, the United States Department of Education (c/o 1980s), and most all "State Government Educational Departments" and regulators work to make sure no one is left out. This is only done successfully by consistent observation, and reviewed educational issues. Therefore these procedures are to balance the factual challenges that make education productive for all ages, in all regions, and places in the United States of America.

Education and liability is some of the oldest values of mankind that consist of learning what will or will not work, and or who or who did not; even if the liability of it was written or signed in "stone tablets" contrary to wood, and paper. This format of educated liability subjects within the United States has also advanced with technologically equipped facilities, and factors that consist of cost, and evaluated decisions in numerous ways. Considering elementary schools, and up to the high school level within students these are only logical expenses that are left to tax payers, and citizens that is substantially offered free of tuition to the students, and parents. Then the people only have minor expense's that are personnel items, and supplies of value to support educational disciplines of most all school attending children as citizens. Although some elementary private or parochial schools have a tuition, the overall system of education in America are "occasionally" without excessive cost, except when applicable like's are within the higher standards of others. Therefore even with tax income duties for all school employees, and even citizen's the logic of some exemption factors is a personal, and or family balance to manage resourceful concerns.

Observing education, and tax dollars it is logical to say that the American public system of education is similar to a large enterprise. This format of an enterprise is paid for mostly by government funds, and occasional donations with similar legal, and regulatory requirements for private or public education, and schools. This is slightly different from colleges and universities that consist of vast amounts of scholastic values for cost including occupational, and professional learning opportunities. College students, and even work study programs of experience makes the secondary educational process more detailed for the ambition of studies, and even certain lifelong opportunities. Therefore we observe colleges and universities with tuitions, and diversified funding from cost as a vital function in secondary education. Also this applies to occasional alumni contributions with some values of appropriated expense values that applies to all educational systems, and professionalism in America.

Considering the factors of bailout money from the United States government during 2007, and 2008 the concept of school systems throughout America have accumulated certain decisive enrollment problems which makes bailout money non-considerable. This is very different from the mid 2000 economic crisis that most small or large corporations or businesses are dealing with concerning financial operating expenses that can't be compensated with economic losses to their annual budget expenses. The loss, or gain of student enrollments as a budget item is totally different from any small revenue earnings, or donations that may exist in certain businesses or more so organizations. There might be an exception within the Catholic Church as it applies on occasions to Catholic schools, but other private and some public school systems are more coherent to their values of leadership.

Most public schools are funded by the state government strictly, and the losses over decade's from the 1970s has been complex due to inflation, and tremendous conflicts within the people. An example is schools in Gary, Indiana have loss students to the sad extent that budgets have been reduced from over *(an estimated inflated scale of today) $110,000,000.00 to slightly less than $50,000,000.00, which is valued on equity, students, and faculty. Due to inflation and a difference of 15 years these numbers are very close when a school corporation or public school enrollment goes from *27,000 students to less than 11,500 students upon which certain changes must be considered, and made. This problem is similar in Chicago, Illinois as well, but on a larger more complex scale. Theoretically these losses of young student enrollment issue's within the light of regional crime, and a need for less funded expenditures is a serious social, and financial problem of concern. These changes are effected within the school budgets that the state government will review as workable, and non-workable. Therefore school building's that includes the teaching staff, and certain administration officials becomes a logical factor that eliminates their needed amount of equipment, contractors, and employment resources within jobs.

Between the issued subjects of bankruptcies, bailouts, and expenditures as it applies to education in America, a vast amount of good, and occasional bad must be considered for corrections promptly. School systems in America are mainly based on state government tax funded expenditures. The U.S. Constitution only slightly acknowledges the vital issues of education, and upon this relevance most all responsible citizen, and student issue's are valued by the individual state governments. This usually holds the most relevant observation, and duties of budgets, and certification for the applicable state government officials, and professionals that have close understanding of their regions.

From the 1930s to the mid 1970s expenditure cost which has went from $3.2 billion to over $90.0 billion dollars a year for all schools within the United States is a relevant concern as it applies to the vast amount of issues that American school districts are concerned about. It is rear that any school system's, and districts of the United States will not function on a day by day base, but the concept of not enough room, or too much excessive space has lately occurred. This includes similar factors within a lack of occasional funds for new books or the maintenance or repair's of facility's, and equipment that are a vital review issue yearly. Understanding this access within 50 million student's, and close to 3 million teacher's, and staff that operates the schools from government tax expenditure's of money means this managing process is vital with discipline. These expenditures (c/o inflation) which is reviewed, and appropriated from, and by the state government with certain assistance from local school officials is a valued issue of operating liquidity. The United States federal government also has involvement that consist of most vital guild lines for safe, and lawfully productive schools. Therefore the cities, towns, states, and the relevance of the U.S. federal government is applicable with important required limitations, and advancements to provide an equation of education, and business efficiency.

During the years of 1990 to about 2008 a vast amount of intercity school systems have loss student enrollment at record levels. The consolidated issue of education in America has lost young people to vast amounts of crime (c/o youthful gang violence), and family issues of dysfunctional discipline. This also means the asset liquidity of funding, and the need of teachers, and staff has been reduced dramatically during these 1990, and 2000 decade conditions of human losses. Cities such as Baltimore, Chicago, Los Angeles, Gary, Philadelphia, Houston, St. Louis, and even New Orleans have suffered severely within their intercity school systems. New Orleans was a special case due to the additional effect of the 2005 Hurricane Katrina damaging a vast amount of this city's public schools. In retrospect these all around conflicts occurred to include a sad, and low 10% rate of high school graduates that will attend collage per year before this severe hurricane destroyed a vast amount of the city. Considering this the liability, and effort for solutions to improve the schools in New Orleans which has reference to schools in other American cities, this requires far more than just the appropriations of tax dollars. This also outlines why the state government is observed with more authority then the federal government as it applies to a states regulated schools.

Observing this, even the students, teachers, and school expenditure's of the 1970s, and 2008 are not without dramatic change to enrollments, and economics. These changes also effect the asset liquidity to except certain conditions of inflation. Actually in 1973 there were 50 million (grade school & secondary) students, and during 2009 there is 49.8 million students, which means there was more students during 1973 attending schools in America. These student enrollment numbers consisted of cost expenditures in 1973 of $56,031,041.00 (millions), and today during 2009 the expenditures will be about $543,000,000,000.00 (billions) which over 36 years is a large increase, compared to the same enrollment of students. It's not logical to determine the difference within Catholic schools where there is a tuition (c/o economic conflicts) due to the 2009 recession, and economy. This vitally includes the fact that a vast amount of new charter schools have been built in different parts of the country, and more are being planned with certain amounts of these cost expenditures, and levels of enrollment that have normally increased. Therefore the full value of tax dollar expenditures in certain regions has issues of accountability that has to improve.

The intercity school systems such as in Detroit, Michigan, Gary, Indiana, and Chicago, Illinois are closing vast amounts of school facilities contrary to a few newly built charter schools that are diverse from lower levels of enrollment problems. Throughout the Gary School Corporation in Gary, Indiana more than 50% of the school buildings have been closed, and are now unoccupied. The Detroit, Michigan schools have been compounded with issues that suffered some of the same drastic problems including crime, and high dropout rates which includes school closings. During 1973 Detroit had 325 public schools, and today there is 175 Detroit public schools which is a reduction of more than 45%. Occasionally in some rural areas a few school districts have increased in numbers, and even expenditure cost to appropriate logical operating budgets. Contrary to the business, and budget operating concerns due to those vast few issues of liability, this is a valid concern for students, and liquidity that is still very sad, complex, and serious.

Every year within certain American regions, different school buildings, and facilities suffer damage or must be considered for renovation or construction improvements for a diversified outlook of precautions, and reasonable standards. Mismanagement, and contingent liability factors occasionally become some of the most common reasons that a school district may go bankrupt, or suffer financial problems along with regional difficulties. Observing the distinct level of government, and engineering insecurity within the 2005 Hurricane Katrina this was a severe setback "with some positive repercussions" for a vast amount of young people as students in the New Orleans school system. It is important to understand that this hurricane could not be ignored which included other parts of the state's of Mississippi, and Louisiana, and therefore the schools where damaged, but when schools reopened they had smaller, and more efficient classroom conditions.

In some capacity certain people would say a vital lesson of liability was disciplined, and factored during certain tornado's, and hurricanes with flooding that effected an enormous amount of people in America. Considering other places, and concerns in America that realize that certain obsolete infrastructure issues can one day possibly destroy their livable regions with large expense liability issues of precaution this problem had conditions of caution to become a very important concern. Certain New Orleans schools where damaged during Hurricane Katrina (2005), and could not operate for the young children due to the vast amount of damages. Also within this concern a high percentage of the residential, and other types of facilities, and assets where severely effected, and then they were not fit for human accommodation.

Insurance, and "State of Emergency" funds, and now government bailout issues have been a 100% consolidated factor, and resource to restructure New Orleans, and the 9th Ward schools. This effort of government help is for all parts of the city of New Orleans, but the 9th Ward was hit worse including other school districts within the city of New Orleans that may not be revised any time soon. Considering this issue, the state and federal government has appropriated vast amounts of money, but with tens of thousands of homes destroyed, including hundreds of commercial facilities this consolidated effort will take more than just the govern appropriations that have been committed. Most young, and old people have loss home's, and everything that was established as equity. Considering these issues within problems of maintenance for schools, the government, and or public utility infrastructure's of these assets where vital concerns to the long-term existence of a productive, and safe society. There is no part of America where a school or the overall infrastructure does not need regular maintenance, and occasional renovated up-grades, therefore this becomes important within reviewed planning, and future budgets.

Contrary to the vast amount of economic concerns within the schools of America, the tax dollars that apply to other assets surrounding the issue to educate children in the United States has been threatened by foreign interest. This becomes an issue of childhood self-esteem for young adults and children that requires additional financial support after, and before school. The hundreds of billions of dollars (c/o the 1990s) that the state, and federal government has applied within expenditures is considered an investment, but when illegal immigrants compiled millions of American jobs more than young Americans we must ask; didn't we appropriate money to educate the young American's for a vast amount of those opportunities to work? This means that in 5 to 10 years with 10 million to 15 million illegal aliens working in small, or large businesses as full or part-time worker's a vast amount of opportunities, and education have been misapplied to students born in America. Upon this relevant fact these educated young Americans are not able to achieve or use those positive educational, and social values in certain American places of employment. For hundreds of years young American's in most social concerns have been involved in these before school, and or after school jobs, and work duties. In addition this also includes working during certain school vacations. Theoretically the lack of these issues is an observation within the format of resources that has become an American business factor of failure concerning issues that requires tax dollar bailouts. This is important to restructure the economic tax base within businesses that have suffered from bad, or misguided U.S. domestic, and some foreign relation concerns.

School age children, and even college students working in certain businesses as a vital learning experience is within the understanding of important social business values. Even thou there is laws that restrict children or young adults from doing certain jobs until they reach a certain age, the grooming of honest, and work integrity is a vital developed skill. These values of discipline are also applied to their studies in school. One of the vital examples is that during the 1960s, and 1970s hundreds of high school students in certain regions worked at U.S. Steel Corporation, and other steel plants. In addition during that time young high school juniors, and seniors worked at certain automobile plants within Chrysler Corporation, Ford Motor Company, and General Motors Corporation. These jobs and other conditions of employment, and educational issues of after high school work for students was becoming a vital working part at these companies. Throughout many states within the American society this provided value, and added to the economy in a productive way. From the mid 1970s and 1980s this concept of work opportunities came to a sad slow down with vast amounts of layoffs. This lead a vast amount of young American's from the work force into very indecisive lively hoods upon restructuring their lives.

Considering massive layoffs during the 1970s, and 1980s in most American regions, and especially throughout Indiana, Illinois, Ohio, and Michigan these unemployed workers had to severely change their spending, and budget managing habits. This was another learning experience within the factors of business, which included social adjustments to cut employment needs with budget factors that had to be considered in an overall capacity. Considerably there was other small, and large businesses that provided the same opportunities, and this concept of work employment duties helped change the prosperity, and tax revenue base within most overall issues of business, and values of government. Problems, and solutions had to be considered within the governed economy including tax revenue that had the right issues of changes, and discipline. This level of discipline is factored with observation of the future of business growth, and the changing times of most industry values, and government concerning most American cities, and towns.

These issues of employment apart from education are just as important to remember, and understand that the business has a purpose to achieve overall productive results. Considering the liability within the high school age employees, and all other people working for certain businesses, and corporations the training of these young people is a manageable factor to make the products, services, and most taxable revenue productively good. This means that all employees have a duty or concern to continue working together productively to achieve the goals of the business. Also this is relevant to satisfy the resource's within all others involved or throughout other logical parts of the American society. Therefore the public, private businesses, and even most government procedures can maintain the best workable solutions, which can achieve better efficiency on a year by year factor of progress.

The concentration of American local, state, and federal government concerns also believe in this process of outreach that from time to time offers seasonal employment to good students from their local schools. Whether the concern is government or local business it's usually an understanding that the student must attend school concerning lawful, and acceptable obligations along with some agreements of a student's parents or guardians. The concept of even a newspaper company concerning most American regions has consisted of these work values which have existed for years. Lately within comparing the opportunities for students to work for a city or state government, the numbers have not been as productive during 2000 as it existed to be during the early 1970s. Applicable newspaper delivery has maintained a level of long-term stability of school age people having a part-time job. As we look, and understand industry during the late months of the year 2007, a vast amount of the major newspaper companies are filing for bankruptcy, and this has increased during 2009. These are critical factor's that occasionally effect's all conditions of a business operation, and various parts of America. Concerning this issue within business factors of failure, the effect is quite broad within certain community values. Therefore even this concern exist especially considering how newspaper delivery students don't normally earn enough to pay taxes. Then the government allows them slightly exempt from business, and government conflicts that apply to tax filing duties.

The severe loss of American people in certain regions has been a bad social effect due to the decreasing factor of newspaper subscribed customers, and readers that they sell newspapers to. This effect's the newspapers ordered for delivery (apart from internet subscribed customers), and even the company's tax revenue earning conditions. This becomes the circumference of losses to young people between the schools, the newspaper companies, and other community businesses to understand these economic values of a social recession. My opinion of a social recession is that America is losing more valuable people then the logical United States Census of populated gains of productive American people. These long-term problems within adjustments to survive these financial, and economic hard times has logical concern to reconfigure most all important values. The values of concern (c/o resources) are applicable even more so to the relevant disciplines of the liability of American educational standards of people working together productively. When some people consider the educated standards of social studies within people, they will observe a more detailed understanding that throughout the 2008 American economic recession it's also part of a critical social recession or depression of people for long-term improvements. Therefore within the course of a recovery, most issues will depend on the long-term commitments, and the stability of obligated agreements with liability issues concerning most American standards of society.

Within the decades of the past, and the concerned future, the American system of education, and tax revenue between the government, and society will be factored as it always has with the workable changes, and commitments that lawfully work constructively. These values within taxes to support the education of young people within the population will be understood within the future years of 2000 which is balanced on the social values that lawfully compensate their long-term educational needs. This evaluation is determined by the many changing times that can be sometimes recognized from the decisions of the government. These governed activities, and powers are conducted by executive, legislative, and judicial decisions of the American system of government, and a society that is most times productively workable. Some of the subjects of discipline that will be consistently valued are energy, healthcare, labor, national security applicable to defense, law, engineering, economics, computer programming, internal medicine, agriculture, religion, farming, construction, and other conditions of managing public, private business, and government. Concerning these issued occupations, and professions the prosperity, and sovereign society of America will be balanced with taxable adjustments, lawful leadership, and a funded money circulation that will keep most of the young, and old American people living productive lives.

CHAPTER TWELVE

STATE & FEDERAL TAXES, LIQUIDITY, & REVENUE

The American system of state, and federal taxes that includes the annual filing process is one of the United States government's most critical factors of liability to increase the liquidity of governed assets, and the stability of America in many ways. These taxable income earning issues within tax payable factors declares citizenship values of good standards on a year by year concept of procedures for individuals, and businesses. It also gives each American state government, and all local sectors (c/o regulators and contractors) a resource of government funding for manageable government duties by, and for the people.

In a long-term observation the format of state, and federal taxes is determined by certain legislative government officials, and enforced by certain agencies with the Department of Justice. This process also includes long-term commitments that creates the base of liquidity in all forms of government for future years of contingent liabilities, and U.S. Constitutional obligations. Within the concern of the years of 2007, 2008, and 2009 the U.S. Constitution does not outline laws about bailing out American businesses, or how they maintained liquidity, and disciplines within contingent liabilities. These are contingent business, and corporate issues that an enormous amount of citizens are concerned about, although better business disciplines should have been considered years before this problem. Most of these contingencies, and issues of liability are valued lawfully from the relevance of the individual state Constitution's, and the United States Constitution to have ethical, and lawful procedures of equity within economic opportunities. This becomes the value within employment, and business resource's of future consideration. Therefore certain Constitutional Amendments that apply to other laws of the American establishment's of government become important, and relevant to help this government process of lawful financial, and economic accumulation. Then we observe business liquidity becoming tax revenue of value for the people.

Concerning the relevant obligations that individual states, and the U.S. federal government is committed too, these resources of tax revenue liquidity is a valued issue of importance. These issues consist of a vast amount of assets, and support for government employees, and elected officials upon which this benefit's the citizens. This also includes the citizen concerns within most issues that can be appropriated for useful, and lawful services within all levels of government access. Understanding this, each year within the tens of millions of American people working within the provisions of tax revenue this is applicable to the best duties, and liability resources that the individual states, and the U.S. federal government can offer. It has changed a vast amount sense the George Washington Presidential days as well the other 40 plus U.S. Presidents that followed as of today. Upon these factors theoretically each state, and region has state and federal government officials, and duties that apply to the use of the tax dollar format of funds. These tax funded issues are the general operating assets throughout the executive, legislative, and judicial branches of government that have consistent resource's of duties shared between local, state, and federal employees, and officials. Therefore as each state government has a legislative branch that makes the laws applicable to the state Constitution, and the U.S. Congress making laws from the United States federal government and Constitution this is part of a variation of subjects, and laws for the all citizens. This is when a jurisdiction of land, certain professional subjects, applicable laws, and or people with government must manage to keep compliance of discipline within all American government powers, and duties.

Within a clear understanding of how the United States Constitution is applied to the American "Income Tax" system, and other issues of taxation this was established in America based on a number of different parts of the entire U.S. Constitutional document that was passed into law during 1787. The logical purpose was for the U.S. government to also have funds, and liquidity to conduct business, and government duties within serving the people of America. This is more so observed after certain agreements within the U.S. federal government of 1913, and the affects of Article 1- Section 8, Article 1- Section 9, and the 16th Amendment to the United States Constitution. These laws imply by Article 1 - Section 8 that states: The U.S. Congress shall have power; To lay and collect taxes, duties, imports and excises, to pay the debts, and provide for the common defense and the general welfare of the United States; but all duties, imports and excises shall be uniform throughout the United States. Also Article 1 - Section 9 states that; The migration or importation of such persons as any of the states now existing shall think proper to admit, shall not be prohibited by the Congress prior the year one thousand eight hundred and eight (1808), but a tax or duty may be imposed on such importation, not exceeding ten dollars for each person. Within the value of the 16th Amendment (c/o Income Taxes) this was proposed on July 12, 1909 and ratified on February 3, 1913: and that is stated as; The Congress shall have power to lay and collect taxes on incomes, from whatever source derived, without apportionment among the several states, and without regard to any census or enumeration. The only other factors within relevant parts of certain revision's, or exemption's of the United States government with these separation's of power is the U.S. Supreme Court, and the executive branch of the President.

During 1894 the U.S. Congress passed an income tax law, but the United States Supreme Court declared it unconstitutional. This ruling and declaration by the United States Supreme Court gave format for the 16th Amendment (c/o 1913) of the U.S. Constitution to be authorized by the United States Congress to levy such a tax. These have become the taxable conditions of revenue from individuals, public or private businesses, and the diversified concept of corporations in America. This also includes certain organizations that serve different purposes in the American society that occasionally apply to liability factors of property, and or certain tax exemptions. Property taxes are also within these important issues for most property owners, and that includes the estates that a family may value for a vast amount of years, and therefore govern prosperity is valued.

Property taxes are levied thru the concept of cities, towns, counties, and some school districts within the format of established governments in America. During the years of 2000 the factor of property taxes have caused great harm due to the economic factors of businesses, and households that suffered failure with some falling into bankruptcy. Observing 1929 this is why in 2009, the American economy and all small, and large business have become an economic vital concern for the people, and their income earnings which maintains prosperity. Occasionally losses of young people to violent crime, and this time of war has been a factor that has misappropriated a concerned issue of taxation. Some Midwest cities are suffering to the extent of not having enough funds to operate at 90% to 100% capacity as government. Apart from property tax revenue, certain state tax revenue issues are also a vital part of that suffering. This is due to the loss of businesses like department stores (c/o now some internet shopping), and a variation of other businesses. Even banking has suffered tremendously with the increase of foreign business owners whom are exempt from paying income tax for a variation of at least 7 years. This has instituted a large economic loss to most all levels of the American system of government as it applies to economics, and especially all levels of government liquidity.

The losses which in 2002 seem to be approaching the tune of more than $50 billion dollars easily within loss government tax revenue effected various amounts of individual state governments. During the following years that includes losses of liquidity to the system of American government, and the businesses that support people in the American society, these became subjects of a recession, and possible depression. A billion dollars a year is a large amount of money within losses for one state government, and the people with these conflicts which have eliminated police, and fire department officials, including certain others all over America. One small town mayor in Iowa who's town lost various corporate businesses during 2008, lately (c/o 2010) is working without any executive office government salary. This is the problem from accumulated losses of business, and income tax revenue for local, and some state government establishments, and their duties to increase efficiency with issues such as the infrastructure, and various secured concerns that government should supply. Considering these factors it also includes the federal government, and therefore this negative economic, and social effect within the loss of people, and projected income tax revenue is occasionally passed on with suffering to the other rich or poor taxpaying citizens.

Understanding the U.S. federal government where loss business tax revenue will not be replaced by individual citizens paying state, and federal combined taxes is a subject of American owned businesses that believe in paying logical taxes. As the logical fact of government is concerned about making good investments for the future is vital, this can establish government liquidity. Even TARP funding loans have been considered as good government investments which in 2010 the U.S. government has made a profit from some corporations paying back TARP bailout loan. The lack of American owned businesses which are applicable to the U.S. Constitution, and other laws providing tax revenue is part of the federal, and state tax revenue accumulations of government liquidity. Therefore tax revenue liquidity will continue to be complex due to the increasing problems within foreign interest to be solved at the state, and more so U.S. federal government level. This even includes U.S. Corporations that have paid out large sums of bailout money to foreign businesses.

The asset liquidity of American people with taxable income earning revenue has possibly become an issue within the economic fairness of society as it applies to comparable property tax issues. These are the calculated equations that compensate the logical funding of certain government values from a lawful and logical percentage rate. This vitally includes issues from the citizens that suffered occasional violations within unjust or unfair "Constitutional" legal disciplines concerning their rights of justice being served that are factored on issues of liability. Considering local government depends on property taxes to help finance education, police and fire protection, street and sewer repairs, and other services within important government details these vital asset concerns have been ignored, and put off. These unresolved government asset issues have consisted of the concept within obsolete utility infrastructures in a vast number of American regions.

Other problems have become a losing factor of this lack of format within government liquidity, and liability that is critical to a well developed society. Certain cities (c/o Ford Heights, IL) have even went to the extent of eliminating their local police department (c/o the county sheriff support) due to severe crime, corruption, and vital economic, and financial difficulties. This is a perfect example of businesses not paying taxes for 7 years, and needed or perpetuating vital conflicts or help from government services. Another issue of city service subjects such as sewers that are severely obsolete in a vast amount of regions causing residential backup flooding, and other facility values of out of control cost conditions are exceeding the valued price of a vast amount of homes. This fully describes a concept of contingent liabilities within unworkable government conditions that causes residential citizens, and businesses a lack of liquidity.

These conflicts within the diversion of individual citizens, families, businesses and the issued duties of government with losses of liquidity, and truly good citizen business ownership "equity" in the American society are the judgment, and opinions that occasionally belong in the courts. Within the consideration of how bad some county, and state governments have become which even includes the problem of housing foreclosures within equity, some courts are laying off employed people. Even worse some county courts are being considered to be closed for government business. More so observing the American system of courts, the tax laws, and rates of percentages are from time to time an issue to be Constitutionally evaluated, but budget matters exist so court's must work productively. Some may have taken this for granted years ago, and now it has came back to them, and us as a larger problem. Considering this, even certain deduction's, and exemption's apply, and this is beneficial to the governed citizens, families, businesses, and other logical issues within establishments, but the discipline of government liquidity must be aggressively managed. Within certain economic problems from a lack of government liability most valued hardworking American citizens observe these concerned efforts when the percentage rate of taxes needs to be redressed by government. This occasionally includes the state or federal system of courts, and certain government issues that also apply to various appointed, and occasionally some elected government officials.

The issues of the courts, and the other two branches of government that are understood, and routinely observed having individual state Department's of Treasury, and the U.S. Department of Treasury as a constituent of economic review has duties within issues to apply themselves, and the lower levels of government adequate financial appropriated funds. Managing government funds has various disciplines consisting of state, and federal budgets with liquidity requirements. These tax appropriations are taxes levied within the citizenship commitments to most individual local or county government establishments with the consideration of various federal jurisdictions. The full discipline within most valid concerns of government duties must be free of any civil or criminal issues of crime that will factor higher cost, and issues of corruption. It's sad to say upon understanding, but issue's of corrupt government in America has been the other record braking problem within this bad equation of the American economy during the first decade of 2000. Within the concept of a well developed, and more so lawfully governed society, these factors of low or logical taxes becomes an inflation adjustment concern by the executive, legislative, and judicial branches of government. These tax decision's, and separations of government power provide commitment to their duties, the American people, and society with logical liquidity assets of value. Therefore the entire resource of citizens working together, and forming a (more) perfect union is the valid objective for progress, and the economic changing times of society.

Upon the consideration of the U.S. Constitutions definition of a more "perfect union", the largest cities can be compared financially to the smallest cities, and towns as government tax revenue business concerns are valued with economic, and financial supportive disciplines. Within the different regions of American small, and large businesses with their expanded success is part of the cities, and or towns value of required cost of living standards, and expenses. This becomes appropriate when they consistently boost the tax revenue commitment to local, state, and even federal taxing unites of the Treasury. The larger the city, the more complex the cost of living, and inflation will exist, and this is occasionally factored within tax revenue due to the population, and the vast amount of employer's including citizens, and government assets. A considered "Perfect Union" observing business, politics, and other vital differences is a concept of logical values respectfully, but the state of an economy may become a controlled factor. This becomes relatively diverse by the largest employer, and a vast amount of small businesses that value steady earnings, and progress. The changing times of various American regional businesses have consisted of some moving out, and others occasionally moving in, but now lately this only implies that a money circulation exist. Understanding this long-term production, and business growth issue, it includes stability that is a highly questionable process. Contrary to procedures this is more so observed by the satisfaction of the local people of a city, town, or region.

During the 1990s certain company's with the likes of DHL a Package Shipping Company moved to the small remote regional town of Wilmington, Ohio. This town in Ohio had suffered economically, but this new company only lasted for 10 to 15 years as a productive business for that region in Ohio. More than 5,000 wage earning, and taxpaying employees were affected by this DHL business closer, and they were then removed from the DHL Corporate payroll. Granite City, Illinois being a small city with a U.S. Steel Corporation plant has established certain levels of economic disciplines (c/o good and bad issues) within tax revenue earnings, and economic stability. The U.S. Steel Corporation has been around sense the late 1890s with its headquarters in Pittsburgh, Pennsylvania which gives them workable, and logical experience about certain American regions, and government. Certain whisky distillery farms throughout a few small towns in the State's of Kentucky, and Tennessee have maintained certain small town levels of economic prosperity along with issues of farming, and coal mining. These factors display the good, bad, or successful effort of business, and government to come together with a "Prefect Union" for the American society, and people.

Within certain small coal mining towns throughout state's like Kentucky, West Virginia, Pennsylvania, and others including Utah coal mining, and certain commodities similar to coal is part of a taxpaying business of prosperity, and is valued for "Energy" in America. These industry resource's of standard work production appropriate the small town, and regional government tax revenue that is valuable to government and communities of value. The combined factor of coal is vital to various American utility companies, and distinctively the steel manufacturing industry, and a few other's of importance. These issues, and industry values of tax revenue maintains stability until certain issues may factor rational business, and government discrepancies which are usually the people's work with argumentative factors to respectfully control.

Observing various state, and federal tax paying industries of America certain business factors are occasionally the regional town economy, and money circulation upon which business environments have business growth that is, and becomes perceptional. This includes values within the concern that most times the highest wages are not the most argumentative factor, but they do occur within certain job duties. Even the danger of working in the coal mines is understood with logical values of "technological principals, and moral issues of faith" which also applies to the valued resources of business, and labor. This is part of the alternative that coal is an important commodity for the American society, and others throughout the world. Considering this commodity within coal, and it's taxable factors that are similar to oil drilling, most conditions exist with good employee wages, and business progress that usually exist at productive levels. Therefore the tax revenue factor is compensated with a vast amount of financial, and economic values as it applies to these American regions, and government.

Concerning the issue of the largest to the smallest cities, and towns, the bigger the "population", and "land" the more government expense's for these resource's become necessary to the metropolitan area. This is economically important within society being controlled with established format for applicable disciplines within the larger financial government budgets. In certain markets (c/o 2008) like the banking industry this is a regional observation that may require accountable government TARP bailout money due to the population percentage of people effected by similar financial, and economic problems. The budget within liquidity throughout Cook County, Illinois during 2007 was estimated at about $3 billion dollars a year. Considering this Cook County budget (c/o the population of Chicago, IL.) apart from some smaller or more idol counties in rural areas that may require about $0 to $50,000.00 dollars a year, considerably this resource consist of combined social, and urban conditions. The various combined conditions consist of ratified issues observing most state government populated, and geological difference's. This (Cook County, IL.) is one of the largest counties in the United States comparing the city population of Chicago, Illinois, then there is New York, NY., Los Angeles, CA., and Houston, TX. which are similar regions with large county budgets, and large populations of people to manage, and govern. These regions also consist of large tax revenue earnings, and liquidity that are appropriated from the vast amounts of small, and large businesses. Then there are certain wealthy individuals upon which also become applicable to support a percent of the population which includes employed people, a capacity of donations, and sometimes helpful concerns to others such as children, and the elderly.

Observing that these cities which are heavily concentrated within state and federal tax revenue, they usually consisted of city, state, and federal agencies with jurisdictions to keep applicable liquidity within various assets of government procurements. Other tax dollar procurements consist of county government buildings for courtrooms, clerk's offices, assessors, surveyors, and others within law enforcement including government professional duties. Also it is important to remember that cost applies to everything from cars, helicopters to paper clips, paper, and even utilities and other items as logical government procurements. This becomes an important government discipline observing the vast amount of businesses, and diversified industries that require proper regulatory concerns, or issues of enforcement. Considering these regional tax, and government issues, the large cities can maintain the liability factors of state and federal Constitutional laws. A vital factor for business supportive matters is valued for issues of anti-competitive business responsibilities within U.S. Anti-Trust laws that would destroy small productive business growth, and opportunities if not enforced.

The American format of business growth, and certain opportunities are an important subject lawfully. This also includes not just the disciplines for state and federal revenue within taxes, but also the prosperity of the employees, people, and most all business owners. Observing the productive growth, and opportunities of a business some of the vital factors consist of understanding taxation, and managing their business asset liquidity with revenue earning's. Also, the more consistent a business is within good products, and or service, the more valued equity they establish annually within their business including the provisions of "tax planning and revenue". America has thousands of small, and large public, or private businesses, and corporations that consist of these disciplines throughout America's many regions. They also work with the American people, professionals, and government to be productive in their own intellectual, but lawful way. A factual problem has been observed, and considered during 2003 to 2009 when over 565 businesses in America have filed for bankruptcy protection. These business failures with accumulated values of more than $448.4 billion dollars in assets became a big problem for future business, and employment. Considering the expansion of businesses from 1920 to 2005 it seems that during the early 1990s this was the destructive start within misunderstanding the logical hard work it takes to start, and operate a productive or new business. Therefore besides the American taxpaying citizens within 1000s (thousands) of businesses that are a resource for these factors, the state, and federal income taxes with issues of "legislature that are considered, and becomes important". Also this includes the resource's, from the American system of government. Considering most resources these duties have a vital part occasionally, and lawfully with or more so without illegal interruption unless normal business, or government conflicts occur.

During 1990 to 1995 a vast amount of large corporations where created that would have generated large tax revenue values for certain individual states, and the United States federal government. Apart from the corporations that where started from honest hard work, there were other companies that spent time violating anti-trust laws against others, and because of that a vast amount of businesses did not do good long-term. Without certain commitments to products, and services certain large businesses, and corporation's like Ameritech, Enron, WorldCom, and a few other's accumulated vast amounts of problems. These 3 large corporations, and others were created from large corporate merger cash transactions with certain capital gain taxes to pay. Due to their tax payment, and large cash holdings Ameritech, Enron, WorldCom, and a few others took illegal advantage of some smaller businesses, and therefore this increased the amount of taxable businesses that failed along with those corporate bullies. The concept of capital gain taxes which means a financial asset is held for 6 months before taxes are paid is a government understanding value of maturity. This, and even more so a corporate or individual tax advantage occurs with some corporations continuously having discussion's to merge with, or acquire another corporation. The process here also gives them additional leverage on the liquidity of capital assets they control, or that they have the ability to manage. From this managing control of liquidity within corporate assets this includes their "income tax, and property tax" status as a business of good, and hopeful future values of productive social, and business integrity.

These corporation's within Ameritech, Enron, WorldCom, and other's paid income taxes in access of hundreds of millions of dollars before they vanished as businesses in the American society. Ameritech Corporation did have a logical resource within productive business service's that consisted of commercial, and residential telephone service agreements with a vast amount of employees, but they lacked certain professional business disciplines. Enron and WorldCom Corporation used some of the same disciplines within products, and services that have an interest to millions of American citizens in each of most all regions. Contrary to monopolies in the "Electric Utility" markets in California, and other states like Texas, and Portland, Oregon they had not managed valued ethic's, and market business transactions carefully. These government concerns with Gray Davis the Governor of California, and these corporations with business procedures, and certain transactions within businesses consisted of large, and out of control product, and technological services. This then lead financial, and economic matters to be unprofitable contrary to if they were doing what it takes to earn a profit. In addition this lack of asset management concerns of business control to maintain expanded business equity occurred to a vast amount of businesses during 1990 thru the 2000 decade, and times. Observing this, the businesses, and certain issues of government legislature appropriated these businesses to have no real value of long term business product, and service liability disciplines.

As it is considered when a corporation has a "business plan, and process" that is out of control like the people, and the United States government has recognized from the 2009 troubles of American International Group Inc. (AIG) various concerns, and corrections are vital. Considering the AIG Inc. business concerns a vast amount of American taxpayers where effected. AIG Incorporated has suffered differently from a vast amount of other corporation's sense September 11, 2001 during the George Bush Presidential administration. Now AIG Incorporated has had severe up's and down's similar to the problems of United Airlines Corporation after the 9-11 Report Terrorist attacks, and other attacks that were applied to the United States Anti-Trust laws applicable to the small, and large businesses of America. In addition a vast amount of businesses found themselves troubled with issues concerning the new capacity of bankruptcy. Observing these two companies, and their financial issues of trouble's AIG Incorporated, and United Airlines Corporation both have totally different concerns, and planning of restructuring.

The United States government with the Barack Obama Presidential administration, and the U.S. Congress appropriated over $170 billion dollars to AIG Incorporated during 2009. Passing this legislature was very mixed with anger throughout the United States Congress, and the people. These out of control U.S. government bailout issues includes their business in the United States, and (c/o U.S. tax dollars) business activities, and agreements with a vast amount of other foreign, and U.S. domestic corporate businesses. Another important concern consisted of other international countries within business concerns with extensive AIG Inc. employee bonus. These are the "TARP" funds from pass American tax collected assets that established cash liquidity throughout the American system of government. A vital consideration of this problem is that the United States government has given AIG Incorporated more money than AIG Incorporated has paid, and or appropriated in state, and federal taxes in those last few years after 2001, and 2002. Therefore their repayment of these loans will take longer than most other corporate businesses involved in these bailouts.

The company AIG Incorporated unlike some other insurance company's like State Farm Insurance Company, Allstate Insurance Company, and even Berkshire Hathaway are part of American businesses that have paid out large sums of insurance claims from 2001 up to 2007. Considering the two events of the 9-11 Report Terrorist attacks, and Hurricane Katrina a vast amount of insured assets, and people were destroyed. During this 2000 decade New York City where AIG is located as its headquarters, the City of New York seemed to have suffered the most which included destructively fatal terrorist attacks, but Hurricane Katrina destroyed a vast amount of people's homes, and businesses. In retrospect observing other disasters the people, and government suffering from these levels of destruction even includes the insurance clam's paid out for the 2007 Minnesota bridge collapse. These tragic events upon which some people affected by the Minnesota bridge collapse in automobiles that fell into the Mississippi River, a vast amount of people could not be recovered, or rescued. Theoretically, all three of these tragic events of destruction consisted of assets, and people that could not be recovered from losses, and only the near survivors whom accumulated injuries.

The observation upon how the American society of people, and insurance company's maintained a workable good, and bad relationship, this sadly effected vast amounts of people, and businesses from doing their part as American employees, and providing tax revenue contributions. Upon these facts that various insurance companies have a consistent flow of borrowing money (c/o cash liquidity holdings) to pay clam's with little maturity, these insurance companies are losing equity. These vital conditions of equity are similar to AIG with very little gains of additional liquidity during 2007. Within complex relevance that the American liquidity problem issue during the first decade of 2000 will cause, is turmoil for various American insurance companies in the years to come. Even before this American corporate "bailout, and liquidity" crisis some insurance company's before the year 2000 had tremendous issues to restructure, and earn more money in more stable markets "maybe" like banking.

Contrary to this understanding, the banking markets became very complex with various insurance business concerns with certain banks going out of business or being taken over by other bank businesses. Therefore the less negative activity there is on insurance companies, this is applicable to taxable revenue that causes them to reduce or increase budget spending with logic. One factor that can be observed from their business taxable compensations to government is that occasionally during certain times this consist of certain clam's which are disputed in the courts, but this is additional money, and asset management "conflicts" as well. Therefore the equation of the state and federal tax revenue is applicable to the American Constitutional standards of law, and the society of the people, and businesses providing their best solutions possible.

Observing the state and federal tax revenue that investment banks, and insurance companies have appropriated in their taxable business procedures over the years of the 1st decade of 2000, and the late 1990s has consisted of questionable legal, and business conflicts that occurred with "some" terrorizing greed. Upon this observation these businesses, and public corporations do try to apply with government duties of lawful value. Most American businesses, and some professional offices (c/o even doctors, lawyers, accountants, engineers, architects, or other people) over the last 7 decades after the 1930s, businesses have earned additional money from their personal investments. This process is done inside, and outside of the business with procedures of them also operating a small or large productive business plan of sacrifice, and efficiency. As a vast amount of American people observed some company's which have allowed or pursued these additional money, and or investment earnings to be important for their business process, various issues of decision making by government, and corporate officials had became too complacent. These complacent factors has, and consist of certain conflicts upon which has earnings, and business matters becoming slightly insecure within certain commitments as it applies to the American gross national product rates, and sacrifices to be good ethical businesses for the general public.

Another consideration as it applies to ethic's within investment banking, and insurance consist of their main course of business, and earnings as it applies to good products, and business decisions that was not truly established as a conglomerate, but a select discipline of business may have increased their work load to an inefficient level of quality. Some investment banks, insurance companies, and certain other businesses have taken this subject too lightly with some years of prosperous earnings or income, but also lacking in their core type of business. Apart from one or two corporation's like the activity at General Electric Corporation that became a conglomerate, upon which they were different by trying to keep their core business productive. Contrary to their corporate differences various other businesses needed to make a better effort to keep their core business levels of production within a format of discipline. Therefore even with the productive work of Jack Welch the former CEO of GE Corp, these others would need to continue to restructure, and this would possibly make taxable, and business revenue reliable, and also fully productive.

These non-conglomerate business issue factors that become important to remember, and recognize that the phone companies, insurance companies, and some others are not established to be investment brokerage businesses. Observing Enron Corporation, WorldCom Corporation including a few others with a vast amount of their business activity which were not established as a lawful, and ethical investment bank, or as it applied to the "Enron Corporations Case" of not being a utility company, certain true business values were ignored. Actually the Enron former CEO Jeffery Skilling with the work of others such as the Chairman and their last CEO Ken Lay with their "west coast business of energy traders" manipulated more than $30 billion's dollars from the state of California. The liquid capacity of money came from the Electric Utility Companies, and a majority of utility customers throughout California, and various levels of government. Observing this economic, and liability hurt for people, businesses, and government in California, this problem finally reached the attention of more so the U.S. federal government. Upon their negligent, and manipulated fraud the Securities & Exchange Commission (after the Enron Bankruptcy filing) only took observation with no immediate corrective action. Then additional conflicts within transactions were discovered from most of these destructive junk bond corporate buyouts.

The Governor of California Gray Davis was fairly observant, but he had a level of confusion on this complex level of financial, and utility destruction. My personal (J. Reeves) opinion is that I considered this a severe violation of the U.S. Public Utility

Company Holding Act with some U.S. Anti-Trust law violated concerns. Over five or ten years I thought that maybe the entire government did not no longer care about manipulated fraud, and upon which could be a severe problem. The issue of financial service businesses, and employees of other professions occasionally find issues within the U.S. Anti-Trust laws which has given illegitimate complacency to various businesses, and government.

As WorldCom apart from Enron has been too involved in corporate junk bond markets that became out of control during the 1990s U.S. Anti-Trust laws were ignored with complacency. This seems to be more cognitive from major oil companies, and certain franchise businesses engaged in bad foreign relation issues with national security concerns. Contrary to the fact some oil company's found a good reason for the corporate merger process after certain economic conflicts, or expensive accidents that could have been prevented. This is similar to the vast amount of American bank's with the high rate of delinquent lending that have caused bank failures (c/o over 650) with reorganizing control from the FDIC. Therefore the overall logic is when to many financial companies own the largest stakes in most small, and or large American corporate businesses that don't maintain the right idea, then the right professional issues must be addressed. This also has occasionally given bad, and complacent control to people outside of the productive business operation for various issues as it applies to those of the original business duties of discipline that where established.

One important reason liquidity was established during the years following the 1929 Great Depression is that "Anti-Trust" laws where established with government enforcement to give more oil businesses, and other industry businesses including individuals fair market opportunities. The Social Security Administration was established, and this became a commitment of liquidity to American citizens who worked, and paid taxes up to retirement age, or as a concept of being (c/o the 1980s) disable. This level of cash liquidity, and health benefits were also applicable to their family members such as the children and spouse, but it did not exist before the Great Depression "upon which more suffering was evident"! Tax dollars were also appropriated from the United States government to enforce these laws, but during the 1990s it became an issue for some people to think violating these laws where important to succeed in business. This even included some government officials, just like some rap artist (c/o instigating violence) which is totally destructive, and "Anti-Competitive"; causing long term insecurity if no laws are enforced, or corrected as it applies to compensating other hard working victims. Considering these factors a business is destroyed, and the basic level of format within state and federal taxes has been applied with severe or logical sacrifices of hardship. This means the whole circumference of business, and government procedures has been part of manipulation, and then the revenue, and liquidity resources are valued at their lowest levels of capacity (c/o a recession or depression) in the American society.

As it has been described the concentration of changes by government after the 1929 economic depression where tremendously important for the restructuring of the American society, and economy throughout America. Comparing these issues of social, business, and more so governed change these key elements appropriated values, and laws within legislature. This gave the American society a balance of control, and discipline that was important to value between the people, government, and the diversified concentration of businesses. Also a provision of security was established within investments, and savings that the American people depend on, which was factored with improved resources for the long-term of lifetime commitments. Then these various financial matters to use money consisted of accumulated asset gained liquidity, and interest over the time of sacrificed commitments. When individuals work hard to sacrifice, and manage savings in banking establishments, these commitments are some of the most important resources of fairness that go along with opportunities, education, and appropriate values of determination.

During 2010, and the future of the American society including businesses, and government these people, and their process of business must keep most all professional or occupational values within the quality of improved disciplines. These factors therefore become important, and productive for the stability of revenue earnings. Upon these factors this vitally includes the state, and federal taxable commitments, and the liquidity that help people live a productive life with a dependable money circulation within the standard values of American liberty.

CHAPTER THIRTEEN

War, Taxes, & The American Economy

Within this first decade of 2000 (c/o 2009) which now in America is a "time of war", this vitally includes the concept of the American economy fighting a financial battle to improve businesses, and local governments from a recession, or even worse a depression. This has become a question of when businesses, and government tax revenue will recover to overall economic, and financial stability. Most logical American households, and businesses are hoping that a recession does not become an economic depression, and "even worse" during this, or any "time of war". Upon this concern which implies that there is no other time "worse" then the "war time" issues for a developed nation, and country to have an economic depression with returning (c/o some injured) military personal. This means the effort American's have within work is cut out for them to pursue economic, and social disciplines. Understanding these American military veterans of war, and their families this would be drastic, and would instigate additional social problems! This becomes the fact of what will public, private, small, and large American businesses including government do to produce winning, or profitable solutions that will achieve a productive economy in America during the future years after 2010, 2011, and the future? Therefore this concept, and present observation consist of certain American economic challenge's, and more so this is part of one of the "Worse War Time Economy's" in American history.

Considering pass American wars, the only other time that war (c/o the U.S.) consisted of tax dollar conflicting issues, and more so a distinctive bad economy was during the economic liquidity conflicts after World War I. These became the factual year's between 1918 to 1929 considering the start of the Great Depression. Upon observing the Vietnam War, which the economy was a productive issue with corporate businesses such as U.S. Steel Corporation, Union Tank Corporation, Standard (Amoco) Oil Company, LTV Corporation, and a few like Ely Lilly Corporation, and 3M Corporation with others these defense contractors made levels of progress day after day. This vitally includes companies that develop products, evaluate research, and manufacture ammunition, uniforms, medicine, medical products, and food products including many other diversified items for the American military services. Chrysler Corporation was one of the first well known U.S. Defense Contractors (c/o making Army jeeps) that started to financially suffer after the Vietnam War due to some of their other automobile products that did not sale, or perform the best during the 1970s. Considering that the Vietnam War with sad condition's of agony, the U.S. economy consisted of certain prosperous times in America with hard work. Contrary to the American economy during this Vietnam conflict, and years of war following certain "war time agreements" the late 1970s economy did suffer a few hard setbacks. This was relevant to say observing that the "financial, and economic" times had improved a slight bit over the decades, but the loss of some "Defense Contractors" with other war's has factored certain unmanageable governed disciplines, and progresses.

Various sad, but slightly productive years, and times came with a price for the United States to win wars, fight, and or defend the air, land, water, and other assets as it applies for the people of the United States including some allied military forces, and countries. This was factually understood with these wars, and the losses of American military solders of war with high expenses. Considering these expenses such as those within the U.S. government's recent Defense Department budget, and cost consisted of appropriated money that was estimated at over $186 billion dollars. During these times of conflict from 1914 to 1918 upon review of the American forces fighting World War I, a vast amount of concerns continuously consisted of valued government duties of international affairs.

Considering other war time partners, "World War I" also consisted of costing over a "trillion and a half dollars" for all allied forces combined, and the United States appropriated over $22 billion dollars. World War II as it applies to the United States government was estimated at a cost of over $3.9 trillion dollars, which was one of the most expensive foreign wars fought up until the 1950s, and 1960s. The Korean War (c/o 1950 to 1953) cost the U.S. government over $320 billion dollars. The Vietnam War (covering 1959 thru 1975) cost in excess of over $680 billion dollars, and now the hundreds of billions of dollars that the "Iraq & Afghanistan" War is costing the United States government, and other countries even more. These disciplines of the U.S. Treasury are being observed within American defense subjects of review, and action to defend national security. All these foreign war's consisted of thousands of dead, and wounded casualties that truly outline's the other sad conditions of war. Basically it is more cost efficient, and morally sound to defend the United States, and its people against any threat of war, and destruction to the American society, and the people which should relieve the pursuit of a violent war.

During the 1775 to 1783 Revolutionary War an international concern between America with Paul Revere, and U.S. General George Washington against the Britain Army from England created a part of the established society of America. Contrary to the difference from the Civil War atrocity in America during 1861 to 1865 they both settled with different terms of agreements known as the Declaration of Independence. This Civil War was different from most "foreign wars" that the United States has fought lately considering the Civil War was divided domestically (c/o the north & south states) appropriating conflict agreements by President Abraham Lincoln within different financial, territorial, and social concerns. Also during the Civil War times it consisted of Black American slaves fighting for their freedom, and prosperity to support the future of American life. A strong regiment of black solders was named the Buffalo Solders whom was slightly organized by Hiram Revels (later appointed to the U.S. Senate), upon fighting with other southern commanders. This Civil War, and President Abraham Lincoln also abolished slavery. The Civil War, and the Revolutionary War that was "decades and century's" ago and apart is observed different from the recent times of change from over a century ago with very different conditions of today. Both of these wars exceeded into a fractional cost above a billion dollars each, considering equipment, and war time values which have changed quite a bit. Another observation is that these are some the basic values upon which America's Army and Navy disciplines for governed Defense where established.

These diversified considerations of today's (2001 thru 2009) engagement of war has reached the extent that America is also fighting the struggles of appropriating funds, and loans to failing "large" businesses, and banks during this first decade of the 2000 millennium. Considering this, and even the Barack Obama Presidential administration a recession has occurred. Contrary to the former George Bush Presidential administration a depression is something that no logical American should support or what's to allow within their power as it applies to any branch of government, and the better value of American citizens. Considering the U.S. economy, and war time economic evaluations consist of American public, private, small, and large businesses it becomes vital that they observe the importance to restructure if necessary. This is severely because the Iraq, and Afghanistan U.S. wars are coming to a conflicting end, but a lack of government tax revenue, and high unemployment is giving most parts of America an unsupportive bad outlook for all American's concerned about a prosperous life.

Upon these factors of the economy all small, large and corporate American businesses have a vital role to play with these diversified effects of war, and considerably the economy. This has factored the arrangement of the Troubled Asset Relief Program (TARP) consolidated by the former President George Bush, and the Federal Reserve Chairman Ben Bernanke which was established from the U.S. government with the 2008 Emergency Economic Stabilization Act "passed" by the U.S. Congress. The TARP is the main government bailout program of economic, and finance procedural incentives to support additional economic stability within the guaranteed FDIC insured system of local or commerce bank support for depositors. Also TARP funding support includes helping certain financial institutions, and certain businesses with other economic "emergency grants, and lending" matters. These have become the vital issues that citizens are faced with considering the future of certain factors of war, and other social, and business conflicts. Therefore the American society of citizens and government must work together better than they did before the September 11, 2001 attacks which provided financial, and social distress.

America's economic struggle during 2008 and 2009 to keep banks from closing, and or filing bankruptcy has included a enormous amount of foreclosed properties during this time of war. Contrary to the fact, hundreds of banking institutions closed their business operations. This becomes a lack of insecurity that is only slightly matched from centuries ago when solders would return home, and need support if anything still existed. Observing the Civil War of America, money was spent, and lives were loss, but the American Civil War came to a solution with vital amendments to the U.S. Constitution that was singed years before in 1787, not long after the Declaration of Independence in 1776. Contrary to sad losses of American's in the Civil War, and the Revolutionary War a various amount of people are contingently observant for what was achieved, and established. During that time it also created a workable commitment between the North and South (c/o the Union and Confederate Army) states of America, upon which got more "State" governments established to become the United States of America. These issues of civil war in America also consisted of problems including jurisdictions within eliminating slave state issues, and appropriating a U.S. presidential, and government leadership outline of constitutional rules. Now in America with these changing times, and a new foreign war during the 2000s this conflict consist of national security issues that America must consolidate properly. Therefore these changing times must consist of the best possible economic, and social decisions within the lawful, and productive use of technology with logical defense including the overall format of American resources for today, and the future.

Considering 2009 these American issues of the economy, the leadership within the federal government, and the people which consist of most every man, woman, and family of children, the logic of inflation, technology, and business growth has been active socially, and financially. A vast amount of households with various good, and bad economic concerns are not all guaranteed to live above the poverty level. American families living above the poverty level besides conditions of corporate welfare or with certain discrepancies where families that can buy food, and other items is part of the decade 2000, and 2010 determination to survive. Other people depending on a food bank offering for any level of generous or conditional support, is also becoming a vital conflict. One objective why, is because during 2009 food banks are running low on money, and food, including the theoretical fact that this does not just include the present economic problems effecting the poorest of families. During the 2009 economic crisis of resource in America a vast amount of households are having financial troubles that keep them from their freedom of purchase's, and with strict budgets to pay, and receive a lack of logical goods, and services they desire, or vitally need. Therefore the relevance of personal income must improve for the citizens of America, and not just those people of a new citizenship capacity to become a top level of wealth, and ignore the Constitutional commitments of the United States, and the people throughout most American regions of concern.

As American citizens that own businesses, or occasionally invest in businesses upon being applicable to the investment underwriting business concerns of different public corporations, this is a vital resource of professional conditions to improve the American economy. Throughout American investment brokerage firms which consist of these market business "traders and or managers" these professionals cannot go in any simple, or logical direction without publicly held corporations or businesses to invest in. This becomes slightly applicable to U.S. defense contract businesses, and corporations in America that are offered in the "securities and exchange" financial stock markets. These are factual businesses that are considered with the discipline that these corporations consist of for good profitable earnings, and managing liquidity which vitally applies to the underwriting brokers or managers, and a few others concerned about investment returns to earn money. Theoretically its important also that nonpublic, and publicly traded American company's must earn profits as well! Even investments in commodities (c/o certain markets) the overall business concept of things must be considered as it applies to farms, and most natural resources with commodities regionally, and geographically. This also means that they generate a vast amount of government tax revenue annually with networks of people, and businesses working together.

Certain business sacrifice's, and investment's offset detailed extra liquidity needs of the business, and corporate earnings during most war time economy issues. This also included a resource of good conditions of employment, the consolidation of profitable business earnings, and wage income for a variety of U.S. Department of Defense contractors, and other businesses. The increase (c/o limitations) within work of U.S. Defense contractors vitally includes the American progress of people working together that is very much so vital for the stability effects of asset liquidity, and the prosperity of American employees. As this consideration of economic facts, managing liquidity, and sacrifices by hard working business owners, investors, employees, and others is pursued, a better war time U.S. economy of prosperity could have been achieved. These good, and more so bad issues of business, and even employment are applicable to occasionally review caution "due to the American Economy" that occasionally suffers these cycled economic problems.

This concept of business, and even government tax revenue more so includes the vital fact of how some productive Americans where illegally excluded by destructive animosity during the 1990, and 2000 years of manipulation throughout different markets in America. During these years of manipulation, conflicts (c/o an Endless Loop Crisis) within department stores like Montgomery Ward's, Service Merchandise, other professional offices, and even hospitals which have suffered conflicts, and then went out of business was a tremendous economic problem. This was a slow process beginning during the (1st) first Persian Gulf War observing 1989, and 1990 which was not a very extensive war time with cost. These corporations going out of business had issues due to what seemed like anti-trust legal conflicts upon which also included their operating funds to pay expenses. This was the result of small, and some large businesses having to deplete their business profits to operate. Competitors in business, and certain outside individuals obtaining "Information ILLEGALLY" may have been the conflict. This was destructive considering a few within bad government officials wanting the amended passage of a more powerful "Freedom of Information Act" which seem to support more foreign enemy's has help disclose critical business information that I believe lead to destructive competitive business rights.

Observing the Sherman Anti-Trust Act concerning the U.S. government this is the fact or concept for persons to combine or conspire to acquire, or the power that they are able as a group, to exclude actual or potential competition, and provide issue that they have intent, and purpose to exercise that power, "is illegal". The years of excluding competition before the American economy became worse off during 2009, consisted of issues which did not seem to be helpful from the Freedom of Information Act, U.S. Anti-Trust law concerns, and certain other laws. Observing this matter various American businesses of vital concern where transformed to destructive foreign ownership. Some small businesses acquired by bad foreign people where found, and convicted of financially supporting, and conspiring with middle east terrorist, and war time conflicts.

The 2009 economic recession occurred with vast amounts of American money, and foreign business operations becoming the roots of foreign business competitors from American acquired assets, and commodities within the likes of coal processing, and steel plants. Understanding this lack of American control within small, and "more so" large business which occasionally means U.S. national security can be threatened became a tremendous issue, and problem especially as Enron failed leaving enormous business assets, and liquidity in these conflicting countries. India, and some concerns of Saudi Arabia are countries where Enron Corporation took from American's, and gave billions to foreign countries that are closely connected to people like Usama Bin Ladin from Saudi Arabia (c/o al Qeada), and Saddam Hussein of Iraq, and others. More American dollars going to other countries also occasionally weakens the currency rate of the dollar in America, and therefore American's most times get less product for their dollars. One of the major factors of excluding productive American people, upon which lately includes support applicable to foreign business owners is the unlawful activities that are applicable to certain U.S. Anti-Trust laws that have been ignored.

These U.S. Anti-Trust laws are within a vital anti-competitive, and price conditional concept of laws that had been established after the Great Depression, which followed World War II being a hard fought, and expensive war. Now during today this violent American war in the Middle East consisting of new issues seems to be partly the cause within factors leading into another (2009) recession, and possible depression. This is vitally an issue when the state, and federal courts, including some judicial districts ignored, laugh, joked (c/o even court room TV), and pursue defamation of character against certain productive people. Considering these taxable losses occurred, and then a lack of full sovereignty was accumulated with other unlawful issues of technology, the concept of legislature was incomplete especially as it applies to the duty of the courts. These factors of economic losses then endured the most critical issues of when American small businesses where unable to achieve different levels of business growth, and expansion with a vast amount of business filing's of bankruptcy. This becomes an American down fall within asset liquidity, and future opportunities. Therefore a vast amount of professional, and occupational businesses (c/o overall business communities) with productive tax revenue helping society was loss, and then they were excluded as prosperous people of various communities. This was similar to the productive people, and things that certain other's (c/o bad results) wanted to exclude due to animosity, and other conflicts. Although all is not cheating, but; "When you have to cheat all the time, it always seems to come back" to the people (c/o businesses) that "Cheat the most"!

Understanding U.S. Anti-Trust laws with multiple "criminal counts of law violations" ignored by certain government officials of the courts, and judiciary, this has become the "manipulation" (c/o laws) that has exceeded profitable businesses, and most employment earnings. WorldCom, and more so Ameritech Corporation was observed as businesses including some individuals that caused a vast amount of harm with financial, and social manipulation. This was the economic manipulation of people's personal lives, and professional lives at home, and at work including other places such as even in the church. Observing the beginning of the WorldCom Corporation, and Ameritech Corporation (c/o the 1990s) in the United States these businesses including certain individuals with a few government officials allowed the instigated death, or killing of certain people, destroyed marriage and families, and especially other businesses. Contrary to the billions of dollars that these corporations had, and then loss, the fair opposition of other businesses has proven to be economically important to the American society. The end result continued to be similar to "war like conflicts" in foreign places such as the former Yugoslavia, or even the Africa region of Rwanda, but in this American version of tragedy "No" tanks or very few burials in forest (c/o people being mutilated) within remote areas where used.

Mass murders occurred in the United States, and this more so had an effect of being Aggravated Assault that instigated certain death rate issues of all ages of people. This destruction to human life was "occasionally" pursued with Illegal & Hazardous Operated Satellites (c/o some gang violence) which became their "Honor to destroy" American citizen's, businesses (c/o Anti-Trust laws), and life. Most of these additional acts of terrible violence due to cost, and life in the United States consisted of domestic murder suicide, and homicide killings of some individuals, and family members, and or certain vary complex deadly illnesses. Some families suffered to the extent that there is not enough time in this life to recover. Considering these sad effects which means death was instigated not prevented in our American society has issues of justice to solve. Some of these problems could be criminal negligence which can be of "financial, and or fatal harm", but a vast amount was a vicious level of intent to commit, instigate, or conspire to pursue a destructive act of crime being evident. With additional bad foreign (c/o occasional domestic) relations these become the pretences to how war is declared upon which treason, and espionage has played a vital part.

These levels of manipulation by WorldCom Corporation, Ameritech Corporation, and Enron Corporation (c/o Anti-Trust law violations) instigated exclusion of asset liquidity advancements by American people if they survived. This, more so occurred, with most small, and some large businesses, including certain people that even occasionally supported gang violence. The format within complex foreign business, and relations becomes a controlling factor within born-in-America-citizenship losses of businesses in complex way's. One vital observation is that all three of these corporations were established from corporate mergers, and or buyouts, but the phone company issue had slightly different considerations. This is one of the main reasons why I have acknowledged that certain Junk Bond Markets (c/o issues) "have been lately" Out Of Control, especially with the losses applied to American businesses.

This problem of "U.S. Anti-Trust law violations", and even with certain Junk Bond-Merger issues that have been considered with no logical future solution except overall business failures, massive bank failures, and some effort within market reorganizing becomes complex. If you take close notice there was hardly any public utility companies that failed during these years of corporate welfare! Some of the corporation's that could not get things right seem to be WorldCom Corp with U.S. Anti-Trust law violations, and other concerns including the RJ Reynolds Tobacco Company which has taken up to 20 years to recover from a corporate buyout. A massive amount of victims is another problem of people that did not receive "justice" from hardly any American court or if necessary the Securities and Exchanges Commission. Each time a small or more so large business or market has to reorganize by way of law, and more so economics, you can bet "the pain, is to seek a profitable gain". This becomes a relevant, and aggressive business duty to lawfully survive. Certain improved progress still vaguely exist without extensive work that includes sadly the courts, legislature, and good professionals if things are pursued properly.

Some businesses and markets are now being taken control of by foreign "troubled" businesses, and people which is bad for American businesses. Upon this factual observation the people including their families, and distinctively most American regional economies are suffering. If certain American business owners have a hard time occasionally with the U.S. Constitutional rights of U.S. citizens as customers, and employees, you should clearly understand that foreign business owners in America could do worse! Observing this in America, like foreign dictators from badly governed country's this will cause a ration of problems with additional money, and controlling support that is worse than the concern of being "Un-Constitutional". Basically their respect, and understanding of the U.S. Constitution is rated low, if any rating exist at all. This becomes a very serious social problem in America especially affecting other various businesses, people, and a massive concept of employees that depend on U.S. businesses for American social values of progress.

Considerably government, and social issues of troubled business, and U.S. Constitutional disciplines applies to the overall concept of small, large, public, or private businesses throughout most American communities. Also this includes the effect of lower tax revenue which is accumulated through any form of business, and households that consist of important survival issues. Upon the business, and tax issues which means numerous citizens, and government suffer because of certain groups of people needing illogical acceptance, our American society has loss balance. Most of these problems are from a destructive condition within their contingent business loss (c/o lazy), or employment factors of insecurity. This vitally includes what financial tax revenue is not provided to the individual regions of local government, the U.S. government, and a select few others. This money circulation within business, and taxable revenue (c/o dollars) that exist from the U.S. that is foreign connected when people send it "out" of the United States is a severe loss within the circulation to businesses, people, and government. Then all levels of the American system of government must debate critical government budget matters which effect various government services, the people, and even the employees.

This concept of the American economic recession of 2008, and 2009 within public, private business, and more so government tax revenue is not just a default of people that won't file, and or pay taxes. This also consist of the people that pursued animosity, and hate against the kindness, and hard work of others. These are factual concerns of when the U.S. Constitution is clearly being abused, observing businesses, or government. The U.S. Supreme Court statement that the U.S. Constitution "Grants Power, Limits Power, and Protects against the Abuse of Power", should have become more vital to understand. As American's observe war, and the economic factors of the International Monetary Fund a person can review certain time's, and atrocious acts in certain parts throughout the world like Africa, and "Europe. At certain times" this seriously includes the Middle East which is factual to various social problems. These become "war, and defense" issues that include humanitarian support, contrary to a few bad issues that are slightly transferred by foreign people. It is even more a concern coming from Mexico, and therefore certain U.S. Constitutional values are taken away from American's if the U.S. government doesn't enforce the laws. This applies to some American's that use foreign people, and issues as a criminal deterrent of opposition. What this also amounts to is that some business management officials, along with even government officials instigated conflicts, and then they would refuse to hire the best, or manage Americans productively. Therefore some foreign people became the subject of inexpensive labor, and employment which most times consist of a negative impact on businesses if danger or conflicts occur. Concerning this logic "no matter" how bad or low the quality of service or professional discipline may have been, the results occasionally go backwards similar to the severe increase in manufacturing, and refinery fatal explosion's. This means there were also certain long-term problems applied. In addition this vitally is a subject of when the best American people possible, and workable "are not part of making an efficient workable American economy".

Between the observation of certain state's (c/o Indiana and a few others), with state and federal Attorney General's that clam they don't enforce the individual "State", and or U.S. Constitution as appropriate, and enforceable laws, certain new problems have become evident. This is the conflict of when groups of people violate the state and federal "Anti-Trust laws" against any American's to support various foreign businesses, and this has killed off the American concept of business. After businesses are, and were destroyed this caused a problem to the U.S. economy for many, many years to come. In some conditions of being vulnerable this is what has instigated, funded, and or allowed terror attacks against the American people, and some businesses applicable to U.S. Anti-Trust laws, and now with the engagement's of war.

Contrary to the conflicts of industry in Indiana as it applies to steel mill processes, manufacturing, and oil refineries with liquid storage facilities, a vast amount of small businesses are in financial trouble, or they are closing due to bankruptcy or a lack of earnings. Therefore the state and federal government as it applies to agencies such as the U.S. Department of Justice's Anti-Trust Division to enforce U.S. Anti-Trust laws is inactive, but they (c/o government) are earning a wage with appropriations. This also means the American businesses, and the people are losing thru a bad system of economic conditions that are sadly supported by most levels of complacent government that must be corrected. A vast amount of American's do good, but most economic issues of indication look bad for a growing majority. Upon this evaluation of losses in various American businesses, and society each day within losses over the years becomes equal to more "time", and make-up work "time" then some people, and professionals can ever imagine in life.

CHAPTER FOURTEEN

THE CHANGING TIMES OF CORPORATE AMERICA & BAILOUT'S

American tax dollars as government liquidity, and tax revenue values are established from small businesses as well the theoretical disciplines of Corporate America. During the 1930s to 1950 corporations in America recognized severe change's with the concentration of certain small businesses that expanded into sometimes various productive, and large corporations. This was a valid level of commitment by various people in the 1950s considering 20 years after the Great Depression "which" the United States government had established various laws like the Glass-Steagall Act that changed the way a certain amount of businesses (c/o bankers, investors, and others) operate. This also included their provision of paying state and federal income taxes, and even what's considered, and determined as corporate taxes. Therefore between the 50 to 100 years that certain investment markets, and publicly traded companies have provided taxable revenue with their products, and or services a vast amount of good, and bad decisions, and government issues where structured throughout the American society. Then these changing times are the conditions of our discipline, and commitment of the people's hard work.

Understanding the United States government and corporation's in America during the year 2000 the term's "Bankruptcy and Bailout" for a variation of a few banks, insurance companies, and corporate businesses (c/o automobile and air travel businesses) managed to create an uncoordinated atmosphere within corporate business conditions. These uncoordinated issues of business including some international business conflicts decided on a discrepancy upon which American businesses were considered to important, or too big to fail. These factors also became complacent, and socially worse when it was considered that most of these businesses hire the best, and brightest of educated (c/o American) people, but they can't seem to lawfully keep the business in productive control. Upon this important consideration of educated professionals which is vital in our American society, this includes even sometimes certain businesses being totally informal, and sometimes unlawful to the business concerns of others. Upon these issues all American citizens should be considered important no matter how much education they have, "especially" when they make the best decisions, and sacrifices to achieve certain goals in their work, or effort in business. Considering these factors of business applicable to the educated, and the "not so" educated of American's, all citizens can suffer from the changing times of bankruptcy with a bad American economy.

A format of aggressive business, and even government decisions to survive at all lawful conditions of effort are relevant in America, but this is also considered an issue for the state, and federal courts. This vitally becomes the need to correct issues within the legislative branches of government, which also can make mistakes. Contrary to this lawful concept of consideration's various businesses, including businesspeople transformed, and pushed the people, and American system of government backwards. People like Bernard Madoff (c/o fraudulent investments), Bernard Ebbers (c/o WorldCom) and William Daly (c/o Ameritech Corp.)

including others that discovered the undisputable resource of manipulation to take from the sacrifice, and wealth gaining prosperity of innocence of American's! A level of manipulation at this magnitude is a government concern for the executive, legislative, and judicial powers of the American government is to help the people prevail. This vitally included violations within U.S. Anti-Trust laws against the planning, and commitment of smaller businesses, and their effort to expand has caused insecurity in other markets, and business opportunities.

Observing the bad within U.S. domestic business operations that consist of financial crimes, and severe negligence this has provided an enormous set back with need to create certain laws that apply to the U.S. Constitution. Understanding financial crimes, and issues of new technology such as text massaging has also become an alienation to the U.S. Constitutional rights of citizens, and businesses to protect their assets, and decisions of sacrifice. There is some good in these advancements of society, but legislature and the common good of the people still has some restructuring to establish. These laws that are important to keep up with the concerning good, and bad of all corporation's in America keeps business, and the American general public most times in lawful order. These are the factors of the American society with the changing times that becomes very much so relevant with logical judgment, including overall business, and government decisions.

Throughout the last century more so starting around, and before 1898 with the Bankruptcy Act (c/o 1898), and then the Bankruptcy Code of 1978 having conditions of economic rehabilitation, reorganization, and issues of liquidation, these matters have been vital factors between debt, and credit. American banks, businesses, and individuals have observed the discipline of "credit, and debt" with the U.S. government establishing the Consumer Credit Protection Act, the Equal Credit Opportunity Acts, and the Truth-In-Lending Act to provide orderly, and lawful control in most U.S. business concerns. These have become the business, and individual credit concerns that occasionally factor issues of bankruptcy if people, businesses, and government are not extremely careful. These values of care, and concern of budgeting are vitally relevant within managing their economic disciplines throughout business, and habits of spending.

Understanding money management concerns as it applies to small, and sometimes various large business operations similar to Chrysler Corp (c/o the 1970s) in America, this becomes the hard work, and sacrifices that are "not" to be left idol. The changing times within the use of more computers, and the internet including text, and video messages has made some money management, and social concerns to comfortable to obtain the evaluation of (good and bad) accessible information. Some would include robotics' which is programmed with computers to operate in various manufacturing processes. Contrary to this fact these values of computer user friendly technology still consist of needed legislative concerns, and oversight technology adjustments. This basically also means that more than 90% of the businesses should "not" think, or make logical plans about a "bailout" contrary to any uninsured (c/o insured) contingencies upon which may include good values of technology. A comparison of the Chrysler Corporation, and the Continental Bank of Chicago (IL) had logical contingencies, but both of these businesses became idol with the capacity of not earning a profit in a timely or productive period of concern. These factors lead to issues upon which only Chrysler Corp was the one within the 1970s of these two upon comparison to restructure their business, and that included bankruptcy, and even the corporation asking for a federal bailout. Considering other businesses with contingent liability factors that where ignored until financial distress, these complex losses from management lead to a bankruptcy environment during late 2008. This bankruptcy environment was lead by Bear Stearns Investments, Merrill Lynch, and Lehman Brothers upon which included other investment bankers. Then the American effort of these bad economic times consisted of counter effects in the 2008 markets of real estate, construction, insurance, and banking that suffered in the United States.

The small and large businesses, and corporation's of America work to stay evenly consistent with the changing technology, and the times within lawful business that are applicable to industry, and the government system of tax revenue. Within the concept of expanding businesses various small business operations have suffered "when" some large corporations pursued business expansion values with merger / buyout transactions to become larger, and more aggressive businesses. Understanding this with a junk bond market that was out of control with other problems throughout corporations like Enron, WorldCom, Ameritech, and a few other large businesses, this caused severe social, and local government debt. These businesses had large sums of money, and they ruined other businesses considering the fact that then their businesses did not work properly themselves. This tremendous problem caused long term manipulated debt (c/o liquidity), and conflicts of interest that was also inflicted on some smaller businesses, and citizens that are now occasionally in need of U.S. government help such as with certain stimulus funding. Corporations such as General Electric Corp, United States Steel Corp, Johnson & Johnson Company, 3M Corp, Ely Lilly & Company, ExxonMobil Corp, and a few others managed to suffer minor losses to conditionally recover from in this failing economic issue within time. More so ExxonMobil Corp, Microsoft Corp, Apple Computer Corp, and certain pharmaceutical and food company's where not hurt by the economic recession of the first decade of 2000, but some smaller businesses will be more complex within time to manage a good recovery.

Within the changing markets of the United States various corporations, and some small businesses are finding themselves in trouble which are now effected by too much negative foreign interest. As America maintains social values of foreign relations the good, and more so bad of foreign conflicts has been the largest hurt with fatalities, and financial losses. These issues consist of problems such as the concerns at United Airlines Corporation whom has been pondered with numerous problems, and therefore the business has operated in bankruptcy for the last 10 years observing 2001 thru 2010. This is mostly due to the September 11, 2001 terrorist attacks including the gas, oil, and diversified fuel markets that became out of control with illogical (c/o domestic & foreign) price increases. Even during these times of change in America during 1990, and more so the mid 2000s, this present oil, and gas market upon energy matters is quite different from the 1973 oil embargo that caused problems within supply, and demand. Considering 2008 and 2009 the trucking industry (c/o diesel fuel), the airline industry (c/o jet fuel), and regular trucks including automobiles upon use where severely being effected by these consumer cost issues of fuel. In addition all energy, and fuel usage concerns therefore was a problem to the public, and private sectors of the American society.

Observing recent 2010 business developments concerning the conditions of United Airlines Corporation, and its struggles with bankruptcy, they have decided to merge with Continental Airlines Corporation which is becoming a Corporate America issue of business survival. Understanding the conditions that have effected United Airlines Corporation, and their changing times similar to other corporations have been some of the most radical to achieve good business results. Some details of this are becoming similar to others like ConocoPhillips, ExxonMobile, JPMorgan Chase, Chemical Bank & Manufactures Hanover Bank, including others that decided to merge their corporate businesses for liquidity, and production values of equity. Even as these companies have merged at some point, during the 2008 economic crisis this left the 90 plus year old Bear Stears Investment Bank in financial distress. Considering this Bear Sterns was part of the U.S. government, and the Federal Reserve Banks approved support of a purchase agreement by JPMorgan Chase Co, which only had certain disciplines applicable to the Glass Stegall Act, and other market liquidity requirements. Considering the diverse economic atmosphere, this "United & Continental" Airlines merger undoubtedly is a serious business merger agreement. This transaction, and business deal will create another one of the largest corporations in the world, and within the Airline industry with combined assets, if that helps anything!.

Contrary to decades of pass progress these two corporations (c/o United Airlines & Continental Airlines) agreeing to merge have both eliminated over 135,000 employees with other conflicting problems such a labor agreements. This process of employment elimination and restructuring has lasted a few years sense before 2001, 2004, including now 2010 which therefore the magnitude of restructuring is a critical subject. One fact that I stated about the changing times is that if a 2000 millennium depression occurs applicable to 1929 these could be some of the strong indicators within the new, and different economic depression effects.

Americas conflicting, and changing markets which included some foreign interest which partly had an effect on American insurance companies had to share in the cost of liquidity that effected their businesses for years to come. The company American International Group Inc. (AIG) is and was an American insurance business that is consistently trying to restructure with $85 billion dollars of bailout money upon which at least $20 billion dollars has went to other foreign businesses. American insurance companies had a record capacity of personal, and business clams as they had to compensate for Hurricane Katrina victims, and victims of the September 11, 2001 attacks with the concern of various other asset agreement levels of insured coverage. Considering these factual problems with AIG Inc., other insurance businesses are making changes to prevent bankruptcy knowing a bailout is not a good option.

Before the 9-11 Report of Terrorist attacks the American oil industry had been working between the United States, and certain Middle East countries. This becomes the vital concern that they understood a certain amount of bad foreign relation problems that could effect their business, and the people of America. The

United States government was not totally blind to these national security problems, but very few restrictions, and preventative security measures where applied. Certain insurance company's only had an occasional presence in various other foreign countries which made them slightly vulnerable with serious conflicts. This is becoming a resourceful concern of how the American society of business, and government must understand, and evaluate future resources of a diversified capacity. These resources vitally include oil, and other commodities within most global or foreign business activities with relations, upon which becomes applicable to the diversified resource of American business markets.

ExxonMobil Corporation, six years after the 9-11 Report of Terrorist attacks had its best year of profitable earnings in the history of the company. This concept of economic earnings provided adequate tax revenue to government with minor foreign conflicts. International business from American corporation's consist of corporate office's, and facilities including distribution processes that provides American tax revenue. This is the likely and normal process of businesses like within the expansion of Microsoft Corp products, and Apple Computer Corp products. The product expansion's has a presence in various other countries outside the United States with logically good business earnings. The two companies with the "Founder, and Chairman of the Board" Bill Gates, and the CEO Steven Ballmer; both of Microsoft Corporation, and the CEO Steve Jobs of Apple Computer Corporation whom consistently bring out new products have created massive logical government tax revenue that is supportive. This format of taxable revenue is beneficial to the American society, and it's system of government including "sadly" the bailout within financing of certain other American company's during 2008, and 2009. This bailout money included some foreign businesses from their involvement with certain troubled American company's which resulted in other countries receiving billions of dollars in certain pass agreements. As American citizens, and taxpayers observe these issues from businesses such as AIG Inc., and others the American society of corporate bailout financial issues became an aggravated unpopular issue for other diversified people, and businesses.

Another concept of industry matters consist of corporations including smaller businesses that sale their consumer electronic products that have observed some additional tuff times. Some of the more complex times, and issues consisted of retail stores that have went out of business like the Circuit City Retail Store Corporation. These Circuit City electronic stores lasted for about 10 years before they failed which is slightly, and sadly common for consumer electronic stores if they are not careful, but this is still a very bad or complex concept within business. These are the complex values of what is to be considered as the productive or unproductive changing times in the American society of corporate businesses. Other corporate stores over the years have consisted of Linen And Things, Montgomery Ward's, and Service Merchandise. This includes a few long lasting others that included banking establishments that are a severe part of any changing times for a well developed nation that should be corrected thru government. Upon these factored issues of good, and bad within the concept of management this is always to be considered from the managing of all businesses from the top to the bottom, and with certain logical support from government.

Observing some of the management concern's that America is filtered with, includes some businesses that are having a complex time getting a younger, and more productive resource of professional, and occupational employees. This is vitally important due to the vast amount of people preparing for retirement in the circumference of every few years. This professional and occupational employment concern was expressed by ConocoPhillips Corporation and other oil companies in 2007. During that time ConocoPhillips Corp increased their exploration and production budget by 8% to some $11 billion dollars for domestic, and more so foreign oil extraction projects. The CEO James Mulva is one of the many upper management officials that recognized the need (c/o some difficulties) for construction laborers, project managers, and petroleum engineers. Theoretically I personally don't agree that they should have a hard time finding people that would be good American construction laborers, and occasionally even some engineering professionals. Contrary to this fact maybe this becomes the sad level of risk within how some CEO's don't know how to maintain the managing, and resourceful training of construction labor workers. In addition one of the most vital factors is that most regions of America do have a vital need for more professional engineers, upon whom can be trained for other backgrounds, and disciplines of engineering with adequate studies, or valued training.

ExxonMobil Corp, and ConocoPhillips Corp did try to reorganize their needed stability apart from businesses such as with Amoco Oil Corporation whom was bought out by the British Petroleum Company during the late 1990s. As it applies to American corporations that have been bought out by foreign businesses, and or individuals these become enormous losses within Americas struggle within tax revenue dollars, and government issues to support citizen opportunities. All three of these businesses had involvement in corporate mergers, but Amoco was a loss of U.S. tax dollar revenue for the American system of government. British Petroleum dose pay American taxes with responsible earnings, but an American corporate headquarters of establishment is a big value within whatever United States region they preside in to do business. My observation of this is that certain people in government have taken consideration of these factors upon which some small investors were victimized by un-enforced U.S. Anti-Trust laws, and U.S. SEC rules and regulated laws during the 1990s, and 2000. This becomes the observed problem of conflicting crimes of defamation, and hate that destroyed a vast amount of citizen's, and their domestic tranquility. As people of a foreign and U.S. domestic capacity come together, sometimes they forget or ignore the relevant disciplines of the lawful wording of tranquility, prosperity, and a few other values within the United States Constitution. The people, and the American society providing an obligation to the U.S. Constitutional laws which even includes courtroom enforcement conditions, has appropriated small businesses to expand into larger businesses over the last 50 to 100 years.

As most people will recall oil companies during the 1940s, to the 1980s, and now established very productive growth without bailout money. One consideration of today is that even now "no oil companies in America" has asked for any government bailout money. Contrary to this concern this is more so relevant to the Anti-Trust law court proceedings, and trials of Standard Oil Corp of Indiana. It was also an expanding market within time for automobiles, and even airplanes which use a vast amount of gas, jet fuel, and or oil products. This was just before 1920, and the Standard Oil Company of Indiana with various other state geographical issues, and businesses like Standard Oil of New Jersey & Ohio (c/o Nelson Rockefeller and son's) whom had tremendous control over the American oil markets. These are similar, but different state and federal Anti-Trust law conditions in America "then those that exist today", and the concerning future. The good and bad advancements of technology is the basic Anti-Trust law legal concern observing the "first decade and a half of 2000" throughout certain regions with most American industry, and market disciplines of efficiency. These changing times of American markets consist of computer internet systems, commercial satellites, and even wireless communication activities with good, and some very bad issues. Also with important factors certain internet activity, and communication conflicts, and disturbances are vital for government to regulate for the severe need of corrections.

A large part of corporations that offer commercial satellite (c/o Intelsat & Domsat) services, and wireless communications is consistently a problem with people's rights of privacy, and decency, apart from the good that they provide. This even more so is a problem within small business owners "personal, finance, and business" lively hood decisions, and activities which occasionally requires lawful confidentiality. The vital issue of confidentiality, also consist of lawful affirmation's to achieve certain personal or business goals. The 4th Amendment of the U.S. Constitution outlines this vital law concern within the issued responsibility for the people's houses, papers, and effects (c/o oath or affirmation) with other U.S. Constitutional Amendments, and laws. Some people closely consider this a law that applies to police department and law enforcement officials, but it also applies to the citizen or business rights of privacy in "various project bids", and other "confidential documents" applicable with good personal decisions. This is valued upon being one of the only U.S. Constitutional amendments that discusses personal privacy issues. Therefore just as telephones have changed, issues within the computer data that applies to peoples home, work, and even religious worship including other values must be regulated to appropriate new technology within the boundaries of U.S. Constitutional laws.

Within the hundreds of technology driven companies, corporations, and businesses in the United States including various foreign businesses with oversight technology their activities continue to be vital throughout the American system of government, and society with regulation. Certain examples within the concept of American issues of new technology during 1990, and the 2000s is understood from high speed trains, massive products within (good & bad) video games for computers, and television with some enter-phased thru wireless telephones. Also the massive concept of information technology data that is used for thousands of reasons (c/o television, and communication systems) is not in the same consolidation of the Federal Communication Commission laws that existed during the 1980s, and or especially in the 1970s. Therefore some conditions of the state and federal laws within legislature are due for massive up-grades also.

As certain American's remember the 1st few inventions of computer's with vacuum tubes, and monochrome screens have now changed to become more resourceful which this product has expanded throughout society. These changes consist of microchip's, and video graphic (high resolution) computer screens which has taken these advancements to new levels that have established astute reliability in their capabilities. Contrary to this format of advanced technology the need for government legislature goes further than these advancements. Now in technical format the computer's that have a large data base of input, and output statements of conditions with memory of personal data is the relevant start within maintaining codes of ethics, and privacy matters that become more vital to our American system of laws.

Considering our American system of law's that are established within all city, state, and U.S. federal branches of legislature, it is vital to keep up with business, and technology issues. A vast amount of importance in the subjects of advanced business, and technology in the United States also applies to other places throughout the world. Then this format of governed issues, and literacy means we have a valued understanding on how most all things work. Recognizing the changing times throughout America a full concept of the use of computers as it applies to all professions, occupations, and government is a vital part of legislature, and the future years of life in America. Contrary to the importance of the many advancements that society consist of, certain values of normal life such as pen, pencil, paper, reading, writing, and arithmetic are still very important. In addition this includes the normal conditions of a man and woman having a loving relationship, and or marriage with true values of face to face communication which is vital for most all humans on the earth. Therefore the changing times of society do consist of values of technological advancements, but most all simple values such as respect for other human's that are taught form most conditions of childhood, then are vitally important for the improved changes in society.

How the American concept of citizens within professions such as civil engineering and construction to build roadways, bridges, power plants, dams, and other structures has changed is a part of logical decisions just as old ideas slowly diminish for anything new. These valued issues are balanced with the importance of certain levels of equipment, professionalism, and occupational standards. This vitally still includes the commitment, and hard work attitude within all people involved, but with most basic conditions of caution for logical safety which is still vital. Considering this format, the results should exceed the obsolete projects of the pass, but with occasional improved qualities that provide future understanding of logical advancements.

The best engineers, and construction workers on various construction projects still depend on some of the most obvious, and simple details. These details consist of looking over the progress of work, and then with the evaluation of calculations applicable to drafted plans they develop for this work, then on various occasions they have logical working discussion's until everything is understood, and properly constructed. Upon this resource of discipline they then follow within the good, bad, and vital format of things to be constructed, and considered with as built approved revisions to plans. A vast amount of computer aided drafting, design, and land surveying computer programs are used, and plotted out on paper for detailed calculated diagrams, and this has now given a cleaner approach to reading a conditional set of blueprints, and design details. These factual issues of observation are done in the process of decisions, and professionalism that consist of engineering, and construction duties to format the best solutions possible.

Observing the 2008 Minnesota bridge collapse this was an engineering, construction, and government mistake observed as severe negligence. Government engineers should have observed this very important issue of reduced structural load strength capacities. A licensed professional engineer has a professional duty to provide their best qualities on any project including this Minnesota bridge project which has vital conditions of strength, and materials with live, and dead load capacities. Another vital detail throughout this bridge project is how they could have otherwise rerouted traffic, due to the fact that the bridge was one of the few ways between Minneapolis, and St Paul consisting of two large, and very active cities in Minnesota. So this means the vital problem that occurred was within the vast amount of authorities involved on the project that did not take on the evaluation of excessive equipment (c/o the load capacity) on the bridge during construction. In addition certain lower, and upper load capacity materials where removed, and therefore with cars and trucks passing thru on other parts of the bridge, this became a load weight capacity problem. This exceeded the load capacity of the bridge, and then therefore the structure collapse occurred causing damage to assets, and the sad fatalities to various people.

America has advanced at a slow pace in the construction, and engineering market with only slight conditions of improvements to all issues of the American infrastructure. These factors are maintained within the progress of changes that cannot be taken for granted with statements like "there's nothing to worry about"! This occasionally is a bad statement that I recognized if certain business, and professional engineering duties are not pursued properly. As the concept of engineering, and other professional firms including businesses (c/o even doctors, lawyers, accountants, or construction managers & ect.) is considered, they are liable professionals when accidents occur. This professional liability even includes the validity within issues such as the bridge collapse that occurred in Minnesota during 2008 which has a negative effect to the general public. A government bailout for professional negligence is totally not an issue, but usually there is other court proceeding's occasionally these professionals must be concerned about. A sad, but relevant example is the "BP" (c/o Amoco) Texas City, Texas plant explosion during March of 2005, just as there are court proceedings for the Minnesota bride tragedy, and other's. These become just a few of the American professional liabilities that are important to correct in the American concept of major construction, and mass production industry concerns. This concept within massive construction, and manufacturing in America must continue to work to improve how they conduct business without fatalities to people, and or damage to equipment, and other parts of society.

As we understand as Americans, the changes that have occurred in the concept of businesses, and taxable revenue in the United States will continue to change. The vital resource of these changes is that most all industry, markets, and government changes are for the better of a more productive, and safe business environment. Also without negative conflicts less companies may fall upon the concern of bankruptcy, and even the consideration of bailouts, and therefore the American economy can maintain productive, and prosperous growth.